New, hitherto unseen, first-hand accounts of the battle of Arnhem, the heroic Allied military operation known as 'Market Garden', become rarer as time passes. *Chig: Sky Pilot to the Glider Pilots of Arnhem* is the story of a choir boy, who became a country parson, and went on to take part in Operation 'Market Garden' as Chaplain to the men of the Glider Pilot Regiment. When he left home "Chig" – Rowland Chignell – later the Rev'd Prebendary Chignell, wrote often to his father. Remarkably his father kept those letters written between August 1940 and September 1944 before, post-war, returning them to Chig. Chig died in 1994, and when his effects were being cleared, among them was a small bundle of papers, containing 84 dog-eared letters Chig had written to his father. With them were eight densely-typed foolscap pages. This extraordinary and unique document, Chig's account of his time in Arnhem with the Glider Pilot Regiment (GPR), recounted first-hand conditions which got increasingly hairier before ultimately, under heavy fire, came the withdrawal across the Rhine. The early letters provide almost a social history of war-time rural life in two small parishes in south Shropshire, recounted by a newly-married, newly-appointed country parson. 'Dig for Victory', the establishment of a pig club, and keeping of hens, are on the agenda. The difficulty of obtaining petrol and tyres is noted, and yet Chig's cricket club has petrol for the mowers to maintain pitch and outfield, which allows cricket to be played against the various Service units stationed nearby – good for morale. A Searchlight Battery's arrival led to Chig becoming their unofficial chaplain. His greater awareness of the vital role played by Service Chaplains led, too, to his volunteering himself as a Chaplain to the Forces. Attached initially to the Parachute Regiment's Training Unit – when the use of paratroops in war was still very novel – Chig later was asked to transfer to the GPR. The tenor of the letters change, yet always painting a full and varied picture about his own role (in so far as war-time security allowed) but also about cricket, about bird-life and the scenery, and about music too – a great love shared with his musical father. Padre Chignell's letters tell a story that demands to be told.

Mike Vockins, the author, was a long-time friend of Chig. They met first in 1971 when Mike was appointed Secretary of Worcestershire CCC, where Chig was a member of the committee.

As Worcestershire's chief executive until his retirement in 2001, Mike was awarded the OBE in 1996 for services to the game. Uniquely, in 1988, alongside his career with Worcestershire, he was ordained as a Church of England minister, welcoming the challenge – and privilege – of combining his cricketing and church roles for thirteen years. He continues to assist the country parishes in the Hereford Diocese where he lives, viewing the cricket world as an extra-parochial charge. His service to the diocese was marked in 1999 by his appointment as a Prebendary of Hereford Cathedral. Mike's active involvement within cricket continues as a member of the England and Wales Cricket Board's Major Match Group, and as Secretary of the Hornsby Trust, a charity supporting former professional cricketers.

The love of cricket and the church shared by Mike and Chig cemented their long friendship. That warm bond and Chig's encouragement and wise counsel was (and still is) much cherished by Mike.

Mike and his wife Eileen live on the Herefordshire side of the Malvern Hills, in a cottage formerly used by Sir Edward Elgar as his country retreat. Their two daughters, Helen and Morag, have long since flown the nest but return often with their families, enriching for Mike and Eileen the delights of being grandparents.

CHIG

For
Sue, Judy, and Jenny
Chig's nieces

and for

all who have served, and all who today serve, as Chaplains to the Forces, the 'sky pilots' faithfully ministering to those alongside whom they stand and serve

Chig

Sky Pilot to the Glider Pilots of Arnhem

Mike Vockins

 Helion & Company Limited

Helion & Company Limited
26 Willow Road
Solihull
West Midlands
B91 1UE
England
Tel. 0121 705 3393
Fax 0121 711 4075
Email: info@helion.co.uk
Website: www.helion.co.uk
Twitter: @helionbooks
Visit our blog http://blog.helion.co.uk/

Published by Helion & Company 2017
Designed and typeset by Mach 3 Solutions Ltd (www.mach3solutions.co.uk)
Cover designed by Paul Hewitt, Battlefield Design (www.battlefield-design.co.uk)
Printed by Short Run Press, Exeter, Devon

ISBN 978-1-911512-33-2

British Library Cataloguing-in-Publication Data.
A catalogue record for this book is available from the British Library.

For details of other military history titles published by Helion & Company Limited contact
the above address, or visit our website: http://www.helion.co.uk.

We always welcome receiving book proposals from prospective authors.

Contents

List of Illustrations

1

Knocking at the Door

Rat-tat-tat-tat!! The hammering on the door reverberated around the office. It all but shook the sturdy, steel-framed door off its hinges!

It was a knock I would come to recognise over coming months and years, whenever the Rev'd Prebendary Wilfred Rowland Chignell – Chig to almost anyone and everyone – visited the offices of Worcestershire County Cricket Club, where – in October 1971 – I had just taken up the post of County Secretary (chief executive in today's parlance). Chig, a member of the Club's Committee, had journeyed in to Worcester from his home village of Whitbourne, just over the Herefordshire border, to introduce himself to the new man. Either that, or to suss him out. Perhaps both.

Whichever it was, that first meeting led to us working together occasionally during cricket's close season, and then meeting on his more frequent (but, for him, never frequent enough) summer visits to the Ground and to its Committee Room to watch Worcestershire play.

Such meetings led to a warm and deep friendship not least when, in the late Eighties, I started training for the ministry alongside my continued role with Worcestershire. Chig was a tremendous, but sensible and grounded, encourager as I considered whether this was the right way for me to go. He remained an inspiring encourager during my training, as well as a wonderfully wise counsellor, mentor and guide in the years which followed my ordination. We became very good friends though, by that time, it tended to be me visiting him and knocking on his door – albeit somewhat less vigorously than he had first announced himself to me. But how fortuitous that had been!

Our friendship grew as Chig moved towards the end of his active parish ministry. It was something we both enjoyed nurturing as he moved into retirement. Indeed, at some point in the later years of his life, he asked me to hold power-of-attorney for him (and asked another friend to do the same for his devoted wife, Pauline). In fact neither the friend nor I needed to trigger the powers as both Chig and Pauline kept their faculties to the end, but it had seemed to them both a sensible precaution, and one better prepared thoughtfully and sensibly with time in hand rather than becoming a last-minute and urgent necessity.

When Chig died, on New Year's day in 1994 (Pauline had pre-deceased him), two of his nieces, Jennifer Hirst and Sue Paxton, asked if I would help them clear up his effects. They were both extremely fond of their uncle ('Unc') and knew him well, but they weren't sure about his cricket-related possessions and so wanted advice about what was important and what was not.

It was during this process that we came across a well-thumbed draft of his autobiography (large chunks of which Sue had typed) and also a pile of papers.

The autobiography, a huge bundle of dog-eared foolscap pages, I had read a year or two previously. It had never been published (though I sense he had approached a publisher or two) but, for someone like me, who was immensely fond of him, knew him well and, in some ways, was sharing the same journey, it proved a fascinating read. Mind you not much had been missed out from his eighty-six years. If not the lightest of reading, it was a fascinating tale, illuminating his good and full life.

Alongside the autobiography we found another smaller pile of papers, equally dog-eared. This proved to be a bundle of letters, short letters typed on A5 paper. Some, by now, had become fragile. They dated from the time he'd been appointed to his first living as a clergyman, a regular bulletin to his father. His father had kept them and, at some point, had returned them to Chig, enabling him to look back on the times of which he had written.

A brief scan of the letters readily revealed a remarkable social history, telling of the life and times of a young, newly married, newly-instituted country parson in the years leading up to – and into – the Second World War. That brief scan made one thing abundantly clear: these letters deserved closer study and, almost certainly, a wider audience, not necessarily for any skills of penmanship but because of the story they told.

And then we uncovered yet one more bundle. Bundle is perhaps too generous a term. It was simply eight pages of now well-thumbed paper, with typing so dense one wondered how all the words had been squeezed on to the page. The story these pages told truly was amazing. They offered a first-hand I-was-there account of a major campaign, a notable historical event of Britain's Second World War. It was, again, a story that demanded to be told, and told to a wider audience. Here it was, buried unremarkably amongst Chig's possessions, with no hint of the value or importance of what an outstanding story this collection of papers had to tell.

*   *   *

Rat-tat-tat-tat! That long-ago knock, 'with gusto', was followed by the briefest of pauses as Chig courteously waited to be invited in. Doffing his cap, and putting his pipe, his almost ever-present pipe, into his pocket he stretched out his hand in welcome. From that instant all that follows here would unfold.

Chig was at that time, 1971, sixty-three. He was a country parson, and would have been proud to be called such. It was a priestly vocation he had faithfully fulfilled since his ordination in 1933, and he was now moving towards retirement and the end of his active parish ministry. Not that he was one to take this step carelessly or in a 'demob happy' way. Hale and hearty as by nature he was, his was a dedicated and lively ministry among people who respected and admired him, indeed loved him.

His devoted wife, Pauline, and his parish and his service of God were the prime focuses of his attention. Pushing them close, though, was his love of cricket, and County cricket in particular, and Worcestershire County Cricket most of all. Music, too, was hot on its heels

He – as a Worcester-born lad – had followed the County Cricket Club since he was a young boy. In more recent times he felt very privileged to have been invited to serve on the County's committee as a representative of Herefordshire.

As one characteristically conscientious and dedicated in so much that he did, Chig served the County's committee in exactly that way but recognised – and felt – that his parishes and his ministry must come first. One way in which he was able, however, to serve the Club was as Editor of the County's Year Book. Ever since he had first taken an interest in cricket as a very young boy the statistics of the game (and, of course, of Worcestershire players in particular) had interested him greatly, not quite in an obsessive way but certainly one to which he devoted much enthusiasm and time. Thus his role as Year Book Editor made him a round peg in a round hole. It was in this role that he had come to introduce himself to me. It was a role which necessarily brought him to the County Ground on a fairly regular basis during the winter months. That hearty rat-tat-tat on the door became a familiar signature tune, which a composer might indeed have annotated "with gusto". And there was much gusto about Chig.

From that first moment I enjoyed his company. He was good-hearted and amusing company, with a delightful and slightly mischievous sense of humour, a sense of humour so simple and straightforward, and so devoid of hurt or waywardness that there's a temptation to describe it as schoolboy humour – yet it was better than that.

In those early years I gathered up snippets of information about him as he chatted away, painting for myself a more rounded, more detailed picture of him but, as he seldom spoke about himself to any great extent, it took a re-reading of his drafted life story, those browning pages with their faded type, to be reminded of the fullness of his life.

What follows here then is that story in shorter form, offered with the intention of setting the background and context of the man who was awarded the Parachute Regiment's iconic red beret. How had I missed the significance of such a noble item hanging in his hall-way all those years, a pointer to that part of his life now long-hidden away? It is an account of one whose contribution to the Arnhem campaign and to the Glider Pilot Regiment was recognised in his twice being Mentioned in Despatches.

Here then was no archetypal country parson and yet, in so much that he did, that is exactly what he was, for so many years for so many people. That is how he would best wish to be remembered, but there is that aspect to his life which few, if any, of his parishioners or his cricketing friends, knew. It is time this tale was told.

Let's hear now the first part of his story, before letting the letters to his father weave their own threads in the tapestry of a remarkable life, a tapestry and story with an heroic weft.

2

The Innings Gets Under Way

Wilfred Rowland Chignell was born, in Worcester, into a musical family or, in truth, to a musical father and into a family with firm Christian foundations and convictions. Born on 5 June 1908, he was the youngest of the four offspring of George Street Chignell and his wife Emma Mary.

His older brother, Hugh, was born in 1898; the elder of his two sisters, Margaret, arrived the following year, in 1899. Their younger sister, Robena, drew her first breath in 1903. Initially she was Robin to the family but latterly, after her marriage to Robin Milward, the family re-christened her as Bobbie to avoid confusion. In later years Chig, with characteristic tongue-in-cheek humour concluded "Father and Mother decided that they had had enough when I appeared in 1908 – and who can blame them?"

It says something of Chig, and of the era in which he was born and grew up, that he always referred to his parents as "Father" and "Mother", and usually in that order. Indeed in reading his drafted life story there was no mention of his parents' names; they were always and everywhere referred to as "Father" and "Mother", yet always with affection, always with respect.

What did intrigue Chig when he was old enough to register such thing was that his parents – before marriage – were both Chignells. They were second cousins.

George was born in Havant, the middle child of seven, whilst his wife-to-be hailed from Romsey. She was one of four children, having two sisters and a brother.

George seems to have been destined for a musical life quite early on, for he was sent, as a choral scholar, to St. Michael's College, Tenbury Wells, in Worcestershire, a school with a strong musical reputation. From there he became Assistant Organist at Salisbury Cathedral where he doubled as a junior Master at the Cathedral's Choir School. One challenge this post threw up was trying to maintain discipline among boys who were not much younger than himself, among them his brother Hugh, his junior by only two years.

From Salisbury, via an organ scholarship at Selwyn College, Cambridge, George moved to Worcester, as Assistant Organist at the Cathedral (from 1893 to 1896), and later became a well-regarded and respected music teacher in the city, as well as

Organist and Choirmaster at the parish of St. John in Bedwardine, a growing parish on the western edge of the city. Chig's birth certificate shows his father's occupation as "Professor of Music"

Chig's parents married in 1897. During their engagement George had thought nothing of spending a day cycling to Romsey from Worcester (a round trip of over 200 miles!) for the pleasure of an hour or two in his fiancée's company. That must have meant a very early start and a late return home!

At the time George and Mary married and settled in Worcester, one of the city's favourite sons was coming into his pomp. Edward Elgar, in the last years of the 19th century and those early years of the next, was becoming more widely known. His concert overture, "Froissart" and the much-loved "Serenade for Strings" had begun to win him public fame. Publication of his "Enigma Variations" in 1899 won him acclaim far beyond his home city's boundaries. Elgar, too, taught music and among his many other musical activities was his involvement with Worcester Philharmonic Society (formed in 1897), where he was the conductor – with George as his rehearsal accompanist and assistant conductor. George would later become one of Elgar's trio of friends who acted as his proof-readers. Chig was immensely proud of this family connection with Elgar. His father had passed on to Chig first edition copies of "Caractacus" and "Gerontius" presented to him by Elgar himself. In the hallway of Chig's and Pauline's home, in the years I knew them, there hung a framed page of an original Elgar score – alongside that iconic beret.

A very young Chig standing between his mother Mary and father George,
with other family members.

Of his early homes Chig says "About 1912 the family moved from Braelands" – without saying where that was – "to Hill View on the Bull Ring and shortly after that to Hill House, only two doors away". Houses on the Bull Ring, in the parish of St John's, were substantial, with large gardens and orchards (now long gone and built over). References in Chig's book to "the music room", "family prayers before breakfast" and "the maid" offer a glimpse of life at Hill House. In those years St. John's had the feel of a village on Worcester's outskirts, separated from the city by the River Severn, Worcestershire's county cricket ground and the playing fields of King's School. Those remain a buffer between St. John's and the city today, though the parish has much more of a suburban feel and is now one of Worcester's larger residential areas.

It was very shortly after the outbreak of the First World War (1914-18) when Chig began his schooling. Miss Cavanagh's was a small pre-prep school, in many ways a Dame's School.

One notable event from that time – though perhaps only of very special note to Chig and the other pupil involved – was a pageant at Worcester's Theatre Royal, in Angel Street. He played the part of a class dunce and a clock-advancer (without ever suggesting this was appropriate casting!) who, in the sketch, would be chased and soundly birched by the Dame. Plenty of cardboard padding in the seat of his trousers made the punishment sound effective and thorough!

Another group staged a tableau about Pope Gregory, and the famed incident where he said captives from Britain were 'angels', not 'Angles' as he had been informed. One of the 'angels', a fair-haired little girl, stood out in Chig's memory. Twenty years later and many miles away from Worcester, he would meet her again.

From Miss Cavanagh's he moved, around 1916-17, to Tredennyke School, a well-known prep school just north of the city centre, to which he travelled daily by scooter. It was a time when cars were few, and most people walked or travelled within the city by tram, or by train or bus from the outlying towns and villages. There were still a few carriers, driving horse-drawn waggons in from the country, delivering goods in and out and sometimes undertaking shopping commissions. Young Chig's other great passion then, alongside his blossoming interest in County cricket, was cycling and, again, the limited traffic on the roads made this a safe pastime for a young lad. Aided by a remarkable pocket-book, which had been his father's and which gave details of all the main local roads and lanes, showing their gradients in graph form, he loved setting off, with sandwiches prepared by his mother, exploring just about all of Worcestershire west of the Severn and frequently venturing into Herefordshire.

Tredennyke's Head, Miss Robson, retired soon after Chig became a pupil, to be succeeded by Mr H H Gairdner. Chig considered him "a born teacher, no mean musician, a good and enthusiastic cricketer, a man of delightful humour, serious and convinced in his Anglican Christianity, and a true guide and friend to all in the school". Clearly that was a reflection of later years – but what more could a boy want? It was an idyllic time: "far and away the best years of my school life" he later recalled – a time made even better by Gairdner's appointment of a red-haired and well-built games mistress, Marjorie Pollard, who would become a leading figure in England's

Chig (fifth from right, centre row), towards the end of his time at Tredennyke School.

women's cricket and hockey. It was through Mr Gairdner that Chig gained a life-long love of Charles Dickens' writing and even in later life he often had a Dickens novel beside his chair, for evening reading.

Life was not wholly idyllic. In April 1918, his brother Hugh, who had left Sandhurst the previous year and been commissioned into the Third Worcesters as a Second Lieutenant, was killed in a fierce battle to recapture Mount Kemmel. Hugh was reported missing, presumed dead. His body was never recovered, and his loss was deeply felt by all the family.

Chig's lifelong love of county cricket, and of Worcestershire CCC above all, was whetted in that first post-war summer of 1919. Worcestershire was ill-prepared after the war years to re-enter the County Championship but, nevertheless, a few non-championship games were staged on the County Ground. One of these was a match between Worcestershire and the Australian Imperial Forces XI. Reliving the memories which had created such an impression on him on watching his first serious cricket match, Chig later recalled "I can still see that terrifying run of J M Gregory up to the wicket. I walked out between innings with a great friend who was with me at Tredennyke, Geoffrey Dorrell, to see the marks of his run-up and, no doubt, to discuss with the great experience and wisdom of eleven-year olds, the state of the wicket. Little did either of us imagine then that we should eventually both serve together for years on the Worcestershire County Cricket Club Committee, and that Geoffrey should twice be elected Chairman and later become President, followed a few years later by me!"

Chig's love of the county game developed further when his Headmaster took his two top forms on occasional visits to New Road to watch the likes of Frank Woolley, Philip Mead, and Worcestershire's own Fred Bowley whose batting joyously embraced the grace and charm of cricket's pre-war Golden Age.

By this time Chig, unsurprisingly, was a regular and ready attender at Church. His organist father would encourage his love of both church music and cricket in an unusual way. Returning home at the end of a day's teaching Mr Chignell would often pop in to the County Ground to watch the day's closing overs and, on reaching home, would disclose the score to his son as follows: "'Ye holy angels bright' for six"; or "'Art thou weary, art thou languid' – all out" requiring Chig to remember the hymn's number in Hymns Ancient and Modern or to look them up, to discover the score was 546-6 (surely an opposition score in those days when the County was rebuilding its cricket fortunes?) or 254 all out.

Towards the end of his time at Tredennyke, the School moved to Tibberton Court, near Gloucester. Chig went with them, and thus became a boarder for two terms. He loved the attractive country mansion, with its spacious grounds in which was a delightful little church, surrounded by marvellous countryside with fine views across to May Hill. During this period Chig swotted away hoping to win an Open Scholarship to Worcester Cathedral King's School (King's School, Worcester as it is simply known today).

His swotting was not entirely successful. The Open Scholarship passed him by, but he was offered a House Scholarship. This he would like to have taken up but, financially, even with the benefit of the scholarship, it was too much for his father. He became a day boy instead which, from his family's point of view, must have seemed sensible since their home was barely a mile's walk from school. Looking back Chig later regretted missing out on the major scholarship and the chance to board for he sensed he would have been a more committed pupil as a boarder, and would have been less inclined to just 'get by'.

The School, during his time there, had around 200 boys, nearly half of them, like him, day boys. He felt strongly – again with the benefit of hindsight – that the day boys were apt to take little part in school life outside the classroom. He concluded that "being a day boy, I was only really committed to the things that I fancied, and could escape the rest – and this included work to a large extent."

In his first terms at school he managed to come near the top of the class in exams but, within three years, his enthusiasm had waned, except in certain areas. By his own admission he played vast amounts of paper cricket during Greek and Latin lessons.

The school's campus, however, inspired him, nestling as it did alongside the magnificence of Worcester Cathedral, and College Hall, the old monastic refectory – "the finest school I have ever been in" he declared.

Corporal punishment still prevailed, something which Chig accepted, saying "I never objected to being beaten, though I certainly received my ration! Caning was painful. You knew what it was for. It was soon over. You avoided doing anything to bring it on your head – or your bottom! – if you possibly could, but it was neither cruel nor vengeful". Another form of punishment was the writing of 'lines'. He claimed that "Chignell, take a hundred lines" or "Chignell, take a thousand lines" were fairly common pronouncements.

Experience of these punishments he once turned briefly to his advantage. With an entrepreneurial skill that vanished almost as quickly as it arose he spent one wet school holiday writing batches of 'lines', a hundred at a time. The following term these came in handy, not only for himself but also for others, to whom he sold them at 1p per 100 lines. This worked for a while, with profitable results, until an observant Master noticed a striking similarity between several offenders' writing and that of W R Chignell. Striking might be the appropriate adjective there since, in Chig's own words, "The result was distinctly unpleasant and painful!"

The School's Officer Training Corps, with a good drum and bugle band, did win his enthusiasm. Boxing was another interest at school and, in the Spring of 1925, he reached the final of the house boxing tournament, where he came up against a more skilled opponent who trounced him, breaking his nose in the process. For one who, seemingly, hadn't made much of a mark on the school hitherto, his parents were surprised but pleased when the Headmaster informed them that "He had never thought anything of me until he realised when watching this fight that I had plenty of pluck and had a smile on my face from the beginning to end of the encounter". They had gone to see the Head to discuss what their son might do on leaving School. What they thought of this testimonial is not recorded.

Greater by far than Chig's zeal for the OTC and boxing was his passion for cricket. He won a place in the school's First XI (as he had done at Tredennyke) as a slow left-arm bowler and stubborn batsman, and was thrilled to be awarded his First XI colours in his last term at school, during which he passed his 17th birthday.

Alongside school activities he was becoming ever keener on music. His father patiently taught him the piano and to sing and, although Chig felt his slackness in practising made his father give him up as a bad job, there can be no doubt that his father had indeed sowed some seeds, good seed, which would flourish well in later years. Music was to be one of his greatest joys, with concert-going being a special treat. With a school pal, Douglas Rowe, he shared an enthusiasm for Gilbert and Sullivan, and a gramophone at home introduced him to the music of Beethoven, Wagner, Brahms, Elgar and Smetana in those adolescent years. With Rowe he had joined the church choir at St. George's where his father had become organist and choirmaster – after twenty-four years at St. John in Bedwardine – when the family moved to Thornloe Bank, Barbourne, just north of the city centre.

In Chig's unpublished autobiography, as he looked back at his schooldays, he claimed "Examinations were not all that important to your future". If current generations of parents, pupils and employers find that hard to believe, it certainly proved true in Chig's case, though there would come a time when he regretted having nothing to show for his schooldays.

He had left school without attempting School Certificate, but plainly had enough about him to impress the Manager of the Midland Bank in Malvern. Thus it was that, on 7 September 1925, dressed in bowler hat and dark suit, he set off for his first day's employment as the branch junior.

His duties included admitting staff colleagues as they arrived for work; unlocking the strong room and bringing out the Bank's ledgers along with all the cash that would be required when the branch opened for business. The previous day's blotting paper was replaced, as were nibs of pens which were becoming worn. At 10.00am precisely – 9.30am on Saturdays – he opened the main door for business to begin. With these tasks behind him his main duty was to enter every cheque received that day into the Day Book. His salary was £50 a year.

In his first days with the Bank Chig travelled to Malvern by train, opting for his bike occasionally at such times as the twice-yearly Bank balance, when staff were expected to work longer hours.

The year following Chig's commencement of gainful employment, 1926, was the year of the General Strike. Anticipating that trains might not be running, Chig's father bought him a 350cc side-valve BSA motor-bike. Colleagues of his also bought motor-bikes, and the railways lost custom they never regained. During those days of the General Strike Chig fixed to his bike a notice saying 'Malvern' or 'Worcester', depending on his direction of travel, in the hope of being able to offer a lift to an attractive young lass. All he got was a rather effeminate male hair-dresser who tried to cadge a lift every day, until Chig decided it best to vary his route.

It was around this same time that Chig took up smoking. When the Bank was closed to the public the staff were permitted to smoke, and many did. Chig opted for a pipe, which became an ever-present with him for the remainder of his life (or until his final years). He found it a soothing and calming pleasure – and a definite aid to concentration.

Church and music continued to be important to him. As organist and choirmaster at St. George's Chig's father played at four Services every Sunday, and took two choir practices each week (one for the boys and one for the full choir). It was a big commitment, which Chig lightened for him, on leaving school, by taking over the Sunday afternoon young people's Service.

The Chignell household was firmly Christian. His parents' attendance at the early morning Holy Communion services made an impression on Chig. With all the Services which required his father's attendance, and the Services his mother also regularly attended as a faithful worshipper, it might be thought they did enough. But the early morning Communion was, in a sense, their own; they could worship together, rather than one in the congregation and one in the choir stalls or at the organ stool. That they did so, and greatly valued their shared worship, began to speak to Chig, and he too became a frequent attender at this Service.

A delightful girl, Winifred Grove, helped at St. George's Sunday afternoon Service for young people, alongside Chig and others. She was a lively and amusing companion, and they became good friends. She accompanied Chig, on the back of his motor-bike, to the Three Choirs Festival in Hereford in 1927. Here, in the Cathedral, they heard

Elgar's "Dream of Gerontius" – conducted by the composer himself. It made a terrific impression on them both. Indeed Chig recognised it as a turning point in his musical life, which led him to a decision he never regretted.

He joined the Worcester Festival Choral Society, having heard that they were to perform "The Dream" – and that Elgar would conduct it. This in turn led to him singing with the chorus at the Three Choirs Festival. This long-established and prestigious music festival is staged in the Cathedrals of Gloucester, Hereford and Worcester in annual succession. Chig was a member of the chorus for the festivals in 1928, 1929 and 1930, and relished for many a day long the memories of wonderful music-making.

One incident, a remarkable story of Elgar and the Three Choirs Festival recalled by Chig, is worth recounting here, since, to my knowledge, it has not been recounted anywhere else. During the 1929 Festival, at Worcester, a young man, a keen and talented musician, approached W H Reed, the leader of the London Symphony Orchestra, and asked if he would try, and offer an opinion about, the young man's violin. With great generosity Billy Reed said he'd do better than that, he would use it in the performance that was to follow.

Edward Elgar often favoured listening to Three Choirs' concerts from the Lady Chapel, at the end of the Cathedral farthest from the orchestra and chorus, where he could hear but not see. At the end of the concert George Chignell and Elgar were talking together when they were joined by Billy Reed, one of Elgar's greatest friends. After a moment or so's conversation Elgar said to Reed: "Billy, what violin were you using tonight. It wasn't yours was it?" There had been no solo part for Reed in that evening's performance yet Elgar's finely-tuned ear incredibly had detected the difference.

Aside from work, music and church Chig's sporting interest was to the fore. He watched the County whenever he could. On leaving school he'd been keen to continue playing cricket himself, and in that first summer, he and another school pal, David Littlebury, joined Worcester City Cricket Club. They did not feel welcome. At net practice no-one took the slightest notice of two youngsters, and they were not selected for the Club's matches. It was a closed shop and Chig concluded that, in their callow youth, they probably did not fit into a side noted for its capability at post-match drinking.

Frustrations voiced among themselves during the winter months sparked an idea. They would form their own club. Chig, Douglas Rowe, David Littlebury, and Don Arbuckle, were all of one mind.

Recruiting other players was not difficult. Plenty wanted to play, though not all were talented cricketers. H F George, as an older, more experienced player, was appointed Captain, and Chig's father became its first President.

Their attempts to find a ground were unsuccessful, and so they became a nomadic side. Worcester Nomads CC was formed. The Nomads' first match in 1927 was against Norton Village CC. The players cycled out to Norton's ground, in a park, and went on to win by 7 wickets. They were not always as successful, but Worcester Nomads CC today remains a flourishing club and stands as a wonderful and continuing memorial to their vision and enthusiasm, and their great love of the game

Now, not quite twenty, content with his work at the Bank, and enjoying his music and his cricket, life was good for Chig. All seemed secure, comfortable, and stable. But other voices were calling.

3

Called

As a chorister, Chig was a regular Church attender – even if that attendance sometimes owed more to faithful duty than enthusiasm. Like many in his situation he had heard a good many sermons and, like many of those others, he had probably not *listened* to too many.

One Sunday morning, towards the end of 1928, he settled down into his seat in the choir to have, in his words, " … a lazy time of non-attention to the Vicar's sermon".

The Rev'd D W Maclagan, a dry Scot who, earlier, had been a missionary doctor before entering the priesthood, was speaking about the work of the Bush Brothers in Australia. He was on familiar territory as he enlightened his congregation about the Anglican priests who serve the isolated farmsteads and homes in the Outback, travelling vast distances on horse-back. It was a tough life.

Whether it was the subject matter or the way it was delivered, Chig suddenly found himself – in the middle of the Vicar's sermon – with a strange overpowering feeling, one he'd never experienced before. Whatever it was, however it had come, it was telling him that he had to be ordained. Such was his conviction he could scarcely wait until the end of the Service to tackle Mr Maclagan. With another Service to take, the Vicar could not see him then and suggested Chig should call on him a day or two later.

Come the appointment and with no fore-knowledge of what his visitor wanted, his Vicar asked Chig what he could do for him. Eschewing any preliminary small-talk, Chig blurted out "I think God wants me to be a priest". "Great Scott!" was the Vicar's amazed, if hardly tactful, response. But then, with the wisdom of a good man, he helped Chig unpack his thoughts. "Come back next week", he said, after listening patiently and interestedly to what Chig had to say. "Pray, come back, and we'll see what God has said to us both".

After a week of much prayer Chig returned to the Vicarage, convinced that he was being called, and was relieved to find his Vicar equally convinced.

It was time to tell his parents and, at Rev'd Maclagan's suggestion, immediately to hand in his resignation at the Bank. That would be a real test of his calling.

Returning home Chig found his father in the music room and told him his news, and also discussed with him what he felt would be a real problem, funding his training. On hearing the news, his father's face lit up: "This is wonderful, old boy, come on, we must go and tell Mother. And then I'll tell you something that happened only this morning".

Unsurprisingly Mrs Chignell – whose Christian faith was lived out in a very practical way, faithfully and loyally supporting her husband and family and visiting needy families in the parish, especially poorer families in the slum areas typical of Worcester in those years – declared the news to be marvellous, and warmly hugged her son again and again. Together they then told Chig about a letter they had received that very morning from cousin Mildred. Mildred was about the only wealthy member of the family and she, generously, had previously helped meet the cost of Chig's sister Margaret's nursing training. Since the completion of Margaret's training Mildred had directed her financial support to another trainee nurse. This young lady's instruction was now completed and, out of the blue, Mildred had written wondering if there was anyone else she could help.

The Chignells wrote directly to Mildred, parents and son feeling that God's hand was at work here, for he does move in mysterious ways his wonders to perform! Mildred, thrilled at their news, was delighted to help, making it abundantly clear that nothing would give her greater pleasure than to fund Rowland's training.

Following his Vicar's surprising but wise counsel Chig, on 12 December 1928, gave the Bank one month's notice of his intention of resigning. Whether the swiftness of that action seemed entirely wise to Chig, it is certain that he did it with conviction, confident in the advice he'd been given. How long that confidence remained may be questioned, for his earlier lack of enthusiasm for examination success at school now became a concern and a hurdle.

Two attempts to get into Selwyn, his father's old college, failed as did a subsequent attempt for Hatfield College, Durham. With things getting desperate Selwyn College allowed him one more attempt, on the understanding he would not take up a place there but simply obtain the equivalent of Matriculation. This would open the door to training at a theological college, and Sarum Theological College, at Salisbury, was happy to take him.

The belated pursuit of examination success and the search for a training place occupied the best part of two years, during which he lived at home. With time on his hands he played a great deal of cricket with the Nomads club, and spent many a happy hour watching Worcestershire at their New Road ground. In one of these seasons he captained the Nomads and, long after, recalled an amusing incident when he was bowling. He appealed for a catch behind the wicket: "Owzat?". The umpire looked solicitously at the batsman: "Did you 'it it, Bill?" "No" replied Bill. "That's not out then!" declared the umpire.

There were other brief diversions in Chig's wait to take up his college place. He spent two winter terms at Tormore School, Deal, as an assistant master, in order to earn some money during the frustrating extended wait to begin his studies. He swiftly concluded he was not a 'natural' as a teacher. He decided, too, that east Kent in winter, with its intense cold biting wind was the worst place in England.

It was a relief, at last, to begin his studies and he was delighted to find that his old school pal, Douglas "Tiny" Rowe, was to begin at Sarum at the same time, after completing his degree at Durham.

They travelled south anticipating this would be a period of extreme holiness and 'goody-goodiness' among pasty-faced students of the kind the stage often delights in portraying as clergymen. Reality proved far better than imagination, and they found themselves among a group of lively, talented and remarkable fellow students.

Discipline and petty restrictions aside, Chig found college life full of fun and, alongside work, he found time to play cricket and hockey. Fives was played in the winter and, for some, there was tennis in the summer but the college's main summer game seems to have been Sarum croquet. As the chief object appeared to be to hit their opponent's ball to the furthest point this was not croquet as the pukka players knew it.

There was work too. For those students, like Chig, who were there for three years there was, alongside much good and useful practical training and experience of worship and leading worship, the General Ordination Examination to be passed. After 18 months in college, Part I (consisting of Old Testament, New Testament, Doctrine, Worship, Church History, Latin, and Greek New Testament) was tackled, with Part II (extensions of the same subjects but with Latin and Greek New Testament replaced by Ethics and the Epistles) taken as their college days drew to a close.

Chig's Part I results suggested his academic progress was much the same as at King's School; he was doing just enough. "I just managed to scrape through," he said, "by the skin of my teeth".

In fairness to Chig, and to his continuing love of cricket, it might be right to make a brief diversion here to look at his cricket that summer. During the vacation he played for the Old Vigornians (King's School's Old Boys) against the School XI, and took all 7 wickets that fell. In fact he played against the School's XI three times that summer and, in one game against them, playing for the Nomads, he recorded his only century, the first scored for the club he had helped found. These were pleasing interludes before the serious work of completing his studies got under way again.

A newly motivated Chig successfully negotiated Part II of GOE with immensely better results. His post-exam interview with his Principal was an encouraging and affirming consultation, at the end of which he discussed with Chig his "title". An ordinand's "title" is the parish to which he is appointed at ordination. It is also very much about the parish priest to whom he is appointed, with whom he will work, and who will be such an influence in the early days of his ministry.

Canon Dimont, his College Principal, knew "just the right man", and the right parish for Chig. It was a parish "up north". This would valuably offer a vastly different experience from that Chig had encountered hitherto. More importantly the Rev'd Harold Lancaster Taylor, Vicar of St.Matthew's, Lightcliffe, in the diocese of Wakefield was, in Dimont's eyes, a first-rate trainer of young clerics.

Memories are amazing things, and it's always surprising the minutiae that they sometimes unveil. Of that first interview with Canon Taylor Chig remembered so much – including the fact that on the morning of his meeting, he discovered he had forgotten his razor. Staying overnight with an uncle in Cheshire, he asked to borrow his uncle's razor. But Uncle used an old-fashioned cut-throat razor, and Chig managed to cut himself so many times that, with the amount of cotton wool used to staunch the bleeding, he went to breakfast looking like Father Christmas! A call at a barber's in Manchester en route to Lightcliffe provided a tidier shave, but he arrived at Harold Taylor's vicarage still resembling an escaped client of Sweeney Todd.

The Taylors were delighted to see him, and made him warmly welcome. Even better, Harold Taylor made it abundantly clear that he would welcome Chig onto his staff as an Assistant Curate.

As he returned to Sarum for his final term he knew, subject to the approval of the Bishop of Wakefield, he would serve his title in Lightcliffe.

James Seaton, Bishop of Wakefield, readily gave his approval, and ordained Chig in Wakefield Cathedral on Christmas Eve 1933. The Taylors had kindly invited Chig's parents to stay with them so that they could attend the ordination. Both families afterwards had lunch together, before returning to Lightcliffe where, that same evening, at the first Evensong of Christmas, the newly ordained Curate read a Lesson. He was also required to be part of the Solemn Procession, processing round the church with the choir and his fellow clergy, very conscious – and somewhat embarrassed – that the eyes of a large congregation were taking in their new Curate. His life of ministry and, particularly, his ministry "up north" had begun.

"Up north" was foreign country to Chig. It was a part of the world, and a people, he quickly came to love, greatly aided and encouraged by the Rev'd Harold Taylor and his wife, and their family of two sons and two daughters. Mrs Taylor, in Chig's memory, was "a big woman in every sense, quite tall and with utter Christian dedication to her Lord, her husband and family and to the people of Lightcliffe". She, like her husband, had a wonderful sense of humour. Chig quickly felt at home.

His time at Lightcliffe stayed happily in Chig's memory for the remainder of his life. So too did his clerical formation under Harold Taylor's wise and experienced guidance. Alongside the normal and extensive duties of a curate serving in the parish's two churches, he taught in the C of E junior and senior schools (sometimes trying to teach the elements of Christianity to 60 or 70 children at a time, when two classes were joined together) and in the church's two Sunday schools, and entered fully into the parish's social life. Much, perhaps most, of his time was spent visiting.

In his first year in Lightcliffe Chig joined the local cricket club. Lightcliffe CC played in the renowned Bradford League and, though it had been going through a bad time for a couple of seasons, he thought it would be good to keep up his own cricket. Even if he wasn't selected it would be good to practise in the nets and he'd enjoy watching. It would widen, too, the circle of people he knew in the parish – always good for a Curate.

Somewhat to his surprise he was asked to play in the First XI near the beginning of the season. A useful 27 batting down the order encouraged his captain to put him in first in the next game. As he and his partner walked out to bat he noticed the opposing opening bowler was a very tall, thin man. He also noted he was very elderly. Chig supposed there might be plenty of scoring opportunities.

The venerable bowler ran gently to the wicket, over came his right arm, venomously high and straight, and the ball thudded ominously into the wicket-keeper's gloves without the batsman getting a sniff of it. Chig had not seen the ball. This scenario was repeated with both the second and third balls of the over. The fourth ball was different. Rather than the sound of the ball hitting the keeper's gloves there was a rattle of timber and, with his stumps in disarray, Chig withdrew to the pavilion.

"Sorry, Skipper", Chig said to his captain, "Who the blazes is the old fellow?"

"Didn't tha' know?" grinned the captain. "That's Syd Barnes". Chig may not have *recognised* the sixty-year old Barnes but, keen cricket statistician that he was, he *knew* that Sydney Barnes was considered one of the greatest bowlers the game has known, his 189 Test Match wickets costing him a paltry 16.43 and his 719 first-class wickets costing little more. Most cricketers and students of the game in that period in which Barnes played were agreed he was the bowler of the century. He continued to play to a great age, some believing that he cannily preferred the reward and comparative sloth of Saturday league matches to the continuous daily toil of county cricket.

Though he didn't recognise Barnes as he ran up to the wicket to bowl to him, Chig reckoned that "Chignell, bowled Barnes 0" was definitely an acceptable and note-worthy addition to his cricketing pedigree!

The story has an amusing sequel. Years later, at Worcestershire County Cricket Club, Chig met Barnes in the Committee Room where both were watching Worcestershire play the Australians. Chig diffidently reminded Barnes of the event at Lightcliffe, memorable to Chig but utterly unmemorable for the older and hugely experienced player. Barnes listened politely and impassively to Chig's recollection and then, with a twinkle in his eyes, said "I must have been a bit off form that day for you to have lasted so long!".

Chig's career with Lightcliffe was short-lived, not because of his paucity of runs against Barnes but because Saturdays were seldom free. Weddings, and parish events and diocesan meetings often filled his Saturdays, so cricket took a back seat for a while.

Chig's love of music continued to grow, as he built his record collection. With Friday as his day off, and also the day when Bradford Festival Choral Society rehearsed, he took a voice test for them and was able to join the Society. When he wasn't singing with them he often went to the cinema, in part because his college training (backed by advice from Harold Taylor) had lauded the merits of getting away from things and getting out of the parish on his day off. As Bradford offered two cinemas he often saw an afternoon film in one, an early evening in the other and then had a light supper before choral practices. He reckoned he ate a good many herring roes on toast on those days off!

Warmly welcomed though Chig was by the parish he, like many young curates before and since, found that he didn't get too many invitations out. Would-be hosts were diffident about getting "too familiar" or they believed a curate's waking hours were already wholly filled. One young couple who *did* invite him for supper and for other hospitality was Arthur and Olga Hirst. He, a solicitor in Halifax, had been a good cricketer and rugby player, and both of them were leading members of Halifax Thespians. Olga was a lively and friendly hostess. Both were good and faithful supporters of the church though Chig was amused by Arthur who always seemed to adopt an expression which suggested "he was there under duress".

Olga was the elder daughter of the late Col. Bottomley. His widow lived in Lightcliffe in a charming old stone house called Helliwell Syke, along with her other daughter, Pauline, who was Captain of Lightcliffe's Guides as well as a Sunday School teacher. Pauline was slim and fair with grey eyes and, though quiet, she had a fascinating laugh and a lovely speaking voice. All of this Chig noted as he got to know the family.

When with all the family on one occasion, Chig heard them talk about Worcester, where the Bottomleys had lived for a year or two at the beginning of World War I. Their talk spread to reminiscences of the pageants staged at Worcester's Theatre Royal by Sir Arthur and Lady Carlton. One of these was the scene of Chig's part of clock-advancer and class Dunce. Pauline Bottomley remembered the Dunce, for she too had appeared in the pageant. She, the fair-haired little girl who had stood out in Chig's memory, had been one of the 'angels' not 'Angles'. Twenty years on the Dunce and the Angel had met again.

The autumn of 1934 saw Pauline and a cousin head off to South Africa to visit relations there. Chig found that absence did indeed make the heart grow fonder, and he missed her greatly. He would have liked them to marry immediately but his stipend was only £210 a year (it rose to £220 the following year); it was enough for a curate to live on, but not enough for a clergyman and his wife.

In the summer months they played tennis together and their joint love of music proved another bond between them. In 1935 they signed up for a series of four autumn subscription concerts to be given in Bradford by the Hallé Orchestra. The concert on 22 November was by Myra Hess, who played Brahms Variations on a Theme by Handel and Beethoven's last Piano Sonata. Whether Chig was moved by the music or by other things he felt bold enough to propose. Pauline joyfully accepted. Sometime later she told Chig that, at that First Evensong of Christmas, his first Service in the parish, her eyes had alighted on the new Curate and the thought passed through her mind that if she was to marry she hoped it would be someone like him.

Chig and Pauline married on 10 June 1936, with a packed church, full choir, and a guard of honour formed by the Guides. The reception was small, to avoid any heart-searching among parishioners and because they wanted to hold it at Helliwell Syke. They began their honeymoon with dinner at The Feathers hotel, in Ludlow, before staying at the Green Dragon, Hereford. From there they motored to Woody Bay to

Chig and Pauline on their wedding day, 10 June 1936.

enjoy the quiet of north Devon with its wooded valleys and fine scenery at its high summer best – but not before making one diversion. Chig persuaded Pauline that they might visit Exeter so he could see the GWR Cornish Riviera express, the steam train pulled by a King Class locomotive. Not everyone's idea of a honeymoon essential but, for Chig, it was a sight never to be forgotten.

On his marriage Chig took up the post of Senior Curate of Huddersfield Parish Church, but in charge of St Mark's in Leeds Road. They rented a house in Wentworth Street, number 13. It was one of a row of "solid houses, built of stone and black with years of industrial grime". At some stage it had been used as a private school, and the Chignells had to convert its three storeys (with a basement which, initially, housed their kitchen) back to its original use, to make it more convenient for them and for their maid. Yes, they had a maid in those days, such was the expectation for clergy families.

Chig's new Vicar was Canon Arthur Leeper, a "fine-looking well-built Irishman". He provided a marked contrast to Harold Taylor who, soon after Chig left Lightcliffe, had been made an honorary Canon of Wakefield Cathedral. Whereas the latter disliked change – to the extent he preached the same (or similar) sermons on the same Sundays each year – Canon Leeper, according to Chig, "had no use for anything that had served its purpose". Whilst Taylor had been adept at smoothing the ruffled feathers of difficult or challenging parishioners, Leeper tended to be impatient with them and would tell them what he thought about them. Though different they were also complementary in the sound training and valuable experience they provided for Chig, who concluded "As far as the continuation of my training was concerned no-one could have been better to follow Canon Taylor than Canon Leeper". His life-long regard and respect for these two men was genuine and boundless.

Chig was the senior of *three* curates serving Huddersfield Parish Church in those inter-War years. Splendidly sited, in the centre of town, St. Peter's church, with its gallery on three sides, could seat 2,000, which it often did for major Services and civic occasions. St. Mark's, for which Chig was primarily responsible, had been built in the 1870s, by the parishioners of St. Peter's, "in the very snobby days", when they preferred the poor of the parish to worship elsewhere! It stood in a slum area with the gas works close by and "a filthy canal running, or rather stagnating, close by". St Mark's had a huge advantage in having a good parish hall, which was extensively used for parish and other social events.

Among them was "a magnificent Guides Company that won just about every award possible".

On the countless occasions he walked to St Mark's church hall for a Saturday evening function Chig noticed that the police often patrolled in pairs and, one evening, he tackled them about this. "Well," said the sergeant, "it's tricky on Saturdays for there are so many Irishmen who drink too much and get quarrelsome, and you and the Roman Catholic priest are the only folk who come down here on your own on Saturday nights".

Life for Chig was full, with Services in both churches, church and other social events galore, youth clubs and Bible classes, the staging of plays and other entertainments, the annual sales of work and fetes, and, of course, parish visiting which fruitfully accounted for a huge proportion of clergy time in those days.

With a large population there were many baptisms to conduct and one Wednesday evening, when Chig was on 'baptism duty', expecting to conduct three christenings, he found there was to be a fourth. A young woman had come on her own carrying a very young baby. Chig took her quietly aside to seek her details and discover the baby's names, and was taken aback to discover the infant had been born that very day. Nevertheless he was delighted that the young woman had come along. She was a member of a travelling circus, and had walked three-quarters of a mile to church to ensure her baby could be baptised. Her husband was performing at the circus that evening, which was why she had come alone, and they were to move on the next day.

Weddings featured highly on the task-list for the young curates, especially at Easter and Whitsun. "We had a great many," Chig recalled, "On some Saturdays one of us would have up to five or even six". The curate who had earlier interviewed a couple and discussed with them their wedding plans might not always be the one conducting their wedding.

One Sunday evening early in January 1937 Chig received a call from his father to tell him his mother was very ill. Bronchitis had suddenly taken a turn for the worse. He travelled down overnight, and reached their home early on Monday morning. (George and Mary had moved to Lillington, near Leamington Spa, in rural Warwickshire, to be nearer Chig's sister, Robin, and her husband) His mother was well enough to greet him: "How lovely of you to come, Rowland darling" but she soon slipped into sleep, the sleep of death.

Mary Chignell was buried at Lillington. Chig's memories of her were of one who was "not only a beautiful woman in her youth, but retained a beauty of face all her life, as her magnificent, loving and gentle character shone in her eyes. An utterly convinced Christian, she always seemed to put others next to God and herself last. Thus she was a constantly happy person, despite many difficult times through which she and Father guided their family. She faced death when it came, quite happy to trust in her Saviour and to leave us all in his care".

Chig was encouraged, too, in the way his father responded: "Father was marvellous. They had been a wonderful inspiration to us in their love for each other. His sense of loneliness must have been awful to bear, yet he rarely referred to it. Added to that, was the fact that he had every reason for wanting his beloved wife close to him as his sight deteriorated. Then there was the sorrow of having to give up their comfy little house. The Robins (Chig's sister Robin – or Bobbie – and her husband Robin) had plenty of room and gladly gave him two rooms for himself in their home at Kineton".

As the awful between-Wars years of unemployment (devastatingly felt 'up north') were passing there came a more menacing threat, on a wider scale, with the steady and ominous growth of Nazi power in Germany, under the lead of Adolf Hitler. As he hoodwinked his own people, as well as other nations and statesmen, some spoke out against his threat. Some, like Winston Churchill in our own country, were considered scare-mongers and – initially – went unheeded.

However, by the mid-Thirties, the beginnings of a Civil Defence service were in place, plans that advanced after Neville Chamberlain returned from Munich in 1938, waving a piece of paper and declared "Peace in our time". In Huddersfield Chig, as Curate seeking to set a good example, joined the organisation – "if one could call it that" he said. Gas masks, carried over the shoulder in cloth bags, were issued. The local district Civil Defence branch met fortnightly which, looking back from this distance in time, suggests the perceived urgency of the threat was not immediately apparent. Instruction for the branch included how to deal with bombs and incendiaries, and how to manage people in the area of such attacks. The branch was issued with gas capes, rattles (like football supporters' rattles), whistles and various other bits of kit with which to warn and protect the local populace.

On the night of Sunday 3 September 1939, the day when, over the wireless, Prime Minister Chamberlain had told the nation that as Herr Hitler had not replied to the United Kingdom's protest over his invasion of Poland, Britain had declared war on Germany, air raid alarms sounded in Huddersfield. Chig leapt out of bed, remembering not to put on the light (for blackout regulations were already in place), and pulled on his trousers. In his haste, and in the dark, he put them on back-to-front and needed to restore the situation before, momentarily delayed, he reported for duty. His branch had only one set of equipment and so, as he later remembered, that night he "set out to meet the might of Germany armed with a whistle" as his ration of the branch's kit.

Whilst holidaying in Scotland in late summer – Chig's father was with them – a very efficient postal service (even in the Highlands), had brought an unexpected letter from Herefordshire. The Archdeacon of Ludlow, Archdeacon Dixon, had written offering Chig the living of Cressage, a small rural village in the Diocese of Hereford, though actually in that part of the diocese which embraces huge swathes of south Shropshire.

In those years it was not 'done' for a clergyman (and they were then all men) to apply for a post. Preferment came by invitation or by recommendation. Chig never really knew how Archdeacon Dixon came to hear about him, but here he was inviting him to take on his first parish as Vicar. Exciting though this was, it required prayer on the part of the Chignells, the completion of their holiday, and consultation with Canon Leeper.

A visit to Cressage confirmed for Chig and for Pauline the rightness of acceptance. They loved their first impressions of the place and both felt they were being called to go there. Chig wrote and accepted the living, which was shortly to be united with the neighbouring parish of Sheinton.

His institution and induction (the dear old C of E has some lovely titles for such events and processes, all historically, legally, correct but somehow 'other worldly'!) was planned for 20 September 1939, barely three weeks after Prime Minister Chamberlain's profound and universally life-changing announcement that Britain was at war with Germany. Canon Leeper advised Chig that he and Pauline should get to Cressage as soon as possible, as it was anticipated transport and travel would become problematical fairly quickly. They booked furniture vans from Jim Hoyle's Removals, but were warned that the vehicles might be commandeered by the Army. With help from Pauline's mother and sister everything was swiftly packed and the loaded vans headed for south Shropshire.

Chig and Pauline set off by train, but already war planning markedly upset established timetables. A much-interrupted journey saw them at one stage sitting for three hours on the platform at Crewe, the country's busiest station outside London, without seeing a solitary train. Eventually they reached Shrewsbury to find, in its siding, the 5.30pm Severn Valley train. Chig decided "The train driver had either not been told there was a war on or that he wasn't going to be stopped by the ruddy Germans!"

On arriving – on time – in Cressage the Chignells walked to Old Hall to collect the vicarage keys from Percy Baldwin, one of the Churchwardens. Baldwin, "a fine old man", had earlier been head of the great woollen mill in Huddersfield, Paton and Baldwin's. He had a great many Huddersfield friends and relations. Had they spoken to Percy about Chig? Had Percy Baldwin been the instigation of the Archdeacon's invitation to Chig? The new Vicar never knew. No matter. After collecting the keys from Percy they headed off down the drive towards their new home, just as Jim Hoyle's vans passed by. The removal men were "simply marvellous" and very efficient, and the Chignells were soon settled and at home in The Vicarage.

Little did they realise that for the next thirty-four years (war service excepted) Chig would remain a priest in the Diocese of Hereford and that, for them both, the diocese and county would be 'home' for the next half-century.

Cressage, the Chignells new home, was a small village on the north-facing slopes of Wenlock Edge, four miles north of Much Wenlock and some nine miles south of Shrewsbury. It was most definitely part of beautiful south Shropshire and yet, ecclesiastically, it was part of the Diocese of Hereford, which embraced the whole of Herefordshire, extended out into the Welsh Marches, eastwards across to parts of Worcestershire, and northwards into south Shropshire almost to Shrewsbury and to Ironbridge, Broseley and Coalbrookdale nestling against modern-day Telford.

The village, with its population of 250, was served by a school, pub, two shops, a post office, bakery, and blacksmith's forge, and a resident doctor (though, in this rural spot, his bailiwick extended far beyond the village). There was the church too, of course.

Sheinton, which lay barely a mile eastwards of Cressage, along the banks of the River Severn, would soon also come under Chig's wing. It was a parish of just 89 people – and yet was the biggest parish in which Chig's predecessor, the Rev'd W W Gawn, had ever served! As well as its own church, Sheinton also had a village school.

The Vicarage at Cressage, a well-built house in a garden of excellent size, had been built just before the First World War. The Chignells were delighted with their new home and, not least, with its splendid garden. Years after, Chig recalled the wonderful fruit trees there, and the delicious crops they produced. "Whoever planned this house and garden knew his job and also a lot about plums!", he recalled, "We had a number of gorgeous plums, beginning with Early Prolific, passing through Victorias, Kirk's Blue, Pond's Seedling, Cambridge Gage, Transparent Gage to the supreme plum, in our estimation, Coe's Golden Drop. There were other culinary species, too numerous to mention. Then there were the excellent apples – Worcester Pearmain, Lane's Prince Albert, Grannie (*Did Chig mean Granny Smith perhaps?*), Newton Wonder, Peasgood Nonesuch, Cox's Orange and Bramley Seedlings among others. Whoever saw a more beautiful apple than Peasgood Nonesuch?"

The Chignells seemed to have landed on their feet, but Chig did wonder if he had been properly – and legally – admitted to the living. Even in those very early war-time days transport had become disrupted, or folk anticipated problematical or interrupted journeys and so were reluctant to travel unnecessarily. For such reasons Bishop Lisle Carr, Bishop of Hereford, felt unable to travel up to Cressage from the Bishop's Palace in Hereford. Chig therefore was instituted and inducted to his first 'living' by the newly-appointed Archdeacon of Ludlow, deputising for the Bishop, and by Prebendary Peake, the Rural Dean and Rector of nearby Berrington, who filled the part the Archdeacon would otherwise have taken. As this was the first such ceremony at which Archdeacon Whately had officiated, and as Prebendary Peake was extremely deaf, some parts of the Service were duplicated and others, unintentionally, omitted. Chig claimed he gave the right answers and affirmations at the right points in the Service, so he supposed all was well – in the end.

Very early on in his time at Cressage and Sheinton Chig recognised there was a profound difference between rural ministry and that in towns and cities. In his country parishes he could "easily get to know every parishioner. The work was extremely personal. I knew far more about them, and they knew far more about me, than was ever the case in town or suburbia, as Lightcliffe was, in effect. I found I was concerned with many of the ordinary events of village life. This meant that I met and chatted with people in a very ordinary and natural way. I was one of them.

"Almost invariably there were others who knew a great deal more about the subject under consideration than I did. This was extremely good for me, as it must be for any young priest. One of the great temptations is to think we (clergy) know more than others. 'Priest and people' too often gets translated as though the priest was the officer and the people the other ranks. This may have been the usual state of affairs in the days of the 'squarson' but it certainly is not so today," he reflected.

It was a revelation and recognition which ever after stood him in good stead. He took to rural ministry like the proverbial duck to water and, one diversion and war-time service apart, spent the rest of his ministry in this field.

The people of Cressage and Sheinton took to their new Vicar with similar ease, and greatly valued his ministry among them. He was immensely fortunate in his first Churchwardens, Percy Baldwin and Mr H T Evans. Chig never knew the latter's Christian name. 'Mr Evans' to everyone, he was the schoolmaster, "probably the finest Headmaster I have ever known" Chig declared. "A very quiet, friendly, slow-moving man, he was utterly unflappable. He never spoke in class, or anywhere else, at more than 'mezzo-piano', and this produced superb discipline". Both Wardens were committed Christians who provided tremendous support for Chig and he owed much to their wise and kindly advice and counsel – and, sometimes, diplomatic and discreet correction!

Another source of sage advice and friendship was the Rev'd Adrian Stokes, in the neighbouring parish of Acton Burnell. To Chig he was "a saintly priest, with wisdom and a sense of humour. He had been a Bush Brother in Queensland, and was a man to whom I could go and discuss what to do, how to deal with various problems, and who gave me of his time and wisdom without stint. What he shared was of inestimable value to me". The Chignells enjoyed Stokes' visits when he cycled over to Cressage and called on them before catching a train to go shopping in Shrewsbury.

In his time in Cressage and Sheinton congregations grew. In part this was due to Chig's initiatives of starting a choir at Sheinton Church and building up the choir at Cressage. He started a youth club, and his endeavours to reach out to, and involve, the young people were well-received – by them and by others supportive of his initiatives. His organist at Sheinton, Jim Tilsley, said to him one day: "You've done the right thing, Vicar, for the young. What I always say is that if us old 'uns aren't saved yet you won't do it!"

He worked hard to combine the two parishes which, initially, had not welcomed this coming together. Folk at Sheinton in particular were concerned, fearing they would become the junior partner. Chig was determined this would not happen, not least because Sheinton was in fact the older of the two parishes, Cressage having been carved out of the neighbouring parish of Cound in the more recent past. He arranged for both parishes to have two Services each Sunday and this, and his constant visiting and other pastoral work, drew them happily together

About a year or so after arriving in the parishes, Chig was appointed a Diocesan Inspector of Religious Studies. This required him to make a visit annually to a number of Church of England schools in the north of the diocese, to assess the school's religious teaching and assess, too, its Christian ethos. Dedicating a week to the task he would cycle between schools, and stay locally, often with the local clergy. It was a task he enjoyed enormously, getting to know small schools, some of them in remote areas, as well as one or two larger ones in the more urban areas. He was constantly delighted to find splendid work being done by teachers who were dedicated to their profession and to the children in their care. He only ever felt called to make two poor reports.

One was in a school where the local vicar was a senior, and pompous, member of the Diocesan Board of Religious Education, who regularly visited his local school to conduct worship and teach RE. Chig found the worship offered the children was "dreadful, hurried, quite over the heads of the children and thoroughly uninspiring. The religious teaching in the school apparently was also uninspiring, for the children knew little and seemed not the slightest bit interested". His report reflected his findings, resulting in a great row within the DBRE, but Chig stuck to his guns and not one word of his report was changed.

A small school in a very remote village attracted his other poor report. He stayed with the parish's vicar the evening before his visit. Determinedly tactful though his colleague was, Chig picked up the vibes that the vicar's relationship with the school (or rather the school's relationship with him) was not all he wished it to be. It seemed the vicar was not welcome in school and the Headteacher was wont to make uncomplimentary remarks about him to the children. All this Chig confirmed for himself next day. The morning's opening worship contained no prayers and the Head's talk had little, if anything, to do with Christianity. The staff appeared to walk in fear of the Head, and religious teaching in the school was poor. There was no need for Chig to sell his soul in reporting on what he found. A scathing report led to the Head subsequently receiving a monumental dressing down from the Local Education Authority and also from the National Union of Teachers.

When, a year hence, Chig re-visited the school he anticipated the Headteacher would be fiercely antagonistic or, alternatively, sickeningly ingratiating. He was in for a surprise! On his arrival, the Head invited Chig into his study and, in the most generous, but sincere and warm manner, thanked Chig for what he had done. The Head recognised what a fool he had been and saw the error of his ways. Chig's inspection amply confirmed the change of heart and attitude. The Head's relationship with the Vicar was now excellent, and they had formed a good working partnership. The whole atmosphere of the school, and the quality of teaching, had improved dramatically.

Alongside this role, Chig was fulfilling all the normal tasks of a dedicated country parson, conducting choir practices – for girls, for boys, for the full choir – along with his organists; confirmation classes for children and adults were held; the PCCs (Parochial Church Councils) had to be chaired and parish finances kept on an even keel and, of course, parish visiting featured very high on his agenda. That resounding and firm rat-tat-tat on cottage doors became a familiar, and welcomed, sound around the parishes.

The onset of war brought additional commitments too. He dutifully joined the Local Defence Volunteers (which soon evolved into the Home Guard). On the basis of his earlier signalling experience in King's School's Officer Training Corps, he was immediately regarded as the Volunteers' 'expert' in this sphere. One task of Cressage's LDV was to keep an eye out for enemy parachutists or any other suspicious occurrences. They created a dug-out on Kenley Bank, which provided a terrific view across the Shropshire Plain. Chig's signalling system – using flags (high tech this was not!) – gave the potential to send warnings to those 'higher-ups' who made decisions about such things, but the system was rarely tested. At one stage, when the expected invasion of Britain seemed imminent, the local LDV manned the dug-out post every night. Chig's watch, of four men, included the local poacher and, as Chig recalled "We frequently returned with something pleasant to help out the rations!"

The LDV-Home Guard made their HQ in the village hall, a reconstructed army hut of World War I vintage. Farming folk and gamekeepers could offer their own shotguns as weapons whilst others had to rely on pikes, scythes or stout sticks until the War Office provided more regulation weaponry.

In their planning, preparations and exercises the vulnerability of the Home Guard's HQ had frequently been questioned. Chig's poacher friend held out a challenge. He reckoned he could get from his home four miles away to the Home Guard HQ without being detected. The only conditions he set were that no-one should be stationed within a quarter-mile of his home (he had to get out, after all, if the exercise was to be effective) and those guarding the HQ should not exceed four in number. The challenge was accepted. The poacher won hands down! He got to the HQ from home without once being spotted – but he was able to name all the Home Guard members he had passed on his way. Chig learned a valuable lesson: "Never despise a true poacher – he's far smarter than you!"

To those living in remoter areas like south Shropshire the early months of the war seemed very strange, with so little fighting taking place in the likely battle zones, and thus so little news, yet with much preparation and morale-building propaganda still going on. Chig felt it was like the opening rounds of a boxing match "with two boxers sparring with only an occasional feint here or there" as they sussed out each other's strengths, capabilities and weaknesses. But even on the edge of the Shropshire hills, in this phoney war time, they were heartened when the Royal Navy put the pocket battleship Graf Spee, Germany's heavily-armed warship, out of action in the battle of the River Plate.

Alongside his parochial and community activities there were still daily chores for the country parson. The Vicarage had no mains water supply, and so water came from a well, by pump, and from the rainwater supply.

For relaxation Pauline and Chig played much tennis with other couples in the village, and he also played cricket. Unlike some other cricket clubs which, during the war, had to be moth-balled when denuded of players and without fuel for machinery, Cound Cricket Club was able to maintain its cricket programme. In part this was because of a number of Army and RAF camps and stations in the area. It was deemed good for morale that the men serving there should be able to keep up their sporting activities. This meant, too, that the cricket club received a petrol ration so its machinery could be used to maintain the ground. Cound CC was an above-average club, drawing players from Cound, Cressage and also from Shrewsbury, as well as from the Service units.

With men going off to War, and the growing demand for locally-produced food, many women worked on the land, some with the Land Army. Pauline played her part, working at Park Farm, run by John Wainwright, who later became one of Chig's Churchwardens. John and his wife 'Tommy' were among the Chignells' tennis friends. Pauline became a useful thistle potcher, sugar-beet hoe-er, potato-setter and harvester – all for the princely and hourly sum of a half-penny (old money – about 0.2 pence per hour in new money)!

In late autumn 1940 the patron of the living at Cressage, James Thursby-Pelham, with his cousin Dorothy, moved from London to live at The Lodge. Dorothy had previously worked with the Ministry of Agriculture and Fisheries and, to encourage home food production, she helped set up a Red Cross Garden Show and a Pig Club. Although the Chignells kept hens and ducks in the Vicarage garden there was no pig sty, but they were determined to join the Pig Club and to keep their own pig. Bill Smith, the village blacksmith, let them keep their pig in one of his fields. This meant an addition to Chig's daily clerical, pastoral and household duties, as he staggered down the road carrying two enormous feed buckets with household food waste and pig meal.

Keeping a pig was one thing. Killing it was another. A licensed slaughterer from Much Wenlock despatched their pig in the backyard of the Vicarage. Once the pig was dead, Chig resumed pig-keeper's duties putting the carcase in a copper full of boiling water to scald off its hairs. With some more expert butchering and jointing provided by the slaughter-man, Chig dealt with the innards to be used for sausage meat, pork pies and an excellent supply of lard, before salting the hams and bacon. None of this diminished his appetite in the slightest, and he lunched on "a super casserole of pig's liver, onions and potatoes and so on". He proudly took some to Pauline who was in bed with 'flu. Apparently she turned green and, for the moment, declined the porcine delights!

News of Cressage's Pig Club spread, and even reached the BBC in Birmingham. Dorothy Thursby-Pelham, the club's instigator, was asked to give a talk on air for the

BBC Home Service. Gamely she drafted notes for this, but then got cold feet. Who went in her place? Parson Chignell.

The need to maintain local food production saw Chig also temporarily giving a hand to the village baker, Arthur Cole, when his two assistants went off to war. Baking started at 5.30am each day and Chig would arrive a little earlier to clean the bread tins and prepare them for the dough. He helped roll out the dough mixture before loading the ovens and, later, removed the tins and baked bread. By 8 o'clock it was time for a cup of tea and a cake or two – there had to be some perks! – before Arthur and a young widow, Freda, set off on the first of their two rounds.

Life as a country parson thus was full, and especially so with the added dimensions created on the home front in war-time Britain.

Soon after moving to Cressage Chig began writing a regular letter to his father. George Chignell, after his wife's death, had moved to live with his daughter Robin and son-in-law at Kineton, in the midst of rural Warwickshire countryside bounded by Banbury, Warwick, Leamington Spa and Stratford-upon-Avon. One senses Chig intended they should be weekly letters, but 83 letters in four years suggests that, despite best intentions, he strayed from the target. To be fair, Chig may indeed have written regularly to his father long before moving to Cressage and may have written more frequently whilst there, but the bundle later returned to him by his father (to allow Chig to read the letters again, and to reflect on the times of which he had written) had gaps.

The letters, on small A5 paper and typed, were full of news from the Vicarage and about life in Chig's new parishes. The letters tell the story, and paint a social history, of an archetypal newly-instituted, newly-married young (young-ish) country parson. They paint, too, a picture of rural life in war-time Britain. For both reasons they are important, and deserve to be more widely read.

It's time to let Chig's letters speak for themselves.

4

Letters from Home 1940 and 1941

How revealing Chig's letters are, painting, as they do, a picture of the life of a recently-married clergyman beginning life in a new parish, his first living. And so he wants to share this news with his father, about his churches and his congregations, his church-wardens and his organists and choirs, about parish life where he is.

As if adding pieces to a jigsaw his letters tell about the vicarage, and describe vicarage life and the vicarage garden – and its produce. They tell of village events and activities, of cricket matches and cycling trips. And as these jigsaw pieces fall into place we get a feel of what life in war-time rural Britain was like, with its restrictions; with men and women going off into the Services and leaving gaps – often unfilled gaps – in their communities; with the need to increase food production by making gardens more productive and by turning little used land into allotments.

Of the eighty-three letters written by Chig to his father between August 1940 and September 1944 almost half (38) are very much letters from the vicarage, but they are letters which in their content, and between their lines too, tell us about rural England in that part of the War. The later letters tell a completely different story, to which we shall come later.

From a reading of the collected correspondence it seems there were indeed other letters, but these may have gone astray when his father shared Chig's letters with other members of the family; perhaps there were some, too, he wished to keep. Six letters and part of a letter cover two years from August 1940. Thereafter we have more of the correspondence and so we see more of the jigsaw of war-time rural Britain being painted in.

Chig's first letter from Cressage to his father (overleaf) was written almost a year after their move there (one assumes there had been other letters before this). It embraces war-time travel; the willingness to share food, especially where there was an abundance (in this case plums from the orchard); Home Guard duty; and cricket (a good way for the Vicar to get to know his parishioners better), alongside more usual parochial tasks.

His salutation, "My dearest Father", is how invariably he began these letters. So too his signing off; he customarily ended with "Your loving son, Rowland". When, rarely, he used a different signing-off it was usually in exceptional circumstances, more of which anon.

At this point it might be helpful to look at his name, too. Clearly within the family he was Rowland, his second birth name. It seems that in the Army, and a later letter gives this away, he was sometimes known as Wilf or Wilfred. Then when meeting friends and colleagues from other times in his life and from his post-War times, when he resumed parish ministry, it was readily apparent that he was known almost universally as 'Chig'. In the parish there might have been those who politely called him Mr Chignell or Vicar. Indeed I am hard pressed to remember his wife Pauline calling him Rowland. She may well have done so between themselves but in my company, so far as I can remember, she too called him Chig and, when speaking of him to another, would refer to him as Chig. So ingrained was this in the parishes in which he served that Pauline was often known as Mrs Chig. At my first meeting with him he was introduced as Chig – and that he was ever after, which is why he is most often Chig in this his story.

The second letter we have from Cressage (13 September 1940), was penned nearly a month after its predecessor. It tells of the post being "all over the place" (hardly surprising with war-time transport problems – though it says much for the high regard of the customary efficiency of the postal service when delays become the subject of complaint); of Harvest Festivals, apple picking, the vicarage's water supply, the quality of radio broadcasts during the war and training for the LDV – later the Home Guard.

It may be helpful to paint in the context in which these letters were written. By the time George received those two letters Germany had begun its attack on Great Britain (in July 1940), in what became known as the Battle of Britain. With the fall of France at the end of June 1940, the Nazi leadership sensed that only one major enemy resisted them in Western Europe – Great Britain. With undue confidence but little planning, Germany expected to conquer the UK very quickly. If they could gain control of the airspace they would then be freer to send their ground troops across the English Channel At first they targeted London and the South-East, and especially those airfields which gave the RAF access to Germany, but soon switched to more general bombing, hoping to crush British morale. Unfortunately for the Germans, British morale stayed high, not least among the pilots of Churchill's "Few", and the reprieve allowed the country to take stock. Though the Germans continued to bomb the UK for months, by October 1940 it was clear that Britain's resistance had won the day and there was to be no German sea invasion. The Battle of Britain was a decisive victory for the British, the first time the Germans had faced defeat in World War II.

George VI appointed Winston Churchill Prime Minister in May 1940, when Neville Chamberlain stood down. Germany's decision to attack France made clear to the world that the latter's policy of Appeasement hadn't worked. Just three days into his premiership Churchill made his 'Blood, Toil, Sweat and Tears' speech to the House of Commons, the first of many with which he would inspire the nation.

18.8.40.

My dearest Father,

I'm sorry to be late with this letter, but once again there have been 'extenuating circumstances'! As I think I mentioned last week, Arthur has been here on leave since Monday, and they were off--that is Olga and Arthur--to Halifax on Saturday morning, at the collossal hour of 5.40 a.m. We seized the opportunity to pick some of our tremendous crop of plums to send with them to Mrs. Bottomley, Mrs. Hirst and the Taylor's & Pickles' at Lightcliffe. It took me all the morning to pick them, all the afternoon to sort and pack them. Then immediately after tea I had to go and see a couple of parishioners, then choir practice. I came back from that & had to go out for the night to the observation post to look for a suspicious light that had been reported. I got back about 4.0.a.m. & as Olga & Arthur wanted to be called at 5.30 I stayed up to call them and Heather, and went to bed after they had gone. I slept solidly till just on 1.0 and then off to cricket. Incidently nothing happened about the suspicious light, but an enemy plane was over and it circled about a bit round the alleged area where this light was supposed to be. However, it was in (or is supposed to be) in a dead area, about the only one, as far as we are concerned, and the L.D.V. were out on the watch round there. I don't know whether they found anything. By the way, our post has drawn blood. We reported one night while we were up, a light across the river, but noone took any notice of the report, till about a month later when one of our men reported it again on two successive nights when enemy planes were over. The police were informed and they went to the place, and found the body of a man who had obviously shot himself, as he saw them coming

Turning to more cheerful things, I had a letter from Mrs. Mylne yesterday to say that Mr. Mylne was certainly a bit better after his anointing.

As my congregation were coming out of Church this morning, I saw a face of a non-parishioner that I knew, and on speaking to her discovered that it was Miss Hall who used to be, and I think still is, in Spark' She remembered me and asked after everybody

We have had several cricket matches in the last few weeks, but have not succeeded in winning any of them, though on at least two occasions we were very near winning when time expired. Yesterday, against Broseley we needed 20 to win with two wickets to fall. I got 28 and the week before I got 35 out of a total of 98 against the R.A.P.C.

Our love to you all,

Your loving son,

Chig's letter to his father of 18 August 1940.

13.9.40.

THE VICARAGE
PRESSAGE
SAMBOURN

My dearest Father,

I hope you've had my last letter
by now! Posts are pretty well all over the
place, and small wonder, when you see, as
we can from our observation post, the night
attacks on Birmingham and district. We can
see the flashes of the bombs and the anti-
aircraft fire. I was up last night after
having had our first part of the Harvest
Thanksgiving and followed that up with a
Youth Fellowship meeting.

The Harvest Thanksgiving has
started well. There were only 8 at the early
celebration, but they hadn't had such a thing

on a week day since Mr. Lee died about 6
years ago, so it wasn't so bad; while the
congregation in the evening was much better
than last year. Unfortunately, like so many
places, the gifts consists mainly of very
generous gifts on the part of a few, and
not small gifts on the part of many. I hope
to change that next year by going round &
asking people to give a little of their best
crop. This year, also, we've had no corn,
but that is understandable, for it is just
wasted after, and they haven't got the idea
that an offering to God is not a waste.

The rain has begun to come--
whether the fact that I chose yesterday
to start picking apples was the reason or

not, I don't know, but I had hardly picked
four baskets before it began and stopped me.
By the way, can you tell me why it is
supposed to be harmful to the apples to be
picked in wet weather, so that they say they
will not keep? After all, an apple is nearly
all water in any case, and you wouldn't
think any more could do it any harm. I have
learnt that oats and barley cannot be har-
vested in wet weather because the wet makes
them generate heat when stacked, and so the
stack is liable to catch fire, but that
certainly can't be the reason for not picking
apples. Anyway this rain has done two good
things, it has just saved a good many things
in the garden, and also relieved us of our
'bucket parade', where I pump the outside
pump, and the rest of the household form a

a chain taking the buckets up to the tank at
the top.

Did I ever tell you that we found
that for the first 9 months we were here we
had been drinking rain water!? The outside
pump is the drinking water, not the inside
one! Anyway we don't seem to have suffered
much by it.

It was a year ago yesterday that
we journeyed down here from Hudd. Time goes
very quickly. Except for the great change in
the garden, little else seems to have happened in this village life. I'm certainly not
sorry we came, life here takes on a far
deeper and greater meaning.

Today I'm off to a demonstration
of dive-bombing and also instruction on
the heights of various airoplanes. Then

after that I'm going to go and see the film "Pastor Hall", which, though terrible is certainly one I don't think I ought to miss.

I think it is time that someone started to protest about the absolute tripe that is broadcast for the services. Anyone would think that our soldiers, sailors and airmen hadn't got a mind or a sense of aesthetic beauty between them. This morning after I'd got back from the O.P. I listened first to the 7.0 news and then to the programme summary for the forces for the day, & throughout the day there was apparently to be not one single piece of decent music, not a decent play nor even a good talk, just nothing but Bud Somebody-or-other's Cuban Caballeros or Somebody-else's Tea-time Cabaret etc., except for the various news broadcasts in Allied languages. When I think of poor old Marrian having to listen to that stuff, and porbably countless other chaps to a lesser extent than him, perhaps, but who also like a bit of good stuff, it makes me sick. .

Well, our love to you all,

Your loving son,

Chig's letter to his father of 13 September 1940.

On a more practical level, at the beginning of January 1940 butter, sugar and bacon were rationed in Britain, hence pig-keeping (a subject of some of Chig's later letters) offered ways of overcoming rationing, providing one advantage of rural ministry. Petrol had been rationed since the autumn of 1939 and then, following the rationing of bacon, butter and sugar, successive legislation controlled the purchase of meat, tea, jam, biscuits, breakfast cereals, cheese, eggs, lard, milk and canned and dried fruit.

But back to Chig's correspondence. Having earlier gained a flavour of the style and content of Chig's letters we might look at key points shared in the letters that followed.

25th October 1940

My dearest Father

For the past three days we have been waiting for a couple of time bombs to go off at Cound, about two miles away … the two houses just near them have been evacuated but otherwise nobody seems to bothering very much. These rank as the nearest we've had so far; they were dropped on a very misty night, when the ground all around here must have been invisible from above.

I had a pleasant surprise this week. I applied for a bit of extra petrol for my work. As I had been told that they never granted all you asked for I put down everything I could think of, and worked it out to 14 gallons per month extra. Yesterday I received coupons for the whole amount that I had applied for! On the strength of that I have written to Tiny Rowe (*a fellow clergyman and a close friend from Worcester school days*) and asked if P and I can go and stay with them for a fortnight. If so, of course, I shall have to come back for the Sunday, but it would do us both good to have a few days away from our beloved Cressage, despite all its attractions.

We had the Doctor last night talking to the Youth Fellowship on Miracle of Healing and both he and his wife came and stayed on after for tea and biscuits when the YF had gone.

I think I told you our Church was broken into some weeks back, and that a soldier had been charged with breaking into the offertory box, and also taking from the vestry a small travelling clock of mine and a pair of binoculars belonging to Mr Williams. Well, it so happened that he was brought up for trial before the Magistrates at exactly the same time that I was supposed to be giving my paper to the clergy study circle. Fortunately I had typed it out, so was able to get someone else to read it. Then I went to the Shire Hall. The soldier pleaded guilty, so my evidence was not needed and I got back in time to read most of my paper after all. We had quite a good discussion afterwards. I had gone in by train because I had very little petrol and my coupons had not come through, and so I went to the cinema afterwards to fill in the time till my train was due out. I saw Gordon Harker in 'Saloon Bar', a good, amusing detective story. In addition I saw 'London Can Take It', a Ministry of Information film of how London is standing up to this bombing, and also a marvellous film on Blackheaded Gulls – altogether a good show.

An undated fragment of a letter

We are now in the middle of Sheinton Harvest Fetival, and Pauline and Olga (*her sister*) spent all Wednesday afternoon decorating the Church. It looks really charming, and the Services on Thursday were well attended.

I spent that afternoon cutting down a large dead cherry tree in Sheinton garden. It was the biggest tree I have tackled in my newly found recreation of timber-felling. It had a bole about 2ft in diameter, and rose to about 30 feet I should think. I hacked it down with an axe, and was very pleased when it fell in the exact position I wanted it to. Now I have a job of sawing it up ready for someone to bring over here for firewood.

When I went on duty at our OP (*Observation Post*) last Thursday night, I found it in the clouds, and for the whole night we couldn't see a thing. I think I shall have to see our Company Commander and see whether something can't be done to avoid such a good waste of sleeping time. An OP doesn't seem to me to be of any value if the men can't see! Yes, we have a magnificent dug-out, provided with two home-made beds and plenty of rugs, an oil lamp, and we shall soon have an oil stove. The men made it all themselves.

5.4.41

You seem to have had some excitement with bombs. They must have been quite near enough. We too, had a little excitement on Tuesday. The story begins with the fact that we were out of coal. The firm I am now registered with were anxious not to come out till they had sufficient for a good load, so when I rang up on Tues morning and said we had exhausted all our supply, they asked if I should be in Shrewsbury. I thought I could do all I wanted to do on Tues, as well as any other day, so I went in with the car. The man on the phone had said they had had a warning which was still on as he phoned. Anyway, by the time I got in, that one was over. About 12.00 when I was in the railway goods yard by the side of a railway truck, another warning went off. The two men who were filling a couple of sacks for me took no notice at all, except that the one said "What the dickens do they think they're doing today?" To which the other replied "Well, its April 1st today!" As this took place in the most vulnerable area in the town, I thought it pretty good. As I drove off through the town I noticed that hardly anyone had taken shelter or indeed done anything at all.

You probably saw that the plane was brought down, or rather, crashed on Brown Clee.

We have, as you know, 7 hens. From Nov 1st they laid 601 eggs, and one of them only laid in December and January, after which she went broody. Since she stopped the remaining 6 have averaged 4⅔ eggs a day, and they went on steadily through the bad weather. This, of course, has kept our small household of 3 and sometimes 4 well supplied. In addition Pauline has preserved all she has got room for, and supplied the Vickers across the road as well.

There is then a five month gap in the letters, almost certainly not in their being written and sent but rather in them being saved. As some, perhaps most, of them were sent by George to other members of the family in turn it may be that they did not always get returned to him.

8.9.41

Chig records a few days' holiday in Cambridge, including visiting Heffer's book shop and coming out 27/6d poorer.

Except that Cambridge was full of boys belonging to the Air Training Scheme and that some of the colleges were apparently occupied by RAF and troops, the town doesn't seem to have changed much since I was last there. The glass is being removed from King's College Chapel, but no bombs have been dropped in the town.

We came through Coventry on the run to Birmingham (*on their way home to Cressage*), but saw little of the Blitz – except for the obvious fact that the station itself had had to be repaired, we noticed that there were many factories etc very much in action and apparently quite undamaged. B'ham too, has been well restored though there was a good mess round Snow Hill. Rumour had told us that the Cathedral was more or less a wreck, but except that the windows had either been removed or smashed there was no other damage to see from the outside.

Yesterday, Sunday, we had grand congregations. We had a fair number of communicants including Dr and Mrs Gittins for their first Communion, and then at 11.00 we had a Home Guard parade. They filled up one side of the Church, and the ordinary congregation filled up the other side and the centre and any odd seats up in the gallery, with the result there only 3 vacant places in the whole Church. Afterwards the HG had a march past and the salute was taken by the second-in-command of the Salop HG.

In the afternoon there was quite a good number at Cound, and then in the evening at Sheinton we had another excellent crowd. We gave our offerings for the day to our Bomber Churches Fund and they amounted to just under £6.

Olga and family are shortly leaving us. Arthur has got a permanent – or nearly permanent – post at York and they are going up there.

21.9.41

Our first full week without help (*Heather, their maid, had left to join up*) has gone very well. We are supposed to have a woman for 3 hrs on three mornings a week, but she never came this week, and as she doesn't live in the village we haven't been able to find out what happened. We start the day by my lighting the kitchen fire, and clearing out the drawing room one if we've used it. Then I go up and dress while P gets breakfast. If I have time I feed the pigs before breakfast. Then P does the housework etc while I get coal, pump water, and then do my own work (*his clerical and parish duties – Chig was always very committed and conscientious about his parish duties*). After lunch we wash up, then I prepare the morrow's food for the pigs while P has a bit of a rest. Visiting or gardening takes up the afternoons, while P either gardens or has her WVS (*Women's Voluntary Service, forerunner of the present WRVS*) or takes it easy. We have abandoned afternoon tea and now have a high tea at 5.30pm. After washing that up we then have our evening occupations and a cup of tea and a bit of cake or a biscuit (if we can get them) at about 9.00, and so to bed at 10.00.

I've got about 4cwt of jolly nice potatoes up – they are not monsters, but are a very fair crop and almost clean of any grub or desease (*sic*), and there must be quite another 8cwt to come, though it's going to be difficult to find the time in which to get them up now. I've also had 1cwt of carrots, and I've got more to get up, and about ¾cwt of beetroot, and more to get up, so we shouldn't be short of root crops! I must gather up my French beans which I've grown for haricots – they look a pretty good crop, and leeks are coming on well, but my onions are a complete flop. However I've swapped some carrots for onions with Mrs Mansfield, who can grow onions but can't grow carrots.

I don't know anything about our new Bish(op), except that I gather he is keen on Church music, but I'm afraid he's coming for a rest cure, which is a great pity. It never seems to strike anybody that a country diocese wants a country bishop – one who understands country folk, it's just the same as the idea that only older men should be in the country, and consequently our poor country-folk, the salt of the earth, get left with only broken-downs to minister to them.

Then comes a gap in the bundle of letters, until the first letter of January 1942.

5

Letters from Home 1942

As 1942 unfolded, the Blitz intensified in England, with London and many of our cathedral cities and industrial areas and ports being key targets, but even in rural areas the prospect of bombing existed as returning bombers chose to lighten their loads by releasing unused bombs. In response to Germany's attacks, Britain despatched the first thousand-bomber air raid, on Cologne. The first USA troops began to arrive in the UK as America entered the War. At the end of the summer General Bernard Montgomery had taken command of the Eighth Army in North Africa.

At home soap joined the list of rationed products, and the BBC introduced the Radio Doctor, Dr Charles Hill, who began his regular series of avuncular broadcasts offering health advice to help keep the nation and its people in good shape. At the year's end Sir William Beveridge's influential report led to the founding of the UK's welfare state.

Chig now was beginning to make contact with the local army units, an experience which, ultimately, would lead to a change in his ministry, at least during the war-time years.

31.1.42

I went to dinner with the officers at Buildwas Park (*between Ironbridge and Much Wenlock*) last Sat as I said I was going to. I had to cycle in pouring rain, but I enjoyed myself very much with them. The OC was determined to have some sort of service for the troops on Sunday – it was Cressage Matins – and so I said I'd have a service for them at 12.15. He said he could send a car for me, and we would have it in the canteen, and he said I was to stay to lunch afterwards. All this duly came to pass. We had our service, and afterwards each of the officers came to pull my leg for endangering the discipline of the army by using an illustration in my address, which went something like this. I was talking about prayer and saying that the prayers we learnt in childhood were supposed to be the beginning of our education in prayer, and that we ought to advance on them. 'Just as when we learn that twice one are two, that is not the end of our mathematical knowledge, but the beginning. If we never go further than that, it is a poor look out for us when we get paid.'

The officers said that now all the troops would begin to count their pay, and doubt the efficiency of those who hand it out! It was most amusing how one after the other of them came and pulled my leg about this.

After lunch I walked back to Sheinton for the afternoon service, and then home after that.

Our new Bishop wants to try and get some more men to go as Chaplains. I don't quite know what to do about it myself. I'm quite prepared to go, but if I do, it means that somebody will have at least three parishes to run, and also that these soldiers (*at Buildwas Park*) will have no-one except their proper chaplain who can only come once a month. In addition poor old Cressage has had such a lot of chopping and changing these last 10 years, that it hardly seems right to give them some more.

I'm still without the use of the car and at present there is no prospect of any tyres. Fortunately it looks as though the worst of the weather has gone now, but it is a bit of a nuisance.

9.2.42

It should have been 11.00 Matins at Cressage yesterday, which meant that the Buildwas Park soldiers either had the use of Sheinton for a service of their own or had to do without. Their official chaplain was on leave, so they couldn't fix up a service for themselves. When I came down stairs on Sunday morning I found a note from them in the letter-box saying they were coming to Cressage and could I arrange 40 seats for them. Sure enough, they turned up, having marched all the way. Then they had lorries to take them home. As a matter of fact they expected the lorries to be at Cressage, just around the corner in Sheinton Rd., but I understand from Sheinton folk, that the lorries went to Sheinton Church by mistake, so they had a march of 1½ miles on the homeward journey as well as the three miles down! I don't expect the CO was too pleased!

We had the CO, Major Gillespie, and a Lt Brockenhurst to tea on Tuesday. They have a big job for the WVS to do – something to do with putting camouflage on netting for their stuff. So as the WVS meet here every Tuesday afternoon, I told them to come and explain all about it.

Curiously enough while I was out in the afternoon a car stopped and the occupant asked me where he was and if I knew of any place where he could stay for an indefinite period. The occupant proved to be the Deputy-Assistant Chaplain General for this area. I told him about the Buildwas Park people, and he urged me very strongly to become an Officiating Chaplain to them, so in all probability I shall, as it will apparently clear the air for them, and give me some official position, with a definite permission to use military transport if necessary, and also official permission to visit them when I like. Gillespie said that as far as he was concerned it would have been all right anyway, but that there was always the chance of getting into a row for permitting an unofficial person to have these privileges.

The snow hasn't really been much trouble – it never prevented me getting to Sheinton, though two or three Sundays ago it was not easy. On Feb 1st it certainly was a surprise, but I was the first to go along the Sheinton Rd and so the going was pretty easy. It was not nearly so good coming back, as the thaw had set in, but my good Arthur Cole, the baker, sent a message to say that he would take Mrs Mansfield and myself over for the 11.00 in his bread van! Even on that day with plenty of snow on the ground the troops marched to Church!

It seemed the Bishop's encouragement of his clergy to consider becoming Chaplains to the Forces was, perhaps, taking root with Chig, fostered by his links with the army at Buildwas Park and what seemed, at the time, his chance meeting with the Deputy-Assistant Chaplain General.

16.2.42

Our soldiers turned up yesterday at Sheinton, it was most amusing to hear them coming down the hill from Buildwas, singing at the top of their voices, and knowing that they were coming to Church. It certainly gave the impression they enjoy coming.

Chig wrote of a serious decline in health of Canon Leeper, who had been one of the incumbents with whom he had trained during his curacy. To his father Chig wrote:

I often used to think of him as a man who would shortly be going to more important work. He certainly did a great work in Huddersfield. There are very few people who would have stood a chance of dragging me back to Yorks, but he was one of them.

I've got the form of permission to kill Gloria, and the sad event will take place in about a fortnight's time.

Talking of pigs, I intend to get another one as soon as possible, so as to have it ready for killing sometime round about November or December. I did wonder whether it would be good to get two and keep one of them for you folk at Kineton. The point about this is that two pigs living together usually do better than one, if they are of the same litter. I shall have little difficulty in getting someone to share my sty, but I thought it might be of advantage to you. The main difficulty I see is the question of transport after the pig is dead. It should not be insurmountable to get the bacon and hams to you by rail – we could get the curing done here first – but all the oddments that go to make pork pies, sausages, lard, brawn etc would need using up as soon as possible after the killing. I dare say I could sell this for you. As an economical proposition, it would probably pay. I paid 49/– last time for my pig, and at the moment I believe they are a bit cheaper than that, but are not so easy to get. Meal costs 8/6 a month and there are slight extras such as straw and perhaps some pig potatoes. See what Marco says about it. In any case I strongly urge the keeping of a pig – it is an economical proposition these days, despite what many folk say; the meal ration is sufficient for a moderate-sized pig, if you work it out in proportion to its age. My pig will probably be about 9 score weight, and I've easily managed on my ration of meal – I've even done without 24lbs out of the 63 lbs per month that we get, on one occasion, to help out somebody who didn't get their full allowance.

24.2.42

Chig's next letter told his father that Gloria was not yet dead, but told him of Canon Leeper's death, an account which indicated the challenges of war-time travel.

Canon Leeper died last Sunday week, and I went up to Huddersfield for the funeral. I left here in time to catch the 8.40 from Shrewsbury. This should have got me there at 12.46, but I missed a connection in Stockport and had to wait a couple of hours, so that I eventually got to Huddersfield at 2.40 and the service started at 2.30. I ran to the Church which, as you remember is not far from the station, and arrived in time for most of the service, and went out to Brockholes with the family for the burial.

My main reason for staying on was to give Hazel (Canon Leeper's daughter) a chance to get things a bit straight so that she could come back with me for a few days' rest. We came back on Sat. and again had the exasperating experience of missing a train, this time the local from Shrewsbury to Cressage. There wasn't another for 3 hours, and so I rang up our local garage, and he said he could not leave for another hour but would meet us on the road, so we started to walk. I had agreed to have Bunty (*Canon Leeper's old dog*) for he would be without a home, and we had to bring him along. He is 15 so can't go very fast. We did about 3 miles and then Tom picked us up.

9.3.42

This last week has been really hectic. It was our Warship Week, and Pauline is local Secretary. Last Monday night I returned from our weekly First Aid Class and found her quite poorly with a temperature of 102, and she's been in bed ever since. She's had flu with a cold and nasty cough, but she is much better now, though she won't return to quite normal. This has meant I've had to do what I can for Warships. The whole village has got somewhere round about £500 – we aimed for £350 – and Cressage School got £55.

Then on Monday Gloria was sent off, and returned in pieces on Wednesday. Fortunately two good people came up and helped me with the pieces – Mr & Miss Timmis – he salted the bacon and the hams, and she helped me to make the pork pie meat, which I took down to Arthur Cole next day with 1½lbs of fat and some jelly made from the ears, snout and tail. The result of all this has been a baker's dozen of excellent pork pies! Then there was the putting of the trotters and top half of the head into a brine mixture to be made into brawn, and the slight salting of half a dozen joints such as the ribs etc, so that they would keep for a week or so. I had to do all these and the rendering down of the best lard after the Timmis' had gone, and I only just finished in time for the first of our men's discussion groups at 8.00pm. This went off awfully well, and we are going to meet once a month. On Thursday I roasted a joint of pork, and in the evening fried the kidneys. Since then we have used some of the liver – I made what is called a savoury liver pie, and though I say it as shouldn't, it was jolly good, and we also had an apple custard pie, and today we are going to have roast beef, also cooked by me – the butcher came and left it without us catching him. There has also been a lot of boiling of bones etc.

Just now I seem to be pretty busy in the parish as well, what with two confirmation classes, choir practices and the services for young mothers and babies.

Now that this last dollop of snow has gone I hope to be able to get at the garden, but in the meanwhile I am fast becoming a prize shot! Pigeons have taken a fancy to our greens, and in the last 3 days I've had six shots and killed three, so we shall be having pigeon pie to add to our already overflowing food stocks!

23.3.42

Pretty well every day is full just now. I usually do some gardening and letter-writing on Mondays in the morning and afternoon, and in the evening I have a First Aid Class. Tuesdays I begin to prepare my various sermons and talks during the week, and in the afternoon I dig some of my potato patch over at Sheinton (*the 'Dig for Victory' campaign encouraged people to transform gardens, parks and sports pitches into allotments to grow vegetables. People also kept their own chickens, rabbits and goats. Nine hundred pig clubs were set up and about 6000 pigs were raised in gardens. It seems Chig was setting a good example and had use of a garden at Sheinton, perhaps the old Rectory garden or part of the church-yard?*).

In the evening I have the Youth Fellowship – we are studying St. Matthew's Gospel at present. Wednesday begins with teaching in school, followed by visiting, some reading, and some more preparation for Sunday. I usually manage to keep the evening free. Thursday I teach at Sheinton and spend the rest of the morning visiting either the troops at Buildwas or Sheinton folk. In the afternoon I have my service for young mothers and babies, and in the evening either a confirmation class for boys or the men's discussion group or a garden club meeting. Friday often has to be spent in Shrewsbury, either from 9 to 12.30 or from 12 to 6.00. Then there are choir practices, and a Confirmation class for girls.

Saturday is spent in final preparations for Sunday, and various odd items – for instance last Saturday was almost completely spent in weighing out and distributing seed potatoes to members of the garden club. One Saturday a month is pig meal afternoon, when we hand out the ration for the month. Then comes Sunday … and there is nearly always some extra item – e.g. last week there was a funeral, and I should have gone to a meeting but was unable to do so because of the funeral.

I have now been appointed OCF (Outside Chaplain to the Forces) to the Army units at Buildwas Park and have a badge and a hideous armlet. Yesterday they came to Cressage, marching all the way, ATS and all.

As for the car, I've pretty well given up any idea of running it again during the war.

8.6.42

We have been doing a lot of thistle-potching this last week, but we took the afternoon off on my birthday and went for a picnic by the riverside (*River Severn*) instead but even there, there was no breeze, and we simply stewed.

My Infant Sunday School teacher wanting a holiday, I have started to train two young girls for the job, and yesterday they had their first try out. I went and listened with the object of telling them what I thought about it when they come for the weekly class tonight. As a matter of fact I have very little to say to them, for they did their work astonishingly well.

Chig also wrote about the YF's (Youth Fellowship) annual cycle outing, and their trip to Haughmond Hill, about 3 miles east of Shrewsbury. On reaching their destination they left their bikes at a cottage at the foot of the hill, and climbed to find a picnic spot. On their way home they got caught in a torrential thunderstorm, with rain so intense that they couldn't see where they were going, and attempted to shelter near a tree, the only cover available. "We were absolutely soaked" Chig said, "I don't think I've ever been so wet, even when having a bath!" Eventually the storm abated, and they cycled the 5½ miles home in sunshine and a warm breeze which dried them out. A good time was had by all – and all in the line of duty for a conscientious country parson.

15.6.42

It seems that Chig's father was enjoying a brief mid-summer stay with relatives, near Leominster, and Chig's thought of calling to see his father while he was nearby also gives us an indication about the scarcity of war-time food, and the need to be thoughtful about imposing oneself on someone else's housekeeping.

I have a hopeful idea of cycling over one day to see you, but it largely depends on the weather. If I come I'll bring a bite of food, so that you needn't have any frantic rush to find anything for me.

The roller (*for the garden?*) arrived safely last Thursday, which I thought was pretty good going. The village had some fun seeing me haul it up from the station!

On Thursday evening I went over to the soldiers at Buildwas Park to tea, and a lecture and discussion which they had afterwards. It was very interesting, and in a fortnight's time they are going to try a 'Brains Trust' of which I am to be a member!

We had quite an exciting match on Saturday against a Ministry of Supply team. They batted first and got 142 for 5 before declaring. I kept wicket again and had a couple of catches not allowed! Then we went in for 105 minutes at the most. We seemed to be set for a defeat when we lost 3 good wickets for under 40, for we only had 9 men. I went in and succeeded in staying while the man at the other end got runs, but we found ourselves needing 2 a minute with 45 minutes to go, and hadn't caught up at all when only ½ an hour was left. With 15 minutes to go I decided to have a bang, and when I was caught for 39 we needed 9 runs in 5 minutes, which we got. Thus we won by 6 wickets, 2 minutes from time. A man called Wright got a really excellent 76 – a grand innings, especially as he must be over 50. We are still unbeaten this season.

Again the Vicar is seen to be involved in so many aspects of village life, typical of rural parishes at that time, but perhaps especially so when many other men from the villages had gone off to serve in the forces.

Pauline's mother comes for three weeks beginning today. She is staying until we go off on our holiday. She will need a rest for she has been having to run her house on her own, and has a spell of Olga's children who went there for a bit after their house was damaged in the York raid.

Understand that we now have a large batch of American airmen all round here. I haven't seen anything of them yet but about 1,000 of them turned up at Salop last Wednesday I'm told.

Well, I think that is all the news for this week, except that we are still thistle-potching – a job that seems to go on for ever!

22.6.42

On Saturday we played our local soldiers and after a devastating start when we got 4 of their wickets down for 6 we eased off our bowling – i.e. I went on at one end and they got 90! Then we found they had a couple of good opening bowlers, but were not unduly worried when 50 went up with only 2 wickets down. However at that moment two good wickets fell in one over. I stayed for a few minutes during which another 24 were added and we lost another wicket before winning by 4 wickets. Macy (*a civil servant seconded to the area from London who, with his family, was lodging with the Chignells for a while*) was pleased with himself for he got 6 wickets for 29.

Yesterday we had excellent congregations both at Cressage and Sheinton but I do wish my people would come more regularly and in greater numbers to the Eucharist. They don't compare at all badly with other churches round about, but our country folk are not imbued with much idea as to the necessity of frequent Communion.

One drawback of our holidays is going to be the fact that lots of things like currants, raspberries, peas and beans are just going to be ready while we are away.

20.7.42

Most of this ten-page epistle told the tale of Chig's and Pauline's holiday, for which they based themselves at Ludlow (*all of 25 miles from their Vicarage at Cressage – perhaps yet another indicator of restrictions on war-time travel etc*). They were joined by 'Tiny' Rowe, his pal from King's School and Sarum days and a fellow-cleric, and his wife Hilda, and they spent their time exploring Ludlow as well as walking and cycling and exploring the countryside around (clearly their bicycles were essential for a holiday like this).

Their journey home at the end of their holiday was eventful, and again reflected the vagaries of war-time travel. The Rowes, travelling by train from Ludlow, set off before the Chignells, but had to wait for over an hour for their delayed train, which was then put into a siding to allow an express train through. Chig and Pauline had decided to cycle home, immediately taking what they thought was a short-cut to Bromfield, only to find that they had to turn back as the road was closed by the military. On their new route they found themselves pedaling into a strong head-wind and so opted for a return to Ludlow and the train.

Our train was over half an hour late. We had to stand in the guard's van. We got out at Marshbrook, cycled ½ a mile or so up the road over Cwm Head towards Bishops Castle and had our lunch. It was still overcast but not raining. Then we pushed on to Church Stretton (*where Chig had a Diocesan meeting!*). Here Pauline went on home with the map, while I went to my meeting – a rather futile one … . Then I ambled home, but as it had cleared up a bit I went round by Cound to see how the match against the Buildwas Park folk was progressing. I found that the main match was already over with Cound victorious by 8 wickets, and that a 45 mins each way game was on. This was also won easily, and Cound had also won the previous week. So we are still undefeated with eight wins and one draw.

Everything in the garden seems to have grown vastly while we have been away, especially the apples and pears, but our main trouble now is keeping up with the peas, beans etc that are urgently needing to be eaten.

Yesterday we had our collections for the Merchant Navy's Comforts Fund, and the result is that we can send a cheque for £9 – 6s – 0d, which is pretty good I think.

3.8.42

This letter has scribbled in the top right-hand corner the request "Please return to George", evidence that Chig's letters to his father were doing the rounds of the family, and that George was keen to have them back when all had seen them.

Just at present I am pretty busy. I'm not sure whether I have told you before that we are going to have a Horticultural Show in Cressage this year, both to buck up our local gardening and also to benefit the Red Cross. It is coming off on Sept 19th, and we are now busy doing the preliminary stuff. We have had to decide what classes of vegetables and fruit can be shown, and we have got 29 classes. Then we have to get out entry forms comprising a list of these classes and the rules of showing. I am having to type these out, which takes a lot of time. Unfortunately our duplicating set has worn out. These have to be sent to various people in the neighbouring villages who are going to act as local secretaries, together with posters supplied by the Red Cross, but filled in with particulars by us. Then there are the letters to be written to various folk whom we hope to get as vice-presidents at 10/6d each! Very shortly I have to apply for exemption from entertainments tax, and also for a catering licence for the afternoon. Our good friends the local search light battery are going to give their services at another concert in the evening after the show, and I also have to arrange for side shows and competitions.

Judging for the children's wild flower collection competition had just been completed when Chig wrote this letter to his father. The contents of the collection, whilst generating interest, not least for the large number of species collected would probably arouse considerable concern today, when wild flowers are protected and preserved, and enjoyed in situ.

We have just finished judging the children's wild flower collections. It has been a pretty big job. Seven of them went in for it, and four of them collected over 200 specimens, while two of the other three had well over the hundred. Actually none of them had 200 different species, for they had several in duplicate, but the winning kiddy had 164 different species, which was very good. We gave them marks according to the rarity of the species, 1 mark for very common flowers, 2 for common ones, 3 for flowers which are local, i.e. which are common in certain localities but not widespread, and 5 for very rare flowers. They got a mark for every specimen named correctly, and a maximum of 10 marks for neatness, pressing, and for arrangement. The winner got 356 marks and she was a kiddy of only 10! We have to do the same for Sheinton now, but that will be considerably easier for they have got nothing like the same size of collections.

I am seriously contemplating the writing of a book about the country parson and his work. I have got a grand title, being a quotation quoted in a review of Dr Henley Henson's autobiography (*Henson, a former Bishop of Hereford, had been Bishop of Durham from 1920 to 1939*). In the review the writer quoted the remark made by someone or other that most town clergy thought of their country brethren as living a life of "leisurely tickling of a pig's back". This strikes me as a grand title for such a book.

Was Chig really thinking of responding to the 'townies' – and urban clergy's – view of the country parson by writing a book? Or was this suggestion to his father simply a way of saying that not everyone recognizes the different role a country clergyman is expected to play, knowing all his parishioners as individuals, meeting them (and working and playing with them) in a wide variety of situations so as to have regular contact with them, and having also the opportunities to get to know them and understand them as individuals? The country parson is often expected to give a lead to the community and set an example – as, at this point, Chig seemed to have been doing, in terms of 'Dig for Victory', in fundraising events, and generally keeping morale high, alongside all those special duties and tasks of an ordained minister.

We wondered if you had any of the bombs in the recent raids on the Midlands. We had some of them, but it had not been enough to disturb us – the sound of the planes going over was what we got most of as usual.

Cound had yet another smashing win on Saturday against a local RAF team. We got 220 for 6 and declared, and then got them out for 127. Even so it was pretty exciting for they were battling well – in fact I think they were the best batting team we had played against this year – and it looked all odds on a draw when, with only 15 minutes to go, they had 4 wickets to fall and two good bats going well ….. we won in the last but one over of the match. Macy and I enjoyed ourselves with an unfinished stand of 80. He got 38 not out and I got 40 not out, It is rather curious that I have got an average for the season that is higher than any single score I have made! My average is 44 and I have not scored anything higher than 40! It is, of course, due to the fact that I have had 2 not outs, and have only once made less than 20.

19.8.42

Well, the main excitement has obviously been my broadcasting experience. It all happened suddenly. For some time I have known there was to be a broadcast about Cressage and its Garden and Pig Clubs. Miss Pelham had been asked to write a script for the BBC, and she was to have given it, but she couldn't go to Birmingham to do it. She tried two other people at my suggestion, but neither of them could do anything about it, so on Friday she came to tell me that she had let me in for the job. I got the script on Saturday, and set off first thing on Monday, calling at the Post Office on the way to see if there was any post. There was a letter from the BBC enclosing my card of admission, and also the agreement. I got to Birmingham at 12.15 and set about getting some lunch. After queuing for about 10 mins I got into Patterson's and had an excellent meal. They have had some damage, though it is all temporarily repaired. After lunch I strolled about looking at the waste places. A large area opposite Patterson's has been wiped out, though there is little to see from Corporation Street itself. I got to the BBC for 3.00pm when I was due for a rehearsal. It was good I had called at our local PO and got their letter, for there was a very large policeman at the door armed with a revolver, who would not have let me in but for my pass.

The place had a rather dead appearance, for there didn't seem to be much going on – I think ours was the only broadcast during the afternoon. The rehearsal was to get the timing right, and also to see our voices were OK. The others had broadcast before, so there was not much need to worry about them, and Jukes – who ran the programme – said I was perfectly all right. We found we had to do a bit of cutting in order to get it into 20 mins. We went through the script twice, and then at 4.10 we hastily drank a cup of tea, and then off we went when the red light came on. I always imagined the announcer had a little room with a glass partition. There was such a room, but our announcer stayed with us, and simply walked up and leant over the table round which we sat, when she had to say anything.

I didn't feel at all nervous, the main thought that got into my mind was the shock that some of my friends would have if they happened to turn on their sets and heard me speaking.

After it was over we went to the BBC canteen and had some more tea.

After sharing with his father the excitement and novelty of this visit to Birmingham, Chig reported on more local things, including the harvest.

All round, the farmers are busy cutting the corn, and we are out fire-watching again. That is we only go out on a 'red' warning, which won't be often, It is a wonderful harvest for everything, corn, roots and fruit, though we ourselves haven't got much in the way of plums.

26.8.42

On Monday I had to go into Salop (*Shrewsbury*) to make the arrangements for catering for our Horticultural Show. I applied for a caterers' licence for it but they would not grant it, and so I have got hold of a caterer who will supply the necessary stuff, but we must fetch it. How we are going to do that I don't know yet, but no doubt we shall get somebody to go in for it.

My good churchwarden, Arthur Cole the baker, is now requested to fill in a form stating why he considers himself free from the menace of being called up – or in other words why he thinks he should be reserved. His reply ought to shake them up a bit. He states that other bakers have ceased to supply our district because of petrol shortage. He has two women assisting him, but that there are many jobs they cannot do because of the heavy weights etc to be carried. That he puts in 90 hours a week (!) and that in his spare time he is churchwarden, Special Constable and a qualified St. John's Ambulance man. It really is ridiculous that he should have to waste time filling in such a form, and it would be a good job if one or more of the folk who spend their time sending such forms were to come and do a day or two's work in the bakery. This, as a matter of fact, is what I've been doing this week. One of the assistants is on holiday, so yesterday I turned up at 7.00am (!) and helped till 12. It was most interesting, and jolly hard work. First I weighed out the dough into the correct weights. This takes a long time when there are something like 200 – 300 loaves, of three different weights. Then I helped to put them in and take them out of the ovens, a very warm job. Then I greased the tins and put them away, and helped to load the van. Then there were tarts to make, and helped put them in the little tins, and lastly I swept the place out! I hope to be able to help tomorrow, Friday and Saturday.

It is worth noting that, whilst a country parson was, in many senses, a master of his own destiny (or at least master of his own time) and could juggle his various tasks, Chig was a very conscientious vicar and would not have let his clerical and pastoral duties slip. Additional tasks, such as helping a baker in need, being part of the Home Guard, encouraging others to play parts in the Pig Club, Gardening Club and Horticultural Show, and setting an example in the Dig for Victory campaign had to be fitted in around his own clergy tasks and duties.

22.9.42

Chig began this letter "My dearest Father, I doubt whether I shall have much time to write today, but I'll do as much as I can" and, six densely-typed pages later, he finished "I must stop now, though I'm afraid I've missed the post, and also have not mentioned anything else except the Show. I'll try to remember other bits of news next week." The Show seems to have been a resounding success in so many ways and, not least, as yet one more way of bolstering parishioners' morale in those middle years of the War.

After several minor crises the Show went off and was a great success, The first of many crises had been the indifference of many in the village towards it. The Show was either 'too late' or 'not advertised enough', or the folk said they had nothing to show or, in the case of one small section, they would have nothing to do with the Show because they had not been put on the committee! (So one learns village politics!). The next crisis was that for a time it looked as though there would be hardly any entries, but eventually we had 154 in 28 different classes (*the village's population was around 300 at this time*).

Then came the great crisis. For some time there has been doubt as to the position of the Home Guard and the Village Hall. Owing to the fact that both the secretary and the treasurer of the Village Hall have left the village, this committee has been pretty well non-existent, and no-one knew exactly the terms on which the HG had the Hall, It was commonly thought they had commandeered it (*shades of Captain Mainwaring and 'Dad's Army'!*), but a few weeks before this we found out that such was not the case, but that they have only rented it for certain purposes. Immediately we knew this, I kicked up a row about the dances which were being held under the auspices of the HG every month, and which have been pretty nasty affairs. In addition I mentioned in my letter to the HG HQ that many of us wondered where all the money was going that had been raised at the dances, (It was supposed to be going to HG funds, but I could not see what funds the HG needed, seeing the rent for the Hall – their only expense – was paid by the Territorial Association). The HG HQ jumped on the local CO, who in turn jumped on the main organizer of the dances – a youth of 26 and quite incapable of organizing any such event .... he has been told to furnish a statement of accounts for the past two years – the CO being ignorant of the fact the dances were held for HG funds! – and spread a rumour at the beginning of last week that there were to be no more social events of any kind in the Hall. This rather queered the pitch of the concert which was to be held there on Saturday night. I wrote to the local HG OC who lives in a neighbouring village, and on receiving no reply cycled over to see him on Thursday night. He said it was OK to hold the concert … .

The last crisis was Saturday morning. We woke up to see a day which promised a gradual gathering of rain – in fact it really looked as though all was up. As we got up, the rain began, and continued to gather strength through breakfast. As I went down the village, the rain left off, and the wind rose a bit and broke the clouds slightly.

Now, going back to Thursday – Lewis the blacksmith and I got a band of useful chaps together to clear out the barn in which the exhibits were to be shown, and then on Friday we got the trestle tables up and did various other jobs, and on Saturday morning ... I was down at the barn from 9.45 – 1.45, by which time everything was ready and the judges had come. We had 28 classes as follows, and Pauline and I entered the ones I have underlined: French Beans, Runner Beans, Beetroot, Brussel Sprouts, Autumn Cabbage, Long Carrots, Cauliflower, Cucumber, Kohl Rabi, Cos Lettuce, Cabbage Lettuce, Marrow, Parsnip, Onions, Savoy, Shallots, Outdoor Tomatoes, Turnip, 2nd Early Potatoes, Main Crop Potatoes, Cooking Apples, Eating Apples, Cooking Plums, Eating Plums, Damsons, Bottled Fruit, Vase of Flowers & Vase of Wild Flowers.

My old Sheinton organist, who is a market gardener, ran away with most of the prizes. He showed 17 classes got 11 firsts, 6 seconds and one third. We actually came next with firsts in Cauliflower, Cos Lettuce (the only exhibit!), and the Vase of Flowers, We were very pleased about the last as Jim, my aforementioned organist, has won many a prize in flower decorations. We got second prize with Cooking Plums (Ponds Seedling) & French Beans, and third with Autumn Cabbage, Cooking Apples (Newton Wonders).

The weather had cleared up and it was a pleasant afternoon. Pretty well the whole village turned up and the side-shows did a brisk trade. We had skittles, knocking bottles over, long jump, slow bicycle race, quoits, putting, getting rings over some antlers, throwing pennies on a shilling, rolling croquet balls, walking on a line, guessing the weight of a cake, and also a country dancing display by the girls from school. The Show finished about 6.30, and everyone went home to get ready for the concert.

This was again marvellous – the way Gillespie and his men made use of our rotten little stage was amazing, and they had some good talent too. There was not a weak point in the show. Incidentally the leading trumpeter turned out to be Harry Roy's leading trumpeter! I take my hat off to him for he could play all right.

We all went home soon after 10.00 very tired but very happy, feeling that our first venture in a Horticultural Show had been a great success. What we have raised for the Red Cross I don't know yet, but it will probably be between £20 and £30 at least, and may well be more.

There was then a gap in the letters, again almost certainly in what was retained in the bundle rather than in the faithfulness of Chig's correspondence with his father.

8.12.42

Pauline and Dorothy (*the Chignell's maid*) are both fit and well again, and we have returned to a more normal existence. This wonderful dry and mild weather is giving me a chance to finish my autumn digging. I am manuring at the same time, and for every four or five rows of digging I have to go down to where my pig is and bring up a barrowload of manure! I think the village are rather amused at the sight!

I am now trying to teach the local soldiers and ATS a few carols for Christmas. This is taking place at Buildwas on Saturdays for an hour from 4.30 – 5.30. They aren't much good (*almost certainly said sympathetically, recognising a cause for much encouragement, rather than criticism*) and I also believe it will not be the same crowd each week, which doesn't make it any easier – still it is contact with them, and it is something to entertain them, and make their rather dull life a bit more interesting.

We have just been filling up forms as voluntary blood donors ….

I've been spending a bit of time this last week, discussing drainage and timber-felling with my tenant (*at this period clergy continued to receive rent and income from the glebe land attached to the parish*). He has a glebe field (one of five he rents off me) which is very badly drained, and now he has got to plough it up (*presumably for the war effort*), which means, that if it is to be any use, it must be piped. Fortunately it is only about 100 yards that needs doing. Perhaps Peter could tell you what is the cost with 2½ or 3 inch pipes. It is somewhere round about 12/6 a chain (*22 yards or 20.12 metres*) isn't it? Then there are also a couple of oaks that may have to come down, and I also want to re-plant a couple, for I don't intend to take any down without replacing them.

30.12.42

We had a grand Christmas. From the very beginning it was full of joy. The Midnight Eucharist was most inspiring. We had 31 communicants at it, and several others have said how much they would have liked to come. My one anxiety was about getting up again at 6.30am after it. But that was managed all right, and I was waiting for my transport to take me to Buildwas for 7.30. I only had 8 communicants there, but everything had been delightfully prepared in the canteen and it was a joyful little Service. We should have been more, only the sole C of E officer at Buildwas was away on leave, and that makes as much difference as the absence of parents! I was brought back to Cressage for 8.30 where we had another 16 communicants, and then cycled over to Sheinton for 9.30 where I only had 7. This was rather disappointing, but it is in part understandable as two regulars are always away for the big Feast Days because of School holidays, and another is now a postwoman, while 2 others came to the Midnight at Cressage.

4 others came on Sunday as they had been unable to come on Christmas Day. After the 9.30am I went home for breakfast, and then we had Matins at Cressage with a good congregation. Then we joined forces with the Macy's (*their lodgers*) for Christmas dinner – goose and plum pudding, washed down by sherry and rum which Macy somehow had got hold of. I had to go for Evensong at Sheinton at 3.30, and there was a good little congregation for it. After a peaceful tea, we joined forces again in the evening for guessing and intelligence games, and so to bed. Next day I had a late Celebration (*of holy communion*) for older folk and there were 5 present, so that we topped the 50 for Cressage this year for Christmas. Then after a snack I cycled off to Ironbridge for a Christmas party for the troops. About 200 were present, another 200 having had their party on Christmas Day. After dinner – turkey or goose, plum pudding and mince-pies washed down by beer, we had an excellent entertainment given by members of the Battery. It all finished by 3.30 and I cycled home. We had a quiet evening and early bed.

Then on Sunday instead of Matins at Cressage and Evensong at Sheinton we had a carol service at each Church based on that from King's, Cambridge, only slightly shortened. At Cressage I got Noel Baldwin and Gillespie (the CO of the local searchlight troops) to read three Lessons apiece, and I read the Christmas Gospel at the end. … It was the first time that the Matins (and more elite) congregation had heard our Carol Service, and there was much enthusiasm. Really, though, the choir did exceedingly well. They seem, at last, to have got hold of how to sing carols, and that they are not meant to be sung like hymns.

On Monday we went out to tea with Mrs Beddoes and her daughter *(Mrs Beddoes had attended the same school as Pauline)*. They live at Eyton, a hamlet over the river. We can see their house, a big white one on top of a hill, but to get there is quite a round-about journey. We went on our bikes. We found all sorts of things in common. … When we left we had a rotten ride home in the dark – it was also considerably colder and was raining, but we got home safely, in time for me to go off and MC a Whist Drive at the School in aid of the School. We cleared over £7 at that.

Last night we had the Gittins in to supper to help us eat a brace of pheasants. Then the Macy's came down and we played Sevens. Unfortunately the G's had to leave at 10.00 because of their little maid being all on her own, but we four went on and played contract whist till about 11.30.

That is the full story of our Christmas and now we shall return to a more orderly and ordinary way of life!

The year as far as the Church goes has been mixed. Communicants at Cressage have not been so many as the previous years, though there has been some improvement in the last 3 or 4 months, but financially it has been a record except for last year which was abnormal owing to the £100 raised at the Centenary. Our collections have amounted to £124, of which about £70 has gone to various missions and charities and diocesan activities. At Sheinton our communicants have increased by 3 on last year while financially it has been a record year. But this has been almost entirely due to the soldiers. The collections have been over £50 this year.

In a little place like this, the inability of one or two communicants to come makes a tremendous difference, and certainly the abnormal conditions of life have caused some to be unable to come – e.g. Dr and Mrs Gittins, with a surgery at 8.30 and no-one to get breakfast, and there are others in a similar position. The willingness or rather the desire to come was emphasized by the good attendance at Midnight, for that did mean an effort, and to have more communicants then than during the whole of last Christmas clearly shows the desire is there. It is now up to me to see if I can find some way in which I can meet this desire.

Well I'd better stop now, but not without wishing you all a happy New Year, and may God bless you all during it.

As the War, now into its fourth year, rumbled on many would have echoed these sentiments, and so many would have wondered too what would bring the war to an end.

6

A Shifting Focus – Letters from Home 1943

"When the war is over" or "before the war ends" appear often enough in Chig's letters to his father. Those same thoughts would have been part of countless everyday conversations throughout the country and, indeed, among service-men and women and their families everywhere, as all looked for the ending of hostilities. On 10 November 1942, following the Allies' success at El Alamein. Winston Churchill, in a speech at the Lord Mayor of London's Luncheon, had ventured: "Now this is not the end. It is not even the beginning of the end. but it is, perhaps, the end of the beginning". It was understandable, therefore, that as the war rumbled on those at home began to sense the end might be in sight. Germany suffered a major defeat on the Eastern front with the surrender of their 6th Army at Stalingrad (on the day Chig wrote his third letter of the year to his father). Not long after, General Bernard Montgomery's success in North Africa enabled the invasion of Italy to be launched. The pincer was closing.

An alms dish, a gift from 363 Searchlight Battery, for Cressage Church forms the subject of Chig's first letter in 1943. The dish – presented by the Buildwas-based unit – provides evidence of his increasing link with the military. By autumn indeed he had become part of the military, serving as a Chaplain to the Forces. With that, of course, the focus of his letters changes markedly. The story of the country parson becomes the story of a Padre serving alongside men on active service, or preparing for active service, at a critical point in the war.

12.1.43

I have received two beautiful carved alms dishes made from the cedars that were in front of the entrance to Cressage Church, and which we had to have cut down. 363 Battery have given them to us as a memento of their time here. They have not gone yet – in fact there is no rumour of their going. I shall expect to see the collections go up still more now that people will be able to see what they and their neighbours are giving!

Did I tell you that Selwyn Walker (*a friend from Worcester days*) is now CO of 505 Battery – the people who were here? They are somewhere fairly near you I believe now, – that is they are somewhere outside B'ham on the south-eastern side. I wish he had been CO when they were here.

I have just picked up 5 more old Wisdens (*Wisden Cricketers' Almanack*) 1893-1897. They include many great events: WG's wonderful return to form; MacLaren's 424; Tom Richardson's great years; WG's success in an Australia tour; the admission of Derby, Warwick, Leics, Hants and Essex to the first-class ranks; the coming of Ranji; the tremendous bowling of Richardson in a Test against Australia, when he took 13 wickets of the 17 that fell, and nearly won the match himself; and all sorts of other good things. This makes me complete from 1893-1942 – quite a good slice of cricket history. Now I want the first 30 editions!

I'm booked to give a gramophone recital to the local WI next month.

Last Saturday I went up to see John Wainwright about a bit of business and found they were in the middle of thrashing (*sic*), so I stayed and lent a hand for a couple of hours. You should have seen me when I got back – I was black, and my hair was absolutely full of chaff and dirt. I had to wash my hair before doing anything else.

19.1.43

We had a telegram from Marco (*for no obvious reason Chig often referred to his former Midland Bank colleague and brother-in-law, Robin, as Marco*) saying that your operation had gone off all right ...... we are glad to hear it is over, and hope now, that it won't be long before you will be home again and with your eye-sight once more.

War-time travel restrictions and the endless duties of a parish priest thwarted Chig seeing his father at this stage, a scenario that would have been repeated in many families and in varied ways elsewhere around the country.

I should like to have come and see you, but I don't think it will be possible. It is very busy time just at present – in fact till after Whitsunday I expect. I have quite a lot of Confirmation candidates this year, and I'm booked up every night of the week except Tuesday, with various items I can't very well cancel, because I can't put them in later on. As a matter of fact I'm booked on the next three Tuesdays as well. If I can somehow squeeze a flying visit I will do so though, but I can't promise.

We are having our annual parish meetings in both parishes this month, having changed them from after Easter to the present time because that is more convenient.

A rather amusing thing has happened. The Director of Education for the County is one of those men whom it is almost impossible to see – he is always busy or out when you try to do so. The Education Committee have recently put forward a proposal to appoint a qualified psychologist to assist teachers etc. and to give advice about retarded or difficult children. There was a lot of opposition to this proposal and so I wrote a letter to the local paper supporting the idea. To my surprise I received a letter from the Director of Education, thanking me for my support, and saying that he would be pleased to see me anytime I cared to call! I know how to get into the Holy of Holies now!

Douglas Rowe has written to us suggesting that we should join forces for a holiday again this year. He has the chance of doing duty in the two little parishes of Shipton Cliffe and Shipton Sollars, a few miles from Cheltenham on the Northleach road, just near Andoversford. Olive Hughes of Powick (*near Worcester, and so known to the Chignells senior and junior and to Rowe*) has a brother who is Rector there. 'Tiny' has said that he will exchange if we will join with Hilda and him. The main question as far as we are concerned is to find someone who can take my duty. I have written to Canon Taylor, in Lightcliffe, and suggested that he and Mrs T should come down here. If they can do it, then we shall join with Tiny and Hilda. I don't think I've ever been to Shipton, though very likely I've been very close, for I've certainly been to Northleach. The Shiptons are just off the main road. Perhaps you will be able to tell us something about that part. Anyway there is something to think about during your long hours of doing little.

Our fondest love to you, Father dear. You know our prayers and thoughts are with you.

2.2.43

Pauline and I will be going to hospital next Monday, but not to stay! We are going under the blood transfusion scheme. There are about 20 going from this village, but most of them will not be called to March. (*Chig had, apparently, overcome earlier reservations about Pauline giving blood, feeling she was not robust enough; either that or Pauline herself was determined to make a continuing contribution to the war effort*).

In our present age donating blood is common-place enough (yet still vitally important), but it should be remembered it was still relatively novel at the time Chig was writing. The first voluntary blood donations in the UK took place in 1921, the UK's first blood bank was not opened until 1937 (in Ipswich) but, after the outbreak of war, four large civilian transfusion centres were opened near London and a military one near Bristol. By 1940, as the war continued to rage, the need for blood increased significantly and eight regional transfusion centres were set up by the emergency medical services and the Army. Thousands of civilians were encouraged to donate blood and 'do their bit for the country' to help save the lives of a great many service men and women as well as civilians. It was certainly not surprising, therefore, that Chig's and Pauline's visit to their regional centre to donate blood for the first time, should be a key feature in his letter to his father. In 1946, learning the lessons of war-time, the national Blood Transfusion Service was set up.

But back to parish matters.

It was mighty fortunate that the new scheme of Services, with my extra one at Buildwas Park, began last Sunday. As I think I mentioned, I could only do this if the Army gave me transport, and so I had a car to take me to and fro, and a jolly good job too, for it was pelting with rain nearly all the morning. For all that, it is extraordinary how little the floods are out – I thought we should have really big floods by today, but there are only small patches here and there.

We had the Cressage Annual Meeting this last Thursday – there was a very poor attendance, but it was an awful night. However it all went off all right, and we did two good bits of business. The first was to compose a resolution which we sent off to our local MP urging him to do all in his power to see that all the children of whatever denomination had definite doctrinal teaching according to their denomination in all schools – that is roughly the resolution; and secondly we decided to launch a scheme for setting aside money to buy tubular bells for the Church as a thanks-offering for Victory and Peace. We hope to do this by means of Nat. Savings, and are awaiting a favourable reply.

Financially we had marvellous year for so small a parish. Our balance on the year's working was £44-odd in the Church Expense account alone, while we sent £70 out of the parish for Missions, Diocesan needs and charities from our Church collections. Naturally finance is not particularly important to me, and the fact that communicants were down a bit, was disappointing, especially as other congregations were good.

I got one shock at the meeting. Arthur Cole suddenly suggested that as parish finances were so good, he thought they ought to pay my dilapidations for this year at any rate! This was passed though it is not intended to be a permanent arrangement, but only because of the present healthy state of the accounts.

On Friday last we had a Whist Drive for the Red Cross, the winners of which go on to either the Area final or a County Final. We had a good turn up, and there were many gifts which had been given to the auction. We made over £10 on the auction. Pauline won a small bag of coffee given by HM the King, and for which draw tickets had been sold. This was auctioned again (*Chig skating over the Chignells' typical generosity*), and made 10/6. I believe a bit over £40 will have been raised by the Whist Drive.

10.2.43

It was apparent from Chig's response to his father that the latter's operation on his eyes had proved satisfactory, as Chig began by offering thanks for a letter:

> in your own writing again, and what a terrific improvement on the letters you have been sending lately. We had great difficulty reading them, but this last letter was easy. You must be feeling very bucked.

Chig then gave details of their visit to the Infirmary at Shrewsbury to donate blood, the wealth of detail again emphasising the novelty of this experience (and opportunity) for the ordinary person.

> As I think I told you in my last letter, we went off for a blood transfusion on Monday. There were 5 of us from Cressage, Pauline and I, Mr Cole the baker, Mrs Mansfield and Miss Price from the farm by the Station. Pauline and I began well by nearly missing the train. The others on the platform were beginning to think we were funking it! We got to the Infirmary and were taken up to the top floor, where all the operations take place. We were told they were using an operating theatre for the transfusion. After sitting outside for a few minutes Mrs Mansfield and Miss Price were taken and, shortly after, Pauline and I. We had to take off our coats and roll our sleeves up, and then lie down on a bed. Then the arm is washed just near the inside of the elbow, and a rubber tube about 6 inches wide is bound round the upper part of the arm to tighten it up and make the veins stand out. Then they stick a needle in with a bit of local anaesthetic – at least I was told that was what they had done to me, though I didn't notice it although I was watching and chatting to the nurse all the time. Then they stick a larger needle in attached to a rubber tube, which in its turn is attached to a quart bottle. Then you have to open and close your hand and out flows the blood. It takes different people different times to give a pint – I took about average – 10 or 15 mins I should think, It is quite strange watching the bottle fill up. Then when it is over they bind up the prick after having got you to flex your arm. Then they remove the rubber tube, and put you on a trolley and push you off for a rest in the next room. Here you get a ½ pint of either very sweet tea or beer, and you just rest for 10 or 15 mins or more if you feel like it. The bandage is removed if you've stopped bleeding and a bit of sticky plaster put on and home you go. Miss Price and P and I felt no ill effects afterwards – though P didn't have a very good night. Mrs Mansfield was sick after her tea when she got home, but that was more excitement and nerves than anything else, but Mr Cole's arm wasn't so good – it bled a good deal after and as he had to mix the flour and yeast etc. for the day's baking when he got home, he had a stiff time.
> I went off threshing most of yesterday, so you can see what effect it had on me!

2.3.43

Pauline's mother arrived last Wednesday. She seems very fit and well, and has already got going in the garden. As a matter of fact this amazing weather has got us all on the job. I have dug up every bit I can except one, and have sown my first peas and beans, and have also had to cut the lawn! On Saturday we had quite a little ceremony. Macy has kindly given us a young plum tree – Burbidge's Giant Prune – and he brought it back with him, so we had great fun planting it by the old apple with the mistletoe on it. We hope that it will fertilize two grand eaters we have just near, but which hardly ever produce any decent plums.

Did I tell you we now have choir practice at 8.00pm so that the men can come? They have got very keen now – we have 5 of them – and they all have decent voices, ranging from Macy's really lovely tenor to very fair country voices. Last Sunday we tried Ps(*alm*) 136 in a fancy way. After the first two verses sung in ordinary harmony, the men sang the first half of the odd-numbered verses in unison and the trebles the first half of the even-numbers, everyone joining in in harmony for the second half, until we came to the last two verses, which we sang with the Gloria in harmony. It sounded excellent, and there was terrific competition between the two sections, to see if the one couldn't sing better than the other!

Now we are about to have a Church Council meeting to decide about bringing the choir downstairs, sitting them in the front pews which we shall turn round facing each other as though they were real choir stalls. This will be a temporary measure, for when the war is over, we hope to have a robed choir in oak stalls.

The Ch. Coun. is also going to launch a special savings campaign to buy tubular bells to ring victory in – we hope! Whether we shall be able to get the bells before the war is over or not, I don't know yet, but I'm waiting for a reply.

Little Sheinton held a Red Cross Whist Drive last Friday, which was such a success that we were able to send over £27 to the Red Cross. It wasn't all Whist Drive, for they had draw tickets for grocery parcels, and also an auction of gifts – I had to be auctioneer – I believe the same fate awaits me this Friday at Cressage at a Whist Drive for Mrs. Churchill's Fund for Russia.

On the reverse side of this letter's final page Chig wrote:

I have at present a very regrettable inclination to make up clerihews about every-body *(which seems somewhat un-parsonical, but Chig had a mischievous and quite robust sense of humour; laughter was seldom far away)*. Here are two rude ones:

James Thursby-Pelham JP
Deputy-Lieutenant Salop, 1903,
A fact he hasn't forgotten
Although he was rotten.

> The Baldwins of Old Hall,
> Never do any work at all,
> They just sit around
> And are the gloomiest people I've found.

10.3.43

At this point whist drives seem to feature frequently in Chig's letters to his father, but they provide a sign of the populace working, in various ways, for the war effort, and also to bolster community morale.

Last week we had another colossal whist drive and auction for Mrs Churchill's Aid to Russia Fund and raised £51. People are extraordinarily generous in the things they give for auction, and also the way in which they buy. The auction took over an hour, after the drive was finished. Someone gave a pig for raffle, and it fetched £6-10-0. A washing machine in the auction fetched £7 as well.

On Saturday I went to hear the President of the Board of Education (*equivalent of our Secretary of State for Education today; at the time of Chig's letter it was R A Butler, "the best Prime Minister Britain never had"*) speaking in Shrewsbury. As he was addressing the National Union of Teachers, he hadn't got much to say on religion, but on the whole I thought he seemed pretty good, though I don't share his good opinions on the ATC and other Youth organisations, and I also disagree with him in his view that Senior and Junior schools must be separated. My opinion is that this will mean a further break up of parochial, or more particularly, village community life. I think we want to get back to that community sense.

On Monday we had a Church Council at Cressage, and have passed a scheme to install either 6 swinging bells or 8 chiming bells as soon as possible after the war. A local ringer had given it as his opinion that we ought to be able to get 6 small swinging bells in the tower, and that they ought to be quite safe. I still have my doubts, but I shall write to Mears and Stainbank and try and get them to give their advice.

The same Church Council meeting approved Chig's plans, as previously shared with his father, to bring the choir from the gallery upstairs to choir stalls downstairs in the Church.

We are also going to have a Midnight Eucharist at Easter. I noticed that a few parishes have started this, and as I know some of my folk have considerable difficulty in getting to the early Service, I thought we'd give them a chance to vote about it. They were very nearly all in favour, and those that did not vote (only 2) were not opposed to it, but it would make no difference to them, for they will come at their usual times.

Tomorrow I am trying out a sort of one-man Anvil (*I presume this was to be a discussion group or something similar, a place where things could be hammered out, metaphorically at least, as a means of reaching out to the wider community*), which is going to take place every Thursday night. I've got half a dozen questions for the first effort – I only hope there will be a good turn up.

Now that there will be limited accommodation in the choir, we are going to have voice tests for all the persons who wish to be in the choir. Miss Ethel Jones, who will accompany the applicants, Macy and myself will stand outside the door so that we shan't see who is singing. I expect I shall know the voices, but Macy won't. Naturally we shan't make the test too stiff, but we want to make the choir into something that takes a bit of getting into, instead of being something anyone can get into. We also propose to have an apprentices' pew.

Well I must stop now, as I have a funeral – a sad case of a grand little chap aged 11 who has died of a burst appendix, when, if only the parents had called in the Dr. earlier, they could easily have avoided the death.

At this point we get another indicator of the effect of war even on minor domestic matters. The quality of the paper on which Chig writes his letters becomes very flimsy, such that one can almost see the print on the reverse side (and Chig was still typing on both sides of the page, as densely as his typewriter allowed, in order to be economical with paper).

16.3.43

Much in this letter would have been of special interest to George Chignell, as a former Organist and Choirmaster. Other comments in this letter suggest that Chig's sister (Robin) must have pressed successfully for an Ash Wednesday Service in her home parish and, reading between the lines, it seems the Vicar's address majored on spiritual healing, about which Chig had this to say:

At a guess I should say the Reformation was the main cause of the decline in spiritual healing. Until those days people went largely to the monasteries to be healed, and though many odd preparations were made for curing folk, yet the ministry would have included prayer and Sacrament. When the Reformation bust up the monasteries, it was accompanied by a great increase in lay medical knowledge, and as with education in somewhat later days, painting and various other arts and many other things, men turned from the Church to more secular means. In this sense I should say your Vicar's address was right – the responsibility rests largely with the laity, for if men do not come to you for healing, your skill is likely to decrease with practice.

Well the choir is now downstairs! The voice test has been held! Three boys have failed to pass – two of them having been in the choir before, at least nominally, and peace remains! One of the choirmen who is an estate carpenter, took Friday and Saturday off to do the job, with such assistance as I could give him. We were able to get the pews turned etc. in time for Sunday, but we had not time to make the front of the boys' stalls. The voice test took place in school on Friday at 4.30. Miss Ettie Jones played the accompaniments, and everyone had to sing a verse of a hymn, which they were allowed to choose, and a scale. Mrs Davies, the schoolmistress and myself were in a sort of lobby where we could hear but not see and the three of us allotted marks to each voice. We then pooled them, and as I said, three boys failed to pass. They have been told they can sit in the probationers' pew, but I fancy the aforementioned won't do that. One of them had quite a loud voice, but is always flat and the tone is ghastly, the second really has no voice, while the third – a new-comer – may have a voice in time, but at present he can't stick to a tune.

We have our 'Wings for Victory' week starting on March 27th, and are aiming at £750. The Church Council hopes to raise £250 of this to be put into the PO Savings Bank as a fund for our proposed Church Bells. Our excellent Mr Cole has promised to give one bell!

I'm afraid I shall have to stop now as I have to type out 81 notices about the Bell scheme, and get them round the parish as soon as possible.

6.4.43

Mrs Bottomley (*Pauline's mother*) goes on the 14th of this month, which is Wednesday week – so you could come as soon as you like after that. Trains don't seem to fit in very well with your buses, but my timetable says there are trains as follows:

Leamington 11.15;	Salop	1.00;	depart 1.15	for Cressage
” 1.06;	”	3.00;	depart 5.30	”
” 4.13;	”	6.08;	depart 8.45	”
” 6.11;	”	8.03;	depart 8.45	”

It looks as though the most convenient would be the 11.15 except that you say there is more likely to be room on the bus in the afternoon. I should have to meet that at Salop for I could not get down to L'ton in time – my first train is due to arrive there at 11.22. Only the late train, i.e. the 6.11 from L'ton has a decent connection at Salop apart from this 11.15.

Now for last week's events. They are almost completely taken up with finance! As I told you it was our 'Wings for Victory' week, and we had included a £250 target for the Chiming Bells we hope to install when the war is over – this money was to be invested in PO Savings Bank and thus loaned for the war effort. I actually expected that we should get round about half this target during the week, and then gradually build it up as time went on, but instead we raised £232 during the week, and have another £35 promised. When you think that that is all straight giving, and not saving for themselves it really is a marvellous effort, especially as neither the Pelhams nor the Baldwins gave a penny except their usual collection on the Sunday. Both my Churchwardens gave £45, and one of them has promised another £15 later on. A smallholder and one of my sidesmen gave £20 with a promise of another £20 in the autumn – various others gave £10 or £5 and practically every house in the village gave something. The children at school each gave at least a 6d stamp.

Then there was the actual savings for the 'Wings for Victory' – the target for Cressage and Sheinton was £750 – i.e. £250 more than we raised for 'War Weapons', or whatever the last special week was called, and working out at about 35/– a head of the population. On the first day we got £330, this went to £420 on the Monday, £490 on the Tuesday, £550 on the Wednesday. We passed the target at 3.25pm on Thursday finishing that day with £804. Then the village went mad. Friday night saw us up to £1250, Saturday saw the total at £1641 and we were informed by Lloyds bank at the beginning of this week that they had invested another £800 which was to be allocated to the Cressage total, so that we finished up with a grand total of £2441–17–0! – something like £6 per head, and no factories or business to put a large sum down. It really is amazing. The two schools between them got a bit over £100 – Cressage £72 and Sheinton £30. Now then Kineton, see if you can triple your target.

7.6.43

I have now finished my annual pilgrimage round the schools. Pauline and I went to Wollaston at the foot of the Breidden Hills last Wednesday. We went by train, and after visiting the school we had a picnic on the hills. It was lovely. We had the unusual experience of hearing a stoat killing a rabbit, and then seeing it drag the corpse up the hill towards the nest where its young must have been. We caught an afternoon train home to Salop and after tea went to the cinema.

Chig clearly had adjusted to not using his car because of petrol and tyre shortages, and was happy to use both his bike and trains, often making good use of waiting time. A reference later in this letter seems to suggest his elderly father had resumed cycling also.

We had another win last Saturday against the Sentinel. I was acting captain in the absence of our regular one who was busy harvesting hay. We were all out for 72 and I got a duck. I thought we were for it for their early men seemed good bats, and they got half way for the loss of only two wickets. I was keeping wicket and got a crack below the eye, which necessitated my going off for a bit of repairs. However I was soon back. Changing the bowling I put Macy on, and he got two wickets (one stumped by me) in his first over, and then (*with*) a really brilliant catch right on the boundary with one hand as the ball was going for six dismissed the best batsman on their side, and afterwards we were well on top getting them out for 54.

I have been helping bring in the hay on Monday and Tuesday of this week – unloading wagons and making stacks. This morning we have been in to Shrewsbury – I bought a first aid outfit for the cricket club!

We are now getting busy with the Garden Show. There is a good deal to do, writing round to possible vice-presidents in the hope that they will give us a donation, getting out entry forms, arranging for gatekeepers, teas, sideshows etc., making applications to get off entertainments tax and so on.

The village seems to be having a lot of accidents lately. One dear old farmer nearly cut his arm off, a ganger on the railway nearly sawed his finger off, a farmhand fell off a wagon-load of hay, fortunately only spraining his foot, and then I got this black eye. However, none of us is very serious and we are all getting about again.

It must seem quite strange being on a bicycle again after so many years, but it is a real joy to ride these days, when there is so little traffic, and when it is possible to get on roads again that hardly ever see an internal combustion engine. I came across the guarantee of your old bicycle last week, and found that it is now 20 years old. The bottom gear of the three-speed has gone – whether permanently or not I don't know, but otherwise she goes well.

13.7.43

I wondered what the stop-press news you sent means? I haven't heard of any men in the present Battery coming from Kineton, though I don't know them very well yet. They are coming to Church at Sheinton once a fortnight now, and Harrison and another officer called Prichard who was at Hereford Cathedral School take it in turns to read the lessons, and very well they read them too. I am going to see them tomorrow as they have asked me to see an E.N.S.A. show and have tea with them afterwards.

21.7.43

No, I still can't get any runs, not for Cound anyway. I had two games last week! One on Tuesday evening, a scratch game with two teams made up almost entirely of soldiers, with one or two civilians I succeeded in collecting. I did manage to get 29 not out, out of 70 in that game, but our side lost.

Yesterday I had to go to Shrewsbury, and as there was no chance of me getting back for lunch, I thought I'd go out to Greenfields, where 353 Battery have moved to, and cadge a lunch off them. I found them all right, and after a good lunch Gillespie showed me round. They are about to have a visit from the General in command of A.A. – though you had better not mention this to anyone, as it is information of value to the enemy, I suppose! – and so everything was paint and scrubbing.

11.8.43

Last week was a pretty hectic one. First there was the Show and the preparations for it. Saturday was not a good day for it – there was a fair amount of rain from about 11.00 till 2.00, but it stopped for the afternoon, only setting in again about 7.00. So we got the programme through completely, except that the sideshows didn't have much of a chance. Still, I think we shall have cleared £40 for the Red Cross. The children's sports were a great success and the tea tent was very well patronized. The actual Show was excellent, Fraser, the judge, telling me that it was the best as far as quality was concerned that he had come across this year. As far as we were concerned we were not so successful as last year. Pauline got two firsts, with Cos Lettuce and Red Currants, and she also got a third with Bottled Fruit. I got a second for Broad Beans and for eating Plums, but my potatoes, which I thought were certain to get a first, for they were well-shaped, the largest and also clear-skinned, didn't get anything. I could kick myself that I didn't show either Marrows or Cooking Plums, for when I went round my garden at Sheinton on Sunday I found a beautiful pair of marrows which would certainly have got a 1st or a 2nd, and also masses of good cooking plums ready to pick.

Well, the chief news, and a bit of news which will come as a real surprise to you, is that I am shortly off as an Army Chaplain. The Bishop wrote to me last week to say that there was a great shortage of Anglican Chaplains, and would I consider the matter. I felt pretty strongly that the time had come when I ought to go, and so I wrote back and said 'yes'. I am now busy making arrangements for the parish in my absence. Burgess of Cound has kindly agreed to take 3 Eucharists a month, 2 at Cressage and 1 at Sheinton, and to look after the parish generally. Noel Baldwin is going to see the Bishop about being a Lay Reader, and if that happens, then the parish won't be so badly off. Of course, there are all sorts of other items, such as finding a Correspondent for the Schools, a Secretary for the Village Hall and for the Cricket Club, a Deanery Secretary for the S.P.C.K. and someone to look after various little financial matters, and also Church matters, but no doubt they will all sort themselves out in time. Pauline will stay on here, of course, and will either have her mother, or Olga and the family to be with her. It has all been rather sudden, and I may be off by the end of the month, but things are generally moving so fast now, that it is a question of being of some use immediately or never.

And then Chig, who invariably signed off his letter as 'Your loving son, Rowland' signed off here: 'Good bye for now Father dear, Your loving son, Rowland'

25.8.43

Things were certainly moving a-pace, but there was time still for two further letters from home before Chig joined the Army, and the Vicar became the Padre.

> As for myself, I have now passed my medical – Category A – and am awaiting a notification to appear for an interview at Chester. It is possible I may go somewhere round there for a bit of training, as there is a training school for Chaplains somewhere near Chester, but it is only for three weeks anyway, and I don't expect there will be much free time, for I understand it is a pretty concentrated course.
>
> I have been writing to various people resigning different positions I hold – it has amazed me to find out how many they were. Noel Baldwin has seen the Bishop and is to try himself out as a Lay Reader provisionally, to see how he gets on. I hope he will find he can do it for it will ease the situation here considerably if he can take Matins and Evensong. Tomorrow I am taking Cressage choir to Salop to tea and the cinema, as I promised them an outing some time ago, and I thought I'd better get it in before I went.
>
> We had quite a decent day last Saturday, and we put it across the Sentinel properly. We got 183 for 7 declared and got them out for 45, much to our joy and their chagrin, for they were out for our blood! It looks as though we shall go through the season undefeated, in fact we have so far won every match, not even a draw!

And, again he ended: 'Fondest love to you Father dear, Ever your loving son, Rowland'.

28.8.43 (amended later to 1.9.43)

> Last week I went to the Institution of the new Vicar of Longnor and Leebotwood, a parish in the Deanery, near Church Stretton. I cycled over as I wanted to be present at the Service, for the new man is an old Sarum man who was at Salisbury just a little after I left. He seems a very nice young chap and I hope to see a lot more of him when the war is over, and I have come back here.
>
> On Friday I went with Pauline to Chester for my interview. We got there about 11.00 and as my interview was not till 2.30 we walked about the town first. It hardly seemed as though there was a war on, for the shops seemed very

well stocked, and they had all sorts of things we never see in Shrewsbury. We had an early lunch at Browns of Chester, and then went for a walk on the wall, past King Charles' Tower where I remember we once had a family snap taken. Then we went to the Cathedral which I couldn't remember much. It is a fine one isn't it, and the mosaics on the north wall are magnificent. Then we set out for Curzon Park where my interview was to be held. It is on the other side of the river opposite the race-course, and very pleasant it is there too. When we had crossed the bridge we stopped and asked an elderly civilian how to get there, and his immediate reply was, 'Do you want No 20?' I said 'Yes', and he replied, 'I expect you are Mr Chignell'! It turned out he was a sort of secretary in the Army Chaplains' Dept. As we hoped to catch a train back to Salop at 3.17 and were a long way from the station I got there early, and asked if I could be seen a bit before 2.30. Consequently I was shepherded into the presence of the Assistant Chaplain General, Western Command, at about 2.15. He asked various questions about my experience with troops, and why I wanted to be a Chaplain – to which I replied I didn't want to be one but thought I ought to do the job if wanted! – and then he told me about my possible future.. After this interview, he sent a form to London stating what he thought of me, and if they accepted me, I should have to report to Tidworth on Saturday September 18th. Well that is what happened and I am now about to get busy ordering my kit and finding the best way to Tidworth. The ACG said that normally a chaplain was guaranteed 3 months in England, but that it was possible the guarantee might not be given now. Well, we caught our train back to Salop, which allowed us plenty of time to catch the 5.30 home.

On Saturday, I played what is probably my last match of the season for Cound, as I don't think I shall be able to play next Sat. We won again, though we had a very hard fight. Our opponents were the R.A.P.C. who beat us twice last year. They got 6 of us out for 35, but I managed to stick and Gee and John Wainwright both played useful hitting innings, and we finally reached 89 on a difficult pitch. I only got 15, but managed to smother their best bowler, who is playing for the R.A.P.C. at Lord's this week. Then they fought like blazes, and despite good bowling had got well into the 50s with only 2 wickets down. However, Dickson bowled really well and got a thundering good left-hand bat out with an absolutely first-class ball, and I caught the man at the other end, behind the wicket, almost immediately after, and that unsettled them, though one batsman proved very dangerous. However, we got him out eventually, and succeeded in winning by 24 runs, which doesn't give any idea of the severity of the struggle, which was the toughest match we've had this year.

You may wonder what I'm doing when I say that next Sunday is my last at Cressage & Sheinton for the present, I feel I really need a few days rest and free from parish and other duties, and so we are going to Powick for the following weekend – from Thursday to Tuesday, then we shall come back, and I shall collect my stuff, and settle up any oddments that may have cropped up.

Last Sunday we had a surprise when at Matins at Cressage we found that the Buildwas Park troops had turned up unexpectedly. They had said they would come next Sunday to the Harvest, but it was a pleasant surprise to see them last Sunday.

Last Thursday I took Cressage Choir out to tea and the cinema, and they had a very jolly time, and, fortunately, the whole show was grand for children.

But last week was very gloomy for the village. Dr Gittins got definitely worse; then on top of that the young locum who was doing his work went off his head and had to be taken to a mental hospital, and I'm afraid it is a bad case. Then a child he was attending nearly bled to death, with haemorrhage from a tooth; a dear old woman in the village had to have her leg off, and was quite despaired of, though she has made a good recovery, and looks like getting over it now and, lastly, the son of this old dear got compassionate leave and came down with his wife to look after the old man, and his wife was taken ill just as his leave expired.

It wasn't the happiest of circumstances in which to be leaving his parishes, but Chig's final message, in the Deanery magazine, setting out arrangements during his absence was firmly robust and encouraging, urging everyone to do their Christian duty "now that we have reached a crisis in the history of the world":

CRESSAGE AND SHEINTON

MY DEAR PEOPLE,

I had hoped to be able to give pretty complete details as to the future arrangements for Cressage and Sheinton during my absence, but at present I can only tell you that the Rector of Cound has kindly consented to look after you. I do not yet know the date of my going, except that it is almost certain to be within the next month.

There will have to be a re-arrangement of services when I have gone. At present the arrangements are that there will be a Parish Eucharist at Cressage at 9-30 on the second and fourth Sundays in the month, and at Sheinton on the third Sunday. It is hoped that Matins and Evensong will continue as before, but the final arrangements for this have not yet been made.

The Rector of Cound will visit any who are sick, if he is told of such cases, and I hope you will let him know, for it is extraordinarily easy not to hear of anyone who is ill.

Now that we have reached a crisis in the history of the world, it is more than ever the duty of everyone who calls himself a Christian to witness by his regular Church worship to the power of God which alone can set the world aright, and to keep the promises which he made at Baptism and Confirmation. During the months to come I trust and pray that you will all put God and the worship of Him first, however busy you are, or however difficult it may be. Especially should we seek Him in His own Sacrament of the Eucharist. A big responsibility rests on you in the absence of your parish priest, and

I hope when I return to find the Christian life of Cressage and Sheinton stronger than ever. Those of us who will have been absent, will expect, on our return, to find a strong Christian Fellowship, based on regular Christian worship, into which we can come and take our part. It is you on which the responsibility for such a fellowship lies, and it can only be attained by starting now. It can't be done in a hurry at the last moment. Whether you are 8 or 80, or whatever age you are, you have your part to play, and one absentee will harm and weaken the whole structure. By staying at home because you are tired or because there is something in the house or garden that wants doing, you are putting other things or yourself before God. We have to make time for God, not fit Him in where He is convenient to us. God bless you all.

Your Sincere Friend and Priest,

W. R. GHIGNELL.

Chig's letter to the parishioners of Cressage and and Sheinton about arrangements during his war-time absence.

7

A Padre's Letters to his Father 1943

Chig made the necessary arrangements to leave his parishes in the spiritual care of a neighbouring colleague, and encouraged parishioners to play their part also during his absence. He and Pauline had then taken their short break, following which Pauline returned to the Vicarage at Cressage, and Chig – now 35 years old – set off for Tidworth and his initial training, both in basic military skills and in the duties of a Forces Chaplain.

He was about to become a 'Sky Pilot', as military chaplains colloquially are known.

Tidworth, home to the Royal Army Chaplains' Dept.'s training centre, housed in an old rectory, was known to Chig, both from school-day OTC camps and also from his time at theological college in nearby Salisbury.

Some 20 priests and ministers were his companions for a fortnight's course instructing them how to behave as soldiers. They "marched about the place, saluted hundreds of times, stood smartly to attention thousands of times and were shown how to fill up Army forms millions of times – all very enlightening" he recalled in post-war years. "We learnt to read maps and had one superb practical exercise in this. We were sent off in pairs with a map and a compass, with instructions to get to a given point at such and such a time. We all got to the place to find it was a cottage café and sat down to a well-earned tea, when suddenly we realized our instructor had not arrived. He turned up just as we finished tea, having got lost!"

"This fortnight was quite a lot of fun," Chig remembered, "despite the 'bull'. Amongst our party were two foreign chaplains, a Pole and a Czech, excellent fellows who had escaped to join their respective forces in Britain".

With basic training and induction completed Chig headed for London and the Marylebone Hotel, for instructions on his next move. This move, a brief one, was to Northern Command HQ in York. His brother-in-law, Arthur Bottomley (Olga's husband) was based there, and gave him lunch. From York, Chig headed south again, to Nottingham, and Chilwell.

With the re-armament and the mechanisation of the Army in the 1930s a Central Ordnance Depot (COD) and workshop to support vehicles was established on the site of the First World War National Shell Filling Factory, Chilwell. The COD opened in

1937 and, in 1942, became the home of the RAOC (Royal Army Ordnance Corps). This British Army corps was responsible for both the supply and repair of weapons, armoured vehicles and other military equipment, ammunition and clothing as well as certain minor functions such as laundry, mobile baths and photography. Chilwell also was a training base for servicemen and women, prior to their posting elsewhere, at home or abroad.

Chilwell's huge complement at the time of Chig's arrival included 2,000 ATS (Auxiliary Territorial Service) women, which made him remember a question he had been asked at his interview at Chester. The regular Army chaplains forming his interview panel had not left a favourable impression on him, and when they asked him "What would your reaction be if you were posted to a unit with a large number of ATS in it?". Chig, being something of a 'man's man' with a sense of humour to match, sought to lighten the rather dour atmosphere, and so replied: "I should probably die, but I should have died in a good cause". No-one smiled, and he was allowed to depart to catch his train to Shrewsbury and on to Cressage – but was the Chaplains' Dept. belatedly exercising a sense of humour – or irony – in posting him to a camp with so many women?

Thus, at the beginning of October, Chig resumed writing to his father, now from Highfield Officers Mess, Central Ordnance Depot, Chilwell, Nottingham. All the earlier letters to his father had been typed, but now – still on A5 paper – they were hand-written.

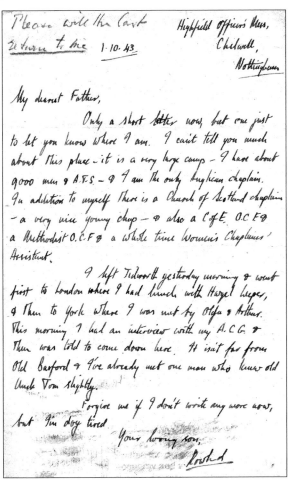

Chig's letter to his father of 1 October 1943.

1.10.43

My dearest Father,

Only a short letter now, but one just to let you know where I am. I can't tell you much about this place – it is a very large camp – I have about 9,000 men and ATS – and I am the only Anglican chaplain. In addition to myself there is a Church of Scotland chaplain – a very nice young chap (*David Easton*) – and also a C of E OCF (Outside Chaplain of Forces) and a Methodist OCF and a whole-time Women's Chaplains' Assistant.

I left Tidworth yesterday morning and went first to London where I had lunch with Hywel Leeper (*son of his training incumbent in Huddersfield*), and then to York where I was met by Olga and Arthur. This morning I had an interview with my ACG (*Assistant Chaplain General*) & then was told to come down here.

Forgive me if I don't write any more now, but I'm dog tired.

Your loving son, Rowland.

6.10.43

I can give you some more of my personal impressions though there is much that I may not tell and there is much that I do not know & probably never shall.

This morning I have been on a sort of Cook's tour of the place, and it has only convinced me of what I had previously suspected – namely that it is going to be incredibly hard to make any sort of personal contact with the men and women. The officers themselves get little chance of this & with the constant flow of men & women, it is going to be nigh impossible for me to touch more than the very outside fringe.

I had a very easy Sunday – a 7.30 Eucharist at one of the two Church Huts – the C of E OCF took one at the other Hut. Then there was a 10.00 Parade Service which has to be held in the cinema because there is not room for it to be held in either Church. The OCF took the Service and I presided. From now on he fades out of the picture & I take over, & it will be up to me to make any other arrangements. The trouble is that Sunday is pretty well an ordinary working day. However there are two little hospitals for slight cases of sickness & the C of S (*Church of Scotland*) Padre and myself joined forces last Sunday in taking a Service at one of these.

On Monday the two of us got together to work out some sort of a programme, & in the afternoon I went to Nottingham to get one or two things. It struck me it was a pretty measly sort of town. I spent the evening getting to know some of the officers in my mess.

Yesterday I spent the morning doing all sorts of jobs in the Church Hut vestry which has to do as my office, & in the afternoon I had to get ready for a Padre's Hour with ATS. I don't know whether you have heard of Padre's Hours, but they are definitely on orders, & consist of an hour's informal talk, discussion and questions. There is a weekly ATS one on Tuesdays at 7.30 & a men's on Wednesday at 4.00. Last night (Tuesday) was a most encouraging start. The numbers are limited to about 50 or 60 so as to be manageable, & I began by talking to them about the attractiveness of Christ & then after about 20 mins we started questions. At first I could get none from them, so I asked them one and off we went. The trouble then was to stop them. We went on over the hour, & got deeper and deeper in our theology. Finally I said anyone who wanted could go, and not a girl went for another 10 mins! Then there was some considerable exit, but even then a batch of about 15 or so remained behind while we discussed reincarnation, the future life & the soul. I eventually got away after about 1½ hours in all, & staggered back to my Mess for dinner, which gradually revived me! Curiously enough, I found in the last couple of minutes that two of the girls who were talking to me had only arrived the day before from Huddersfield! They were not Huddersfield girls, but had been posted there & one was actually billeted in Wentworth St (*where the Chignells had lived during their time there*).

Now later on I have a Padre's Hour with some men. Though I have been told to expect the men to be far more inclined to talk and to question, I can hardly imagine that such will be the case. However I shall soon see!

When peace comes it will be good to be able to talk freely – I shall probably be able to beat even Marco (*his brother-in-law, Robin*) in the tales I shall tell!

14.10.43

I'm now comfortably installed in a bedroom with H & C laid on! I'm sharing this with a Major Nash who comes from Gloucestershire and who knew the Gillespies and also old Lec Williams. He is also a great lover of the countryside, & so you can guess we have plenty to talk about. I'm also getting to know several of the other officers fairly well now & am finding them a very decent crowd.

A good deal of my time is taken with men coming to me with a bewildering variety of problems, some of them are pretty ghastly too. Then the Padre's Hours are a grand opportunity of getting in touch with them, & very lively shows they are too. The ATS ones, too, are very good & I don't seem to be able to get away at the end, men or girls come up to continue asking questions or to discuss some point. My first impressions are that there is a good deal of serious thinking going on these days in men's minds, but that their knowledge of the Christian faith is pretty well nil

We had our Harvest Festival on Sunday & there was an absolute mass of fruit, vegs etc. which I took in a van to various hospitals in Nottingham, on Monday.

I took Monday afternoon off & went to Derby, where after prowling around I had tea & went to the cinema. I saw 'The Moon is Down', a good film about a Nazi-occupied Norwegian village. Cedric Hardwicke was in it. Coming away from the cinema, I passed a V.A.D. (*a member of the Voluntary Aid Detachment, a voluntary organisation set up to provide field nursing services, mainly in hospitals, in the United Kingdom and various other countries in the British Empire; it came into its own during World War I and World War II*) whose face seemed familiar to me, & after passing I realised she was a girl called Joan Berry who used to live at Lightcliffe! Incidentally, last week when I went to a Chaplains' Conference at Nottingham, the first person I met at the Barracks was an ATS who used to be in my Youth Fellowship at Huddersfield! I couldn't for the life of me remember her name though.

We have a Confirmation Class of 15 ATS which I took last night. Miss Allen, who is officially the Chaplains' Assistant, and I share this, taking alternative weeks. Did I tell you she was at Selly Oak and knew Peggy Rolfe through their prayer group? She has been a missionary among the Maoris until, coming home on furlough, she was appointed to this work. She's a good soul, but somewhat overpowering and 'bossy'.

20.10.43

Thank you for your good letter. I find myself eagerly looking for letters these days!, and very bucked when I get some.

Time goes frightfully quickly here – there is so much to do, and so many things simply have to be left. I can't say that I ever found time dragging at Cressage – it was a whole-time job there – but this is about a dozen men's jobs if it is going to be done properly. As if Chilwell itself was not enough, I have been landed with another batch of about 250 men and ATS at Long Eaton, about a couple of miles away. I simply cannot fit in any Services but I shall be going over there once a fortnight to take a Padre's Hour & have a chat with the men. I fancy we must have passed very close to this Depot once when we came over by car to Nottingham – was it on our way to the holiday we had near Ripon? Didn't we pass through Long Eaton and Beeston then? Because, if so, Chilwell lies between them

Last Friday I went to the Depot Choral Society & had a very jolly time. They are a good lot of singers & have a very good chap as conductor, Corporal Freestone who was a London organist. At present they are rehearsing for a BBC test on Nov 10th, when Dr Stanton is coming to hear them. They are rehearsing 'Surely, Surely' & 'The Hallelujah' from 'Messiah', a couple of choruses from 'Merrie England' and 'Rolling Down to Rio' by Quilter(?) (*in fact the words were by Rudyard Kipling and were set to music by Sir Edward German and also by Peter Bellamy*) together with one or two other part songs & they are also practising 'Hiawatha's Wedding Feast'. I hope to be able to get to these fairly frequently.

On the previous night I actually went to a dance! Not to dance, but to potter round talking to those present. They had a 'cabaret' show which included a solo item for the violin, played by a Pte. Kirkland – late of the LPO (*London Philharmonic Orchestra*)! He has fortunately been rescued from the gentle duty of tending tank engines (think of his hands!) and given a job in one of the Battn offices.

Did I tell you that I got landed for umpiring a hockey match ten days ago?! I went to watch & the umpire didn't turn up, so they grabbed me. As I hadn't seen any hockey for about 10 years I felt pretty well at sea; however all went well.

Last Saturday, Easton, the C of S Padre, had to turn out for the opposition at rugger as they were one short. I was very thankful they didn't get hold of me! We have an Irish international called Biggert here, but the others are considerably inferior of course. (*Biggert's name is not listed under Irish internationals; perhaps he was an Ireland trialist, but clearly he was someone whose ability stood out among the others at Chilwell*)

Pauline has had a nasty little attack of gastric 'flu while she has been up in Yorkshire, but she is much better now – at least she says so. It's a good job she got it there with someone to look after her.

27.10.43

Last week I had to go over to Basford on behalf of a man in this Depot, & I went to see old Uncle Tom's Church and also tried to see his successor, but without any luck.

I went for a good walk after tea on Saturday with two extremely nice officers – the Garrison Adjutant & the President of our Mess committee. We went down to the River Trent & walked about 3 miles along the bank. I was surprised how nice it was there – fields on either side & a spot of really nice looking country on the other side, which I must explore sometime. These two men are both about 10 years older than I, & as usual with my friends, are both a good deal taller – it is rather strange how practically all my best friends are tall men. Have you noticed it? – Douglas Rowe, Malcolm Taylor, Tony Fletcher, Dr Gittins, & now these two.

A most extraordinary & unusual experience is coming my way on Thursday – I'm going to a fancy dress dance! I don't want to go, as you can guess, knowing how much I 'love' dancing (!), but I can't very well get out of it & so I might as well make the best of it & go properly dressed. The ATS officers are giving it and Collins & Viyse – the two I've mentioned above – are going & we are getting up a small party. My original idea was to go as "I don't know which way to turn", and I was going to stick a label on myself and put on my uniform back to front! But I realised this would be very uncomfortable, & so instead I've hired a pirate's costume from a shop in Nottingham.

I must stop now as I am going to dinner with a General's wife! Major Nash, my room-mate, & I have been invited – I feel very much among the top shelf!

3.11.43

Well, the weeks go very quickly here – it seems no time at all since I first got here & yet I've been here nearly five weeks. It is very difficult to give you any news, so much of my work is taken up with regular routine items or with personal interviews etc.

The dance was a great success & I even enjoyed it – staying till the bitter end & eventually getting to bed at 2.45am! It really was a treat to see pretty dresses & gay colours after all the drab, dull khaki. Various people took me in hand & very bravely stood the severe trial of dancing with me. I'm afraid, though, that I'm no dancer, & when the war is over I shall once more return to civilian life with no desire to go dancing again.

Easton (*Chig's C of S colleague*) retired to bed on Friday evening & has been there ever since. He has a bad attack of 'flu, & this coming on top of the severe blow on the ribs that he got at rugger the previous Saturday, has laid him up properly. On Saturday I got a touch of it, but managed to stagger around on Sunday when, apart from my normal four Services at 7.00, 8.00. 10.00, & 6.30, I took a Church of Scotland parade Service at 9.00 for Easton & baptised the infant of a Capt. Chidley in the afternoon. Strangely enough, by the evening I was beginning to feel much better, though distinctly wobbly on the legs. However, I have now completely recovered & am full of beans again.

I became all 'Anglo-Catholic' yesterday! (*Chig's own tradition and inclinations were towards that end of the wide spectrum within the Church of England but, typically, clergy serving in rural parishes often have to be 'all things to all people' and to seek something of a common denominator, which is why rural churches, in their worship, are very often 'middle of the road', appealing to – or not offending – as many parishioners as possible.*) I received a mysterious, unsigned card telling me that the Church Union were having a 'Solemn Requiem Mass' on All Souls' day at St. Alban's, Nottingham, & I thought I would like to go, not only, though chiefly, because of the day & the reason, but also to meet some of the Nottingham clergy. So off I went, & after being lost owing to the bus conductress mistaking a Roman Catholic nunnery for St. Alban's Church (!), I eventually got there for a very beautiful Service. The Celebrant turned out to be a Chaplain attached to an AA unit, & we met and had lunch together. He struck me as a very decent bird who, in peace time, has a small parish in Norfolk. He lives quite near Chilwell & has his own house to which he has invited me.

In the evening I had to take two C of E Padre's Hours at 6.30 and 8.30 & was invited to dinner at the ATS Officers' Mess in between. The reason for the two was, of course, that Easton was ill.

I have had a very good long letter from Barbara & also two long letters from girls who come from Cressage. One is now in the ATS and the other was our dear Heather who used to be our maid. I've only recently had two letters from a boy and girl who used to be in my Sunday School at Whaddon. It is amazing how these two have kept up with me.

This letter has a pencilled foot-note, presumably by George Chignell, which reads: "Please return this, as I am keeping all these letters, which will be interesting for you to read in 20 years' time".

10.11.43

The chief news this week is that I'm hoping to get 48 hours leave to go over to Cressage on or about 24th of this month. I am allowed 9 days every 3 months, & this can be taken either in one lump or in two bits – 48 hours after 6 weeks and 7 days after three months are up. I could not make up my mind what to do, but I have just heard from Pauline that Olga has to have a fairly serious operation after Christmas, & as this means, first that the children will be coming to Cressage & secondly that Olga herself will be coming for some time to recuperate, and as my main leave is not due till about then, I thought it would be best to get in a bit beforehand. With luck I shall be able to get over to Shrewsbury by a depot car, for one goes to a sub-depot near there pretty frequently. As a matter of fact that is why I said on the 24th or thereabouts, because I intend to go when the car is going, both to save expense and time.

Last Sunday afternoon I had promised to take Evensong at St. Catherine's, Nottingham for the Vicar as he is ill. The Service was at 3.30 & so to allow myself plenty of time, I set off to catch a bus outside the Depot at 2.15 (it takes about half an hour to get to N). At 3.00 I was still waiting to get on a bus! Four had gone by, 3 full up and one which took 6 people from our stop! I had to rush back & phone up to say I wouldn't get in, which was very sickening. Trying to get into Nottingham on a Saturday or a Sunday is apparently a hopeless business, & when you get there on Saturday, I'm told, it is practically impossible either to get food or to a cinema or theatre.

I met a man last night – an ordinary soldier who has just arrived here, who was organist of Clifton, Brighouse. I must have met him before because when I was at Lightcliffe I preached there, twice I think. Although a lover of straight music and the Church organ, he is very keen on cinema organs, & says they are simply lovely to play, & that if you knock out all the special solo stops used for light music, you couldn't tell the difference in tone etc. from a good Church organ. All I can say is I've never heard anyone playing one who didn't succumb to the awful special effects & stops!

Tonight is the night when our little choral society is having its audition before Dr. Stanton. I'll try to speak to him, but I have to be careful because I'm the only officer in the society.

17.11.43

Once again I have left your letter up in a drawer in my room, & am writing from my office. However, I do remember that you made a remark about the regularity of my letters (!!) now that I am in the Army. The real reason is that I have certain hours when I am always at my little office so that chaps can come & see me if they want to, & I use that time for writing letters, because letters can be more easily interrupted than reading.

Well the Choral Society had its audition from Dr. Stanton last Wed. Apparently the BBC have forbidden their people ever to say anything on the spot as to the likelihood or not of the performers broadcasting, so we don't know the result, but I thought we were pretty good. I spoke to Dr. Stanton afterwards & told him who I was. He asked after you all & said Uncle Tom was a particular friend of his. He was, of course, very sorry to hear of Uncle T's illness.

On Sunday I went to Nottingham to the Anglo-Polish Ballet which was very delightful. I'm afraid I get a bit bored with what I call 'straight' ballet – you know, the usual toe dancing and leaps & the usual white dresses and tights, e.g. Tchaikovsky's 'Swan Lake', but I thoroughly enjoy the more 'national' types.

There followed Chig's response to a question his father had asked previously about how much good music he heard. It was very little, it seemed: "the Mess radio bleats and croons nearly all the time". He did go on to give details of an ATS company concert "the nearest approach for some time to decent music that I've had". It seemed his forthcoming leave would coincide with a visit to Nottingham by the LPO. In other ways he was contributing to various social activities to provide entertainment and keep up morale.

I have been asked to be a member of a Brains Trust (!) on Dec 6th. They had one a month ago, & if the questions are anything like they were then, I fancy I shall be silent all the time! Also I've been asked to give a gramophone recital in the new year, which I shall thoroughly enjoy, as I shall be giving it to the Music Club & shall be able to give them some good stuff, without being too intellectual. At the moment I rather fancy a 20th C programme – Elgar, Sibelius, Strauss, Vaughan Williams, Kodaly, Walton and Dohnanyi, but probably in the end I shall have a completely different idea.

27.11.43

Well here I am again after my short leave. I was very fortunate in my leave, for although it was only officially 48 hrs, I had nearly 72 hrs away from Chilwell. Originally I was to have left here at 5.00pm on Wednesday. There was a conference on here to which various officers were coming from all over the place, including some from round about Shrewsbury. However, Major Buck, in charge of transport, rang me up to say that the officers from Shrewsbury, who were going to take me back, would not be returning until Thursday, but that a vehicle would be leaving here for Shrewsbury on Wednesday afternoon at 3.00pm & would that be any good to me. Easton kindly agreed to take my Padre's Hour which was at 4.00pm so I went & got home about 5.30 in daylight, instead of 8.00 or 9.00 in the blackout. The way home was via Ashby-de-la-Zouch, Tamworth, Lichfield and Wellington. Incidentally I took a new dog home with me! An English Springer Spaniel about a year old. He was remarkably good all the way, although I had only seen him once before for about 5 minutes. He really belongs to a chap who is overseas, & who has been trying, via an ATS officer here, to find a home for him. I think it likely that we shall have him for good – I hope so for he is a dear & Pauline has taken to him very much indeed already.

Pauline had a good surprise when I arrived, for I had told her not to expect me till 8.00 or 9.00, & I had also warned her that we might have to give supper to the officers who would be bringing me. She & her Mother were just about to set out supper when I arrived. They both seemed very well & Cressage seemed absolutely lovely after this place.

In his drafted autobiography Chig recounts that the ATS driver, he and Sam arrived at Cressage to find that Pauline and her mother had tea ready on a two-tiered trolley, with a splendid-looking cake on the lower shelf, a cake which had probably used all Pauline's remaining ration of fruit and other ingredients. Pauline took the ATS driver to show her the bathroom, so she might freshen up after their journey while Chig headed for the downstairs lavatory. When all returned the splendid cake was no more, and Sam looked incredibly pleased with life! No-one had the heart to say more than "Oh, Sam!", but from that one exceptional moment he proved entirely trustworthy in the 12 remaining years he was with the Chignells.

On Thursday morning, I went round the village seeing all the folk I could. They were all disappointed that I was not in my uniform – practically the first thing I did on Wednesday evening was to get out of it. Things seemed very much the same as usual there – my pig is getting very big, everyone is full of praise for the way Noel Baldwin takes the Services & the excellence of his sermons. He, himself, seems a new man with this responsibility & I sincerely hope that in time he may be ordained. Dear Arthur Cole baked me a special seed cake! In the afternoon Pauline & I walked over to Sheinton with Sam, the dog. Poor lad, he's been cooped up in a kennel for the last 7 weeks, & to be free to run about in fields, & the glorious scents he discovered, were a bit of a strain on his obedience, but he was wonderfully good. Both at Sheinton and Cressage congregations seem to be very good, & though Burgess is not, unfortunately, liked very much, people seem to respect him, & to be very loyal.

For the remainder of his leave Chig pottered (with Pauline and Sam), gardened, sawed wood, played the piano, and generally unwound, as well as attending choir practice, where he was heartened by their singing.

> This morning I got a taxi from Cound Lodge garage & caught the 9.25 to B'ham. At B'ham I went to Station St and caught a bus for Nottingham which passes Chilwell & so I arrived at about 1.45. If I had gone all the way by train, I shouldn't have got here till 3.00, as there is no direct line from B'ham to Nottingham – the way is via Derby.
>
> Perhaps the chief news, though, is the letter I received on Wednesday mid-day just before leaving for Cressage. This was to say that I am to leave Chilwell on Wednesday, Dec 1st & report for duty at the Airborne Training Depot & School at Hardwick Hall, Chesterfield. I don't think this means I'm to be attached to the Airborne Division as I am over age for that. I imagine it is a place where they train men for this work, & presumably it will mean that people will be coming & going all the time. I'm really rather fed up about it, for if I'm right about this continual movement, it will mean a pretty hopeless proposition for me, and also it is irritating to be moved from here just when I was beginning to get into my stride. When I got back here today I found another note saying that the chap who is at present at this place (Hardwick Hall) is coming to Chilwell & so it is only to be an exchange, which seems all the sillier. On the other hand Airborne personnel are specially picked people & are a very good grade of soldier, much better than the R.A.O.C. and also Hardwick Hall is one of the Dukeries – it belongs, or belonged, I don't know which, to the Duke of Devonshire, so I imagine I shall be living in a palatial residence with a fine park, & some chance of prowling about in the country during my time off.
>
> As I'm moving on the Wednesday my next letter will also probably be not up to time. I think Airborne Training School Hardwick Hall, Chesterfield will find me, but I'll let you know my address as soon as possible.

3.12.43

Chig's move from Chilwell had come about following a request from the Deputy Assistant Chaplain General. It seemed the chaplain serving the Parachute Regiment's Intake and Rehabilitation Centre at Hardwick Hall was anxious, for family reasons, to have a posting where he and his wife and family could live together. This would be possible at Chilwell, if Chig was willing to transfer.

Chig's last few days at Chilwell were spent clearing up everything and getting things ship-shape for his successor, Price. Chig described him as "a very nice chap, harmless type of fellow, not at all the sort of man for Airborne troops, but a good chap all the same". He had arrived on the Tuesday, at mid-day, allowing Chig plenty of time to brief him about Chilwell and the Padre's role, but for the fact that Price was "a colossal talker & instead of my being able to tell him about Chilwell, I hardly got a chance at all … he, for his part, told me about (Hardwick) about three times over, but without much cohesion!" That evening, 'briefing' gave way to merriment.

> We had a special dinner party for 8 of us – Col. Levick, Collins, Viyne, Ductith, Walker, Thomas, Price and myself – as a farewell to me. Col. Levick made a speech & said all sorts of nice things & they drank my health (in port!), & after I had replied we adjourned for darts etc., and the party finished about 12.00.

That letter, telling his father of his changed location, carried the address: B Mess, Airborne Forces Depot and School, Hardwick Hall, Chesterfield, as a new chapter in his Forces Chaplain's role opened before him. The following months would see him moving to other bases in this new role with the Airborne Forces, moves that would lead to his involvement in one of the most notable campaigns of the Second World War.

8

Airborne Forces Padre's Letters from Hardwick Hall, 1943 and 1944

3.12.43

This letter, hand-written as was now Chig's custom, began by telling of his last few hours at Chilwell Depot, before recounting his arrival at Hardwick Hall. Here, initially, he was attached to the Parachute Regiment.

Chig's writing, miniscule and crammed on small A5 pages, is not easy to read. The letter's key points read as follows:

> In the morning I packed & after an early lunch, caught the 12.42 for Trent where I changed into an express which only stopped at Derby and Chesterfield. For all that, although I saw my kit in at Trent, it was missing when we got to Chesterfield! I reported it both to the Station Master & also the Airborne Forces Rest Centre where I had to report my arrival as well. Then I got on a lorry & came here. After meeting the Adjutant & 2nd in Command, I was taken to my Mess & room. Fortunately most of my stuff arrived later that night, but one small case it still missing, containing my Communion set, surplice, stoles and also my socks and handkerchiefs. This makes it rather awkward for Sunday, unless the things turn up.
>
> Well, my hopes were somewhat dashed when I found that we did not live in the Hall, but in brick huts in the grounds. We certainly don't live in luxury – not even as much as at Chilwell – the huts are pretty gloomy, but the actual mess is quite nice & has a billiard table. The majority of the officers are very young chaps & they are mostly only here for a short while doing special courses – parachute jumping, battle courses or what is called rehabilitation – i.e. getting fit again after either having come back from N. Africa or Italy or from accidents. They are very tough lads, as, of course, are the men – & are probably second in discipline & toughness only to Commandos, even if they are second to them. (They would deny it, I'm sure!)
>
> There is one lot of them over at Clay Cross which is also under me, & I am supposed to look after some Transport Drivers at Chesterfield as well, but how I

morning. I packed & after an early lunch, caught the 12.42 for Trent where I changed into an express which only stopped at Derby between Trent & Chesterfield. For all that, although I had my kit in at Trent, it was missing when we got to Chesterfield. I reported it both to the station master & also the Airborne Forces Rest Centre where I had to report my arrival as well. Then I got on a lorry & came here. After making my report to the Adjutant & 2nd in Command, I was taken to my mess & room. Fortunately most of my stuff arrived later on that night, but one small case is still missing containing my Communion set, surplice, stole & also my robes & hood etc. This makes it rather awkward for Sunday unless the thing turns up.

Well, my hopes were somewhat dashed when I found that we did not live in the Hall but in huts in the grounds. We certainly don't live in luxury - not even as much as at Chilwell - The huts are pretty skimpy but the actual Mess is quite nice & has a billiard table. The majority of the officers are very young chaps & they are mostly only here for a short while, doing special courses - parachute jumping, battle courses or what is called rehabilitation - ie getting fit again after either having come back from N.Africa or Italy or from accidents. They are very tough lads, as, of course, are the men - & are probably second in discipline & toughness only to Commandos, even if they are second to them. (They would deny it, I'm sure!)

There is one lot of them over at Clay Cross which is also under me, & I am supposed to look after some Transport Drivers at Chesterfield as well, but how I am going to manage that I don't know because it is very difficult to get to them & I have no transport.

There is a very nice little chapel here & it has been well furnished. The badge of the Airborne Forces is Pegasus & it looks rather strange to see a Greek god on the Altar Frontal!

It is time I stopped now as I have to visit the C.C.S. (the temporary hospital for slight cases) & then, this afternoon I am going in to Chesterfield to the Hospital, & also to see if I can find out anything more about my missing kit.

Love to you all,

Your loving son,

Newstead

Part of Chig's letter to his father of 3 December 1943.

am going to manage that I don't know because it is very difficult to get to know them & I have no transport.

There is a very nice little chapel here & it has been well furnished. The badge of the Airborne Forces is Pegasus, & it looks rather strange to see a Greek god on the altar frontal!

It is time I stopped now as I have to visit the CRS (the temporary hospital for slight cases) & then, this afternoon, I am going to Chesterfield to the Hospital, & also to see if I can find anything more about my missing kit.

A good many years after the war Chig set about writing his life story where, with the benefit of time and space, he was able to voice further details and more considered reflections than was possible in his letters to his father.

On his arrival at Hardwick Hall, despite not being able to share in the historic luxury of the grand house itself, he recognised it as one of the outstanding architectural beauties of Britain, and was rather relieved that the Services had not taken over the house but occupied huts in the grounds, "sprawled over a fairly large area ... there is something about an Army or RAF unit that is utterly destructive, however nice the individuals are".

"The CO saw me on the morning after my arrival," he went on, "and told me he would leave me free to do what I thought was my job, provided that I discussed it with him first. Then he said that the Parachute Regiment (*then barely twelve months old since its formation, but already with a formidable reputation*) was very proud of having invented 'Padre's Hours' and that he wished to continue them.

"Then he said that though I was not officially a member of the Parachute Regiment I must wear a red beret, or the men would think absolutely nothing of me". So he received the esteemed 'cherry beret', and, as he said at the time of writing his story, "I still have it 31 years later." In all my long friendship with Chig I recall that it hung proudly in his hallway, yet I never thought to ask him about it nor did he seek to mention it, until near the end of his life, when he told me the story just recounted here. He did so recognising that, whilst his award of that beret was slightly unusual, it had been an immense privilege to be invited (ordered!) to wear it. That feeling never left him.

Recalling those days Chig, with typical self-deprecation, remembered: "The job was definitely difficult and I don't think I was much use at it. Trainees came to Hardwick on what was practically a crash course (*I suspect he was wholly unaware of his awful pun!*). All parachutists were still volunteers and they went through an exceedingly arduous course whilst at Hardwick, including assault courses, climbing cliffs, getting across a lake, jumping with a parachute from a tower and then, at Ringway, from an aeroplane. Then there was an exercise to help them should they be trying to escape capture behind enemy lines, for, of course, the essence of parachuting was to be a force behind the main enemy line."

One of Chig's noble virtues was his desire constantly to identify with those he was called to serve and, as far as possible, share their experiences. Characteristically, he

– along with a pal from his mess, the Medical Officer 'Bill' Atkinson – volunteered to join the young troops on one of these escape exercises.

Before starting they were stripped and examined to ensure they had not secreted the odd £1 note about their person. With their underclothes returned together with denim overalls, boots and socks (but without wrist watches) they were loaded on to a covered lorry on a clear, cold, moonlit February night and dropped in the middle of nowhere (or nowhere they knew or recognised) and had to make their way back to a Pennine village not far from their base, between 8.00am and 10pm next day. To make their task more challenging all local police and Service personnel had been instructed to detain them on sight.

Chig and Bill determined they should get off the main road immediately and soon found a two-track railway. Where to go and which way? Chig volunteered his star-gazing knowledge, on the basis of which they set off to their left. After a mile or so, of that testing task of trying to match their normal stride to the distance between the railway sleepers, they spotted a small cottage and risked knocking at the door. It was opened by a railway man, to whom they explained their purpose, and asked if they were on a railway that led to Nottingham. "Yes," he told them, "but you're heading the wrong way; you're heading for Lincoln!" Retracing their steps, again trying to keep pace with the sleepers, they trudged along until reaching a railway goods yard – Newark – where, dodging between the wagons, they avoided detection, decided to abandon the railway line, and found a good road on the town's outskirts.

By now they were pretty tired and hungry and decided it was worth risking knocking at a door in the hope of refreshment. The first door at which they knocked was swiftly shut in their faces when the woman saw the scruffy, denim-clad pair. On they trudged. Against the night sky was silhouetted a large mansion-type building, with turrets and towers, set in parkland. Opposite the park's gates was a pub, and though they suspected closing time had passed, Chig tried the front door. There was no response. Bill had more luck at the back and, trusting to truth, told the land-lord their story. He was a bit dubious but felt that if Bill's companion was a Padre, he should be able to identify the building across the way they had seem silhouetted against the sky. A flash of inspiration told Chig it was Kelham College, the renowned theological college. His answer deservedly won them bread and cheese and freshly-brewed coffee in the pub's kitchen,

Refreshed and armed with good directions they set off for Mansfield, and walked for mile after mile, diving into the hedge whenever a vehicle appeared. At one point they spotted soldiers approaching them in single file, and so jumped into the ditch, lying face down in a couple of inches of very cold, smelly water. As the footsteps approached they heard a voice: "Say, what do you think these guys are doing here lying in this ditch?" It was a platoon of American soldiers on a similar sort of exer-cise, and so they joined company, sharing a good laugh and much chat, and covering some 25 miles all told. As they parted from their American friends they determined to hitch a lift, regardless, from the first vehicle which came along. It was a bus, but not a normal service bus (on which the conductor might have been obliged to report them) but a miners' bus, taking men to their home villages after their coal-face shifts. Chig and Bill were dropped off in Mansfield Woodhouse where they opted to pick up an ordinary service bus. A sympathetic conductor waived the charge (they had no money!) and dropped them off back at Hardwick shortly before 8.00am – mission accomplished!

Amidst such occasional yet special exercises and the never-ending and demanding role of Chaplain Chig continued to make time to write home.

11.12.43

So sorry I had to cut short so suddenly, but I got an urgent telephone call which meant my going to Clay Cross.

I don't really know what I want for Christmas. Things are so difficult to get & my own movements are so uncertain at present. I should like something I can take about with me. Yes, I should like Hugh's glasses (*field glasses?*)– they would be very useful, especially if I go overseas.

As a matter of fact I'm about halfway between Chesterfield and Mansfield – surrounded by coal mines although the actual estate is pretty country. I find I get very dirty here, not just ordinary dirt but the sort of thing I used to meet in Huddersfield.

I'm feeling pretty settled in now & have more or less sorted out those who are regular 'permanent' staff – in so much as anyone is permanent – & those who are passing through on one or other of the courses. I have several Padre's Hours each week, & a lot of men coming to see me &, generally speaking, I'm kept very busy. I find the P.Hs are grand & there is quite a lot of interest shown, though most of the men are woefully ignorant of Christian doctrine and practice.

Goodbye for now, I must go to a CO's Conference, Love to you all.

15.12.43

Amidst all the mess up of last week's letter, I believe I forgot to tell you that on the previous Saturday – Dec 4 – I had been to Nottingham to hear Barbirolli & the Hallé. I had got the ticket before ever I knew that I was leaving Chilwell & naturally I didn't want to miss it if I could help it, so I rushed off after the CO's weekly Conference & caught a bus into Mansfield. There I had a quick lunch & then caught a bus to Nottingham, arriving about 15 mins before the concert was due to start. I met David Easton, the C of S Padre from Chilwell & three ATS officers and two other officers – we had all arranged to go together – &, apart from the concert, it was jolly good seeing them again. The concert was good, the playing excellent. ... I got back here the same way as I came, arriving about 9.00.

I had another journey to Nottingham on Sunday. The 15 ATS whom I'd been preparing for Confirmation were to be confirmed at St. Catherine's Church in the afternoon, & as I am free on Sundays, after 12.15m, I set off again. This time, though, I had lunch before I left, & unfortunately just missed my bus into Mansfield so that I had to wait an hour, & was very late for the Service, which was just ending when I arrived! However I had tea with them all, & they were obviously very pleased that I'd come. I, too, was pleased to see about 8 ATS officers had come with these girls. This time I went back to Chilwell with them & saw my friends at Highfield Mess. I had supper with them & finally caught a train from Nottingham at 9.43. This didn't leave until 10.15 & I had a 3 mile walk from Heath Station back to Hardwick. Luckily it was a topping night with plenty of moon, & I travelled back with a very nice soldier who had been to see some friends in Nottingham, & we found plenty to talk about on the way home. I got into bed just after midnight – easily my latest night since I've been in the Army!

On Sunday morning I had quite a lot of officers at the Parade Service. The reason was that on the first Sunday I was here, there hadn't been a single one, so I went to the Second-in-Command and told him that I thought it pretty poor when the men were detailed to come. Although I hate the compulsory Church Parade business, yet, if the men are compelled, so ought the officers to be. The result was that the Second-in-Command came himself, & about 18 others.

This was not the first time Chig had challenged senior officers on matters of principle. Soon after arriving at Chilwell a young soldier asked Chig if he would hear his Confession, to which Chig naturally agreed. As a consequence, and feeling others might welcome this, he put up a notice in the chapel entrance inviting anyone who wished to make their Confession to get in touch.

Some days later his SCF (Senior Chaplain to the Forces) visited and, when he saw this notice, he went apoplectic, insisting the notice should be taken down immediately. "I'm sorry, Sir, I cannot obey," responded Chig, "there are people here who wish to avail themselves of this sacrament". On being told to obey the SCF's instructions he made his position clear: "No Sir. I am first a priest of the Church of England, and our Prayer Book states three times that it is our duty to hear the confessions of those who wish to make them. I am only a voluntary member of the R.A.Ch.D. and am prepared to resign, if I am forced to disobey the Church".

"You will hear more of this. I shall report it to the DACG (*Deputy Assistant Chaplain General*)."

A few days later the DACG, who proved to be a much more understanding man, visited Chig. He recognised that in war-time all types of churchmen needed to be catered for by the Forces Chaplains, and he insisted Chig should keep the notice displayed. He also pointed out to the SCF that, in so large an establishment as Chilwell, provision of this nature was essential. Chig would have felt no sense of victory here; that was not his way. Rather he was relieved to be able to continue serving his Lord by serving his people.

I've put in for my 7 days leave from Friday the 31st December to Thursday the 6th of Jan. I don't know whether I shall get it, but I hope so, as I'm really due for it on the 18th of this month.

I've been interrupted again with a chap coming to see me, & I can't remember something I was going to say! I get such a lot of poor blighters coming with their troubles, & so often there seems to be practically nothing one can do about these.

It's been bitterly cold here the last few days – a lovely white frost making the park look beautiful, – but it is very treacherous trying to walk about in boots on the concrete etc. when it is so slippery,

Pauline will be busy now with Jennifer & Jeremy (*Olga and Arthur's children*) in addition to her Mother, & Olga and Arthur arriving for Christmas I think.

My fondest love to you Father dear.

20.12.43

My dearest Father,

Just a short note to thank you for the calendar. I haven't found the snaps, but as I didn't discover your letter till this morning, I'll have another look.

This is also my Christmas greeting to you all, God bless you all this Christmas & may it be the last of the war.

I hope you'll like the book – I've dipped into it here and there & found it very amusing.

My love to you all & a very happy Christmas. I'll write again later on this week.

Your loving son, Rowland.

27.12.43

This next letter in the bundle was actually from Chig's wife, Pauline, to George Chignell, "Dear Father Chig". She thanked her father-in-law for his Christmas present and explained that the household had been down with 'flu at various times with their maid, Dorothy, succumbing a week before Christmas, before Pauline herself and her mother went down with it. She also noted that her brother-in-law, Arthur, had taken on the responsibility for the fires "but he is such an untidy man that it almost made more work than if he hadn't done them!" She was also pleased to report that "everyone is better now".

Dorothy is at work again this mid-day so things are looking up. And of course best of all Rowland will be home on Friday.

We didn't have many Services this Xmas. Mr Burgess came over for a midnight one. People turned up well for that. Then Mr Baldwin took a Children's Service at Sheinton at 11 o'clock & here at 2.15 and that was all there was. We had a Carol Service yesterday evening. None of the men (*choristers?*) turned up for it at all. Miss Jones hadn't tried anything new which perhaps was just as well. Rowland will be taking the Services next Sunday.

I think I may go into Birmingham on Friday & meet Rowland. It would mean a few extra hours of him, which all counts these days. Give my love to everyone & much to yourself, Yours affec(*tionately*), Pauline.

Chig's leave enabled him to see in the New Year at home with Pauline. Undoubtedly, like so many others throughout the country and across the world, they hoped this was the year when the war would end (his Christmas letter to his father ten days earlier had echoed these very thoughts). The Allies certainly were making progress, hence raised hopes everywhere.

However confident – or plain wishful – those hopes were, 1944 would see Chig's role as Chaplain taking him in new directions. By late summer he would be in Europe accompanying the Airborne Forces.

His first letter of the year to his father told of his leave, and told, too, of continued troop preparations.

13.1.44

Late again with my letter I'm afraid. Still there is a reason for it, but I'll reach that later. Let me get things in their proper order. First I felt very sad returning from Cressage after my leave. It was grand being home again but the time went so quickly. I went to see Dr Gittins & found him considerably thinner, but amazingly content and able to talk a little. I'm afraid he'll just stay like that for a very long time – it is a colossal strain for his poor dear wife.

We have had our first casualty – the chap who was Sexton & Verger at Cressage, Arthur Manning, has been killed. I never knew him very well as he had been a Territorial & had left the village before ever we got there.

Naturally I felt pretty gloomy coming back here, but I found that some of the chaps had guessed this would happen & had arranged all sorts of things to buck me up. First I went to Canon Paget's to tea on Saturday & he has booked me to preach next Sunday night at Pleasley. On Sunday Atkinson (*Bill Atkinson, his MO colleague*) & I went down to Chilwell in the afternoon & while there fixed up to go to a concert in Nottingham yesterday. On Monday I went over to Ringway, (*then an RAF base, now the location of Manchester Airport*) which is quite near Northenden, with Atkinson, two other officers & 6 sergeants, to watch them jump. It was a very cold journey in an open truck, but a lovely day & the scenery over the Derbyshire moors was wonderful, with the snow glinting in the sun & grand cliffs & hills & valleys. We got there in time for lunch in the very luxurious RAF Mess where I met chaps who had been at Hardwick & had now got to the jumping part of their training. After lunch I went out to Tatton Park where the parachutists actually land & after waiting for a bit, over came the Whitley & out they came. It is a bit frightening to watch at first, but immediately the parachutes are open it is a very graceful sight. Everybody came down well & then we went off to the YMCA for a cup of tea & then set off home. We came back via Buxton & had tea at an excellent WVS canteen there. The roads were very tricky being covered with ice.

On Tuesday I went to Chesterfield for a Padre's Hour & then visited our fellows in hospital. In the evening I went with a party of 11 to a dance at Harlow Wood Orthopaedic Hospital, near Mansfield where we have some more patients. It was a very jolly affair, but we lost our way getting there & wandered about all sorts of roads & lanes in a thin fog, taking 2 hrs to do a journey of about 10 miles – at least it should have been 10 miles!

Yesterday Atkinson and I went off about 4.00 to Nottingham & met our party from Chilwell. After a high tea we went off to the concert – the LPO under a chap called Dr.Heinrich Unger (I think)

Heinrich (also known as Heinz) Unger (1895-1965), was a German-born Jewish conductor, who had left Germany in the early 1930s. Unger often appeared with the LPO and was a keen exponent of Mahler's music. With a very musical father it was not surprising that much of Chig's letter detailed the concert's programme: Mendelssohn's 'Calm Sea and Prosperous Voyage'; Eileen Joyce as the soloist in Schuman's piano Concerto; and what he described as a "topping performance of dear old Brahms' No.4".

We nearly missed our train back as we found we only had 10 mins to get to the station quite a distance away. However we made it all right & then sat in the station for about 40 mins!

I have got my Communion Set again – one of the brighter efforts of the Army! It had been sitting in one of the offices in this camp & the inhabitants of that office never thought that it might belong to me, even though it was clearly labelled!

22.1.44

Chig's next letter to his father indicated he was still doing all he could to share the experiences of the soldiers to whom he was Chaplain and wasn't necessarily settling for a quiet and sheltered life.

I hope Pauline has sent on my long letter describing my adventures with the 'Battle School' last week. As you can guess it was great fun & I thoroughly enjoyed it, even though I got some pretty large blisters! These have practically gone now & are no longer a source of amusement to the Mess.

I've been having a very busy week, though it has been routine stuff & consequently not very interesting from the point of view of letter writing. However I went over to Pleasley last Sunday to preach for Canon Paget, & it was good being in a real Church & preaching to Church people.

Apparently on the Sunday I was away the Second-in-Command here read the Lesson, & coming to the words 'love and kindness' read 'love and kisses' by mistake! It will take him a long time to live that down!

And then Chig was drawn back to domestic matters back at Cressage in his news-telling.

Our pig was killed on the Monday after my leave was over & Pauline (*who, presumably, was left to do the butchering once the animal was despatched*) sent me two magnificent pork pies which didn't last long as you can guess.

26.1.44

I have to go over to Manchester on Monday to see a Toc H man about opening a Toc H branch near Ringway where so many of our men go for their parachute jumping.

The letter is now re-dated 28.1.44.

Two days interruption here I'm afraid. I had a succession of people in to see me, & then I had to go and do something about one or two of them – go & see their company commanders & I never returned to the office.

Then yesterday I was away all day – I had to go to Chesterfield & then to Sheffield about welfare cases & while I was in Sheffield I thought I might as well go to a pantomime as in any case I had to wait about for a long time. So I went & very amusing it was, & wonderfully well dressed and staged considering that it was war time. Of course the comedians were broad Yorkshire – I quite enjoyed hearing it again.

Last Tuesday I had an irritating experience. I go to Chesterfield to take a Padre's Hour, the people there send a car for me. Well, we happened to have a Court Martial on here & the Adjutant of the Chesterfield folk was on it, & took me in at 11.00. When I got there I found that the Padre's Hour was cancelled. The sickening part is that the Adjutant must have known, and was probably responsible for the cancellation.

Today I go to another lot of men in Chesterfield again for a Padre's Hour. Then I shall have to have lunch there & then go to hospital for sick visiting, after which I get on a bus for Bolsover where I am going to have tea with Harold Pickles. He is in charge of the parish of Bolsover which is only about 5 miles from here, but is very much across country, & I expect I shall have to walk home. In the evening I have been invited as one of four to go to dinner at C Mess & play snooker afterwards. C Mess is about 3 miles away & is quite a cosy show. The men there have the advantage of being well away from the camp when they are off duty & the Mess is really a private house. I'm glad I'm going because I don't know the chaps there very well as I don't often get there..

Time goes very quickly in the Army – I've been here exactly 8 weeks today – as long as I was in Chilwell. I wonder how much longer I shall be here? Not very long I expect, for I should think that if I'm to go overseas I shall probably be posted to a division a fairish time before they go overseas, so as to have some chance of getting to know them first.

3.2.44

I have been having quite a good time this week, both as regards work and pleasure. As far as work is concerned, I've been stirring up a hornets' nest. I've been dissatisfied with Padre's Hours in the Depot – when I came there was only one for a small group of men who were recovering from wounds – about 20 men out of the whole camp of 1500 or so. Now I've got a fortnightly one for ATS, and a weekly one for Depot Coy (*Company*) & also for PT Coy (*Paratroops Company*) – Depot Coy are the people who stay here for a fair length of time & are usually men whose morale is rather low; PT Coy are the people who go through here for the jumping course. Also since I came back from Manchester I've had a lot of men to see me about one thing or another. I also got this Toc H Club re-opening near Ringway.

Chig, while in the Manchester area, visited members of his family, one of whom, Marion, "does a lot of Welfare work – visiting homes of soldiers etc", and then stayed overnight with her and her husband Francis. He took a bus to Didsbury next morning with the intention of catching another to Altrincham in order to visit an Uncle and Aunt. However, one bus was 50 minutes late, which delayed his arrival in Altrincham until 2.30pm just half-an-hour before his train back to Chesterfield would depart. This additional family visit had to be aborted. Chig arrived back in camp at 7.30pm.

The following evening he invited himself to the VADs' room to listen to "The Kingdom", a favourite Elgar oratorio.

I knew I shouldn't be able to listen to it in the Mess – in any case our wireless set is awful. It was good wasn't it? I can't think why it isn't done more often. As a matter of fact the VADs did me proud, for they brought me some supper on a tray so that I shouldn't miss any of the broadcast.

Unusually he ended his letter:

No time for more, love, Rowland.

9.2.44

I've now been landed with no less than 8 Padre's Hours a week! The result of my push at the CO's Conference the other day, when I said I wasn't satisfied with the religious provision for the men, has resulted in a veritable boomerang! I have two every Monday, Tuesday, Wednesday and Friday now & I sincerely hope that I shan't stay here long, for I don't fancy my men can stick this for long. These PHs really take it out of you. All the time you know that it is such a golden opportunity to get the Christian faith over, & also that it is probably the only time you're going to have with these chaps. They ask all sorts of questions & it is often very difficult to imagine what is really going on in their minds.

I've been riding about in a Jeep this morning, & very cold they are! I had to go to Mansfield to see a fellow who had his hand blown off by a grenade in an accident the other day. The poor lad is in an awful mess, but he's not dangerously ill now. These Jeeps are pretty good things, terrific horse power & practically no weight to pull. Their acceleration is astonishing & they will go pretty well anywhere.

Last Sunday I preached in the afternoon in Bolsover for Harold Pickles.

In the morning I had had a big Parade Service in the Cinema-Gym with about 700 troops, & the dance band playing the hymns! It was quite good, but I long for my own parish & congregation of real Church folk.

29.2.44

It already seems a very long time since I was, with Pauline, spending that short and happy leave with you all at Kineton. It was good to see you again.

When I got back here I found quite a lot was happening. First my good friend, Atkinson the MO, had been posted. He has got the job he's long been trying to get & will be very happy. He has become a neuro-surgeon at the Military Hospital in Oxford.

Then next I was told that there were to be 5 padres on the next course which was arriving on Saturday. Well they turned up – 2 RCs, 2 C of S & 1 C of E – a very nice crowd & we have a very jolly time together. Already we've had two great brain stretching discussions. One of the RCs enters into these a lot & is, in fact, a man very much after my own heart. The other is rather shy & says very little. The two C of S are grand Scots with a typical theological depth of mind that you don't seem to find in other denominations. The C of E lad is a nice chap too, but I must say it is the one RC I really like best.

Well Sunday was quite exciting. We've had a really heavy fall of snow – about 2 feet deep, & have been nearly snowed in. In addition our electricity supply broke down about 10.00am & was not right again till Monday at about 5.30pm! It was all over NE Derbyshire apparently.

Yesterday I had my second injection, & up to the moment I feel quite good, except for a rather painful arm. I'm supposed to have 48 hrs in bed, but it can't be done, & anyhow it would have been a waste of time today certainly. It's strange how it gets some folk. Now I felt rotten with the first lot, others get it badly the second time, others are nearly laid out both times & a few it hardly affects at all.

Were the injections a sign that Chig was on the move, perhaps to Europe?

Chig's next letter, with a temporary address noted (CRS, Airborne Forces D & S, Hardwick Hall, Chesterfield) and written in pencil might have supported that thought, but the reason was much more prosaic.

8.3.44

The explanation of the temporary address, the reason why I'm writing in pencil, the reason why I have not notified the safe arrival of your parcel – the explanation is all the same – I have been in bed with tonsillitis.

I went to bed last Thursday in my own room & the MO transferred me to here on Saturday, I hadn't had him before. This is a delightful little hospital for people with slight and temporary illnesses & I am well looked after. I am in the Officers' ward which consists of two beds, but I've been by myself all the time. I've been very well looked after, first by my own bat-man who proved himself to be an absolute treasure – he got all sorts of things from strange places, oranges & even a small bag of sweets! Then since I've been in here the VADs have been very good to me, & I've had any number of visitors, officers have been rolling in at all sorts of times. Did I tell you how much I had taken to one of the RC chaplains going through here on a course? (There are 5 chaplains in all on this course, but they will be going on Monday week.) Anyway, this dear chap, Father Good by name, has been in most evenings for a chat. The C of E fellow had to take Sunday's Services. I was very sorry in a way as he was going down to London for the weekend, but I took a very poor view of him, for immediately he knew I was ill the first thing he did was to pop round to see how he could get away without having to take the Services. He never thought of offering to take them, nor did he think of the spiritual needs of this depot. However, I hear he was very good.

Well I got up for tea yesterday & am generally on the improve. The jam (*presumably part of the parcel from home*) has been delicious – it just came at the right time.

17.3.44

I'm sorry to be late with my letter this week. You were, however, quite right, for I got a bit of sick leave & went home on Sunday after taking my Services. As a matter of fact I was let out of CRS on Friday, but being unable to find anyone to take my Services, I had to stay till then, though I felt pretty rotten. Still, I had a lot of good fortune on Sunday. It was one of the Sundays when I have a 9.15 Service in Chesterfield. On my way back I mentioned to the driver of the car who had fetched me that I had been hoping to catch a train at 1.25pm from Chesterfield, but that there was no means of getting there in time. The driver then said he would wait at Hardwick for me & take me after my Services. So I got to Chesterfield at about 12.30 & got a sandwich & some tea & caught the 1.25. It was rather late but I got to Birmingham just before 6.00. I knew that there was no train for Shrewsbury till about 8.30 and that didn't get in until 10.50 after which, I imagined, I would have to walk to Cressage.

Well I didn't see the point of waiting about like that, so I went to see about buses, & found one going to Wolverhampton at about 4.06 – in fact every 15 mins. I caught that and when I got to Wolverhampton, I took a 2½d trolley-bus ride out to Tettenhall & then set off walking, hoping to get a lift. I hadn't gone more than 500 yards when an Army vehicle came along & I signalled it to stop, which it did. I asked where it was going & the driver said Shrewsbury! Well, of course, in I got & he took me to Cressage. I arrived there at 6.15 & found Evensong about to begin, so I popped in, and when Pauline came I went and sat with her. She was very surprised of course, & all the little choir were very amused when they saw her come in & pass the pew I was in without seeing me. Noel Baldwin took the Service & preached really well – he is very good.

Well I didn't do much while I was at home – I was made to stay in bed for breakfast each day, & then I played the piano – a joy I never get now – in the afternoon Pauline & I would take Sam for a walk & in the evening we usually sat and talked. I didn't feel like doing much, but I feel much better now.

Cressage was looking very delightful & I must say I long to be back, not only for my own pleasure & because I love it, but also because I feel I'm wasting such a lot of time here – I can't really do my job in this place.

I must stop now as I have to go & see one of the Company officers, before going to take a Padre's Hour at Chesterfield.

22.3.44

Chig opened this letter by writing of linking up with the Vicar of the parish in which the Camp was situated, and about helping him with an evening Service at Easter. He reported, too, that he was "quite recovered" and was "once more very busy".

On Monday I had a day's travelling. The Adjutant asked me to go & see the parents of one of our trainees at a place called Middleton in Lancs. I got up at 6.00 had breakfast at 6.30 & then a jeep took me to catch the 7.34 from Chesterfield. This was a slow train with two changes & stopped at every station to Manchester! However it went through gorgeous scenery – the line goes just south of the Peaks. I had an early lunch in Manchester & then got to Middleton about 1.00, going by bus. Middleton is about 6 miles west of Rochdale. I had my interview, which must be secret, & caught a bus back to Manchester, catching the 3.50 train back to Sheffield. This time my journey was through Woodhead & Penistone & it brought back memories as I went over the level crossing of the road from Glossop to Huddersfield. As I had no time to look up where Middleton was before I left & had no idea as to whether I should have to wait about a long time, I took a haversack with pyjamas & shaving kit. This I foolishly left on the train when I changed at Sheffield. I don't suppose I shall ever see it again though I've told the railway people. I was in a bit of a fix as razors are hard to get, but after borrowing one yesterday morning, I found a shop that had a 2/6d Wardonia razor in Chesterfield in the afternoon, so I am all right again now, & if I get my old one back I shall actually have a safety to spare!

I have my SCF coming to see me today. I don't expect he has anything in particular to see me about, but I'm going to ask him about a leave after Easter. I must say I didn't really expect that I should get another leave, for I don't imagine that there will be any when the Second Front gets going, but as the time draws on & Easter gets nearer, & nothing has started yet, at least as far as I'm concerned, I'm beginning to have hopes of getting one in

Some of the hedges have got little shoots now & I've heard quite a lot of the commoner birds singing – so that even in this rather bleak part of England there are signs of Spring thank goodness!

5.4.44

Only a short note, I'm afraid, this week. I have already missed Wednesday's post out & am very busy. I have been making arrangements for Good Friday & Easter. Good Friday is an ordinary day in the life of a soldier, but I have been able to arrange a Service here, at Chesterfield and at Clay Cross, all in the men's working hours & the CO has said that any man shall be free to attend, who desires to do so. Also I am sharing a short evening Service here. One rather selfish but nevertheless pleasing thing for me is that I shall be able to attend the majority of the 3 Hours at Chesterfield Parish Church. Easter has not meant much difference in Services except an extra one at Clay Cross. I have looked up last year's Services & find that there were only 20 communicants here, which is pretty awful isn't it? I have, however, promised to preach at Heath at Evensong on Easter Day.

There is not much news to tell you as it happens – more from Cressage than here. The Gittins have moved & we have a new Doctor of about 40-45 who has apparently been invalided out of the Navy. His wife is a Doctor too. Dr Gittins is in a nursing home in Shrewsbury and Mrs G is at present living at her home, but is looking for a little house to take him to.

Another man from the Deanery – the new rector of Longnor & Leebotswood – is becoming a Chaplain; two out of 13 is not a bad number from our little Deanery.

Pauline has some broad beans about a foot high – she planted them in the autumn, & her first peas are through. Good Arthur Cole came, & with two other good chaps, dug up a large part of the garden for her, while Reg Finch is growing sufficient potatoes to last next winter, in one of his fields.

Lots of love to you all, & God bless you this joyful Eastertide.

Chig constantly seeks to make his letters to his father as interesting as possible, but clearly there are restrictions on what he can disclose. In the previous letter the purpose of his visit to the trainee's parents remained confidential. In another he told of having his injections in the expectations of going abroad, without saying why this might be or where he might be going, and in the letter of 22 March he talked of "when the Second Front gets going" – without disclosing how it might affect him and his role.

In the meanwhile his daily routine continued, seeking to provide pastoral and spiritual support for all at the base; liaising with soldiers' families when there were difficulties (perhaps when soldiers were injured or found themselves in others sorts of trouble or facing unwanted challenges); visiting the ill and injured in the sick bay; ensuring all who wanted to could worship; providing worship at the base or in nearby local churches; seeking the support of local clergy (and often helping them too); staging Padres' Hours, often at varied locations; taking whatever opportunities presented themselves to meet and to get to know better the troops and his fellow officers stationed there, and to encourage and support them; and generally looking after and promoting the spiritual welfare and well-being of all the troops who came within his remit.

From week to week there would be much which was routine but, as for clergy everywhere, there was, too, the exceptional, the immediate, the urgent which cast routine aside and, inevitably, took time. All these things in a village parish context require organisation, planning and preparation – and time for that, time gained by necessarily setting aside something else. It is easy to imagine that in the Army, such organisation, planning and administration would similarly be required though, in all probability, with paper-work in triplicate! Life for a conscientious and God-serving Chaplain like Chig would be full, with few idle moments. If, in some of his letters to his father, he suggests it has been "quiet" or "not much is happening" that was merely an indication that little out of the ordinary, little variation of routine, had occurred. Life was chock-full.

9

On the move – with the Glider Pilot Regiment 1944

13.4.44

A postcard addressed to G S Chignell Esq., Estate Lodge, Kineton, Warwickshire, and sent from London:

Postcard from
Chig to his
father written
13th April 1944

I don't know what happened to my letter of a fortnight ago – I actually wrote one, & on the correct day too! This time I'm afraid it is only a p.c. as I am in the process of moving. I can't tell you where yet as I don't know myself till tomorrow, but I'll write as soon as possible & let you know where I am. Holy Week was mainly a sad and dispiriting time – only 7 chaps took any notice of Good Friday, although anyone could come to the Services if they liked at H(eath). But in Chesterfield I had a packed Church at a similar voluntary Service, & men had to go to other Churches as we were full up. Easter again was wretched – only 20 communicants all told. I can't say I'm sorry to have gone except that I had made some good friends round about & in the place despite the latter being almost invariably indifferent to religion.

"I am in the process of moving" Chig's postcard advised. As the Allies' preparations for the Second Front were building up a phone call from the Royal Army Chaplain's Department in London asked if he would be prepared to go as Chaplain to the Glider Pilot Regiment. It was explained to him that it was not a posting he had to take as the GPR was a regiment made up entirely of volunteers. Chig asked for twenty-four hours to think this over, and then consulted friends in the Hardwick Mess. "Don't go to that lot of flying coffins" one counselled. It was guidance overlooked for Chig returned the RACD's call, accepted the posting, and awaited instructions.

16.4.44

This note, in pencil (his pen had run dry!) showed Chig's new address as: No 2 Wing, Glider Pilot Regiment, Home Forces. He had moved.

Well I've had quite an exciting time this last week. First there was the news of my posting. I was told to report in London but had no idea where I would go from there. I travelled down on Thursday & reported at 3.00pm. There I found a lot of other Chaplains, 31 in all. We just had to kick our heels till the following day, after reporting. Then on Friday we were told our destinations. Most of them went off the same day, but I didn't have to report here till yesterday.

With time on his hands Chig phoned a friend from Huddersfield days, now in London, who offered accommodation for the evening. There was time, too, for a stroll round Bethnal Green and Mile End Rd – "a pretty grim part I thought".

Then on Saturday morning I went shopping, & caught a train in the early afternoon. I may not say where I am, but it is quite near a small town which we have often been through on the journey home in the old days. A further hint is that ...... (*frustratingly, the edge of the note-paper is damaged and his writing, so near to*

the edge in order to squeeze in as much as possible, is indecipherable here) …. and there
are only three in the country I think! Can you guess it? Cricklade!!

In fact his destination was Blake Hill Farm RAF Station, near Cricklade, the HQ of
No 2 Wing of GPR. He would serve with the GPR for two and a half years, until his
demobilisation.

His new posting triggered the memory of a remark he had made to Pauline
in the summer of 1943 when in their garden at home. Their reverie had been
broken by the drone of an American Dakota plane overhead (which seemed huge
compared with other planes more commonly seen at that time), towing a glider. "I
wouldn't want to be in that glider", he commented to Pauline, "it looks altogether
too dangerous an occupation!" It was a comment he would often recall, with some
irony, during his time with GPR, where most of his flying was in gliders towed
by Dakotas.

No.2 Wing was seen as the senior Wing of the Regiment. It had been the original
GPR and had seen active service in North Africa and in the Sicily campaign, and in
Italy under the command of Lt.Col (later Brigadier) G H Chatterton, with John Place
(Chig's new CO at Blake Hill Farm) as his second in command.

> Anyway I feel quite happy to be here – the CO, another RC, is very keen on
> the religious side, which is a great change for me, & is also extremely nice, & so
> are the 2nd in Command and the Adjutant. I feel quite at home already, & am
> enjoying the grand soft type of countryside. I've already heard the cuckoo & seen
> 4 or 5 swallows – neither bird having got anywhere near Hardwick yet.
> Frankly I loathed Hardwick & am glad to get away.

That didn't seem to come through in the letters we've just read, but perhaps this was an
indication of Chig's ability and willingness always to get stuck in and make the best of
things, wherever he was and whatever circumstances he found himself in.

> Well I'll stop now as I want to get off to Church this evening. I'll try and write
> on Wednesday, but I don't yet know what my arrangements will be.

At Blake Hill Farm, to which Chig moved on Saturday 15 April, the GPR was
linked to 46 Group RAF, largely a Dakota group whose planes provided the
tugs for GPR's gliders. No 2 Wing GPR had "one very secret squadron, under
Major Alec Dale, which consisted of Hamilcar gliders, capable of loading small
tanks" Chig later recalled elsewhere. "These immense gliders were actually the
largest aircraft in operation and needed Halifax or Stirling Bombers as towing
craft". That particular squadron was based at Tarrant Rushton in Dorset. Other
squadrons of No 2 Wing were stationed at Down Ampney, just up the road from
Cricklade, and at Broadwell, near Burford, the men (and women) at both coming
within Chig's ministry.

Horsa gliders, used by the 1st British Airborne Division, including the Glider Pilot Regiment. Some Horsas had hinged cockpits which allowed the loading and unloading of the gliders; others were designed to come apart amidships.

22.4.44

Just at present I can't guarantee when I will be writing, but I'll try and write as regularly as possible.

Well, this is a topping place & I am thoroughly enjoying my work – whether it is because spring is here, or because I am right in the middle of the vast preparations for invasion, or because the officers & men are such good chaps, or because of the dear RAF Chaplain, or a bit of all these put together, I don't know. At any rate it is grand to be where one really seems to be needed.

The CO is a Roman Catholic again, it is strange that of the 6 COs that I have known – 3 in the Searchlight people (*back home in Cressage and Shropshire*) & 3 since I've been in the Army. 4 have been RCs, 1 Church of Scotland & only 1 C of E, & I only knew him for about a month. However this present one is keen and very nice & helpful & so are all the other officers.

Last Sunday night I went to the local Parish Church – the RAF Chaplain is the Vicar – and we had a very beautiful Solemn Evensong. There were 25 men & girls from the camp & quite a good congregation altogether. The choir consisted of about a dozen boys, well trained, & a couple of RAF officers, not so well trained (!) but keen volunteers, & they have a decent organist.

Monday I went with the RAF Padre round the station & met several RAF people, education officer, adjutant & so on, with whom it is well to be on good terms.

Then on Tuesday I went with the CO to what I believe to be Vaughan Williams' birthplace – anyway one of his famous & lovely hymn tunes (*Down Ampney*) is named after it – where there is another station which I have to look after. The CO asked me if I'd like to go up in a glider & so off we went, he acting as pilot. It was really a small exercise with 18 gliders. The sensation is quite pleasant – I couldn't tell the moment we left the ground it was all so smooth. We cruised about for 65 minutes going over Frome & then to Newbury & back here, keeping around 1500 – 1700 ft. At first the sight of the country below is fascinating, but I can easily understand how soon it becomes boring, for you lose the slight variations in height of valley & low hills etc. Roads & streams & railways however look fascinating winding about. Coming down isn't quite so pleasant, a glider does a very steep descent, but I suffered no ill effects. It was pretty bumpy on the day I went, in fact the CO said it was about the bumpiest day he'd met & that if I could stand that without being sick, I could stand anything.

Wednesday I spent getting a complete list of personnel & next of kin ready – in fact that is what I've been doing most of the time I've been here so far.

On Thursday I went off for the day. I thought I'd see how far I could get comfortably in a day & I landed up at Tewkesbury where I spent a very pleasant afternoon lying in the sun by the Avon. I am hoping that 'Tiny' (*his old friend from Worcester days*) will come down from Powick to meet me in Cheltenham.

Well how are you all at Kineton? Perhaps I shall suddenly appear there one day without warning, so don't be surprised if I suddenly walk in!

It seems Chig might have wished to avoid alarming his father in his recall of his initial flying experiences with his new CO. What he shared with his father was somewhat circumspect and guarded. In his drafted autobiography Chig recalled that soon after his arrival at the Station his CO, discovering Chig had never flown before, took him up in a Tiger Moth. "He put me in the front seat", Chig remembered, "himself taking the pilot's seat behind me. He then took off and, I'm still convinced, the devil tried his utmost to scare the living daylights out of me! He did frightening turns, steep descents straight at woods and lifted just in time to pass over them, and then very steep ascents. I was determined not to appear scared and eventually he decided to land, and we walked back to the Mess where he gave me a very much needed pint! We got on in a friendly manner after that!"

29.4.44

By the way I've just had a fixture list from the new Sec. of the cricket club. Cound have got a complete list for the coming season & start today, lucky dogs! I should love to get up for an odd match.

All those gliders you saw the other day were part of the big exercise that took place round here. I didn't take part in it, but I went to see some of it. A glider is quite a complicated affair, although it has no engine. The pilot can manipulate the wings & rudder and tail fins quite a lot. But it rests with the glider pilot to judge his distance & the angle of descent, for once the tow rope has been cast off, he obviously can't stay up indefinitely. That, of course, is where the skill comes in – & dashed clever they are too. The thing is only made of three-ply wood & consequently doesn't like much bumping.

No, I didn't get home to Cressage. I had put in for leave, but had to come here on the very day I'd hoped to go. I hope to look in at home one day, but it will be literally a flying visit, for it will have to be by plane, I expect.

I did a trip last Tuesday, over to an aerodrome near Norwich. We were going to collect some gliders & set off about 9.30 & were back for lunch. Naturally towing gliders is not a very fast job – not as the RAF think of speed anyway! Still it's considerably faster than I've ever been before, but you don't notice the speed. I went & came back in a plane, as I'd never been in one before. It was very pleasant though I was amused that although I was compelled to have a parachute, nobody thought of telling me either how to put it on or how to work it if necessary! We passed right over Blenheim Palace & the layout of the magnificent park looks very fine. We also went near Ely Cathedral. But most of the journey was rather dull over this flat bit of country.

On Wednesday I went to Cheltenham to meet Tiny (*Rowe*). We had a good lunch & then went to Prestbury & climbed the Cotswolds. Then we just sat and talked till we thought it time to go back for tea & our respective buses. The old lad was in great form & as amusing as ever. He was very taken with my 'cherry beret' (*the distinctive head dress of the Airborne Forces since 1942, when it was first worn by the Parachute Regiment; Chig had been awarded his beret when with the Parachute Training Regiment at the beginning of 1944*).

This letter, and the previous one, and their rather 'breathless' tones about gliders, their construction and use, indicate how novel gliders were and how novel was their use in a war-time context. They had been first used by the Russians and Germans in 1940, the gliders being based on the machines used for sporting purposes in the 1930s. All members of GPR were volunteers from other units in the Army. They were required to pass RAF selection procedures before training as light aircraft pilots. After a 12 week course, they were then given further training on gliders on the General Aircraft Hotspur glider. This glider was commissioned by the Ministry of Aircraft Production as an assault glider. Its compact design, and a change in military tactics for the transporting large numbers of men and equipment, limited its use to training purposes. Trainee glider pilots then undertook a six-week Heavy Glider Conversion course to fly the British Airspeed Horsa or the American Hamilcar.

6.5.44

We have nearly been blown off this aerodrome lately, the wind has been very strong. Otherwise this is still a good spot & I'm enjoying my life here even though I have yet to hold a Service! We can't get anywhere to hold one & so the chaps go of their own free will to the local Church about 2 miles away. Not many go, but there are usually 20 or so in the evening & a dozen or so in the morning.

Let me see now, what is my rough plan of a day? It is rather difficult to describe for each day differs considerably. I'm 'called' at 7.15 & get to breakfast – about a mile away – at about 8.15. We mess with the RAF officers who predominate in numbers considerably. After breakfast another walk of about ½ mile to the office. Here I usually stay most of the morning, writing letters, seeing men & compiling a complete list of personnel & also doing a bit of reading. Back to the Mess for lunch; then in the afternoon I go onto the airfield or walk about the Station chatting to our fellows. Back for tea & another spot down at the office till about 6.00pm. Then a long walk all the way up to my room to change for dinner. Back to the Mess for dinner & then we usually stay & talk or read till soon after 9.00 when we go off to bed. That is a day when I stay here, but very frequently I go off to one or other of the stations where my men are, & sometimes I go somewhere with the CO, as on last Thursday when I went to an aerodrome between Burford & Faringdon, & was away all the morning.

I haven't flown this week, there has been too much to do. I had hoped to go up about once a week.

Cressage got over £2,400 for its 'Salute the Soldier' Week, which was pretty good wasn't it?

I heard a nightingale last Wednesday & have seen or heard about 50 different species since I've been here already.

I went off to Bristol for my day off this week. It has had a bad battering & large areas are derelict including the famous Temple Church, but St. Mary's, Redcliffe is still all right though surrounded by ruins. It is a marvellous Church. I'd never been in before – & compares very favourably with the other leading parish churches of the country, like Ludlow & Cirencester.

PS Your letter arrived on the 4th. Letters seem to take about 3 or 4 days to reach me.

13.5.44

The most exciting event of the week as far as I am concerned has been a journey I did by air up to an aerodrome in north Shropshire. We set off on Tuesday morning about 10.15 & travelled practically the whole journey over familiar landmarks – Cirencester, Cheltenham, Bredon, Worcester, Stourport, Bridgnorth, Cressage, Shrewsbury. It all looked very lovely. I could recognise all sorts of things – the County Ground (*home of Worcestershire County Cricket Club*), Pitchcroft (*Worcester Racecourse*) mostly ploughed up, I even spotted Thornloe Bank (*the family's former home*). Then nearing Cressage we slightly deviated our course so as to fly over it. We circled round once so that I could have a good look. Our house looked minute, but very attractive & the whole village looked charming. Coming back we were a bit pressed for time & so took a straight course which meant going the other side of the Wrekin. The pilot of the plane was a man called Holland-Martin from Bredon! We passed over his lovely house & Col. Place my CO who was with us had also had a house at Bishop's Cleeve which we also saw, so 3 out of the 4 of us saw our homes.

On Thursday I was travelling again, but this time by road and foot. We had a sort of field day on the Berkshire Downs & very lovely they are. It's a part of the country I don't know much, in fact only once have I been through any of it & that was when I was at Sarum & we spent a college holiday by going in a taxi with Whitmill through Newbury & Oxford to his home at Banbury.

Yesterday I was at Vaughan Williams' birthplace. I am holding a Service in the little Church each Friday at 11.00 for our chaps who are stationed there. Yesterday about 20 turned up which wasn't bad for it is quite voluntary & there are only about 100 men all told and several were flying. In the evening I went with the CO after supper to the Hewetsons – a very pleasant house where you feel completely at home. Last time I went I had a long chat over a pig-sty wall with an old chap who has 8 little Saddleback pigs. Last night I had a long chat on gardening with another man – very pleasant & unwarlike it was too!

This place is magnificent for birds – a nightingale sang me to bed the other night, I've seen & heard all sorts of birds & this morning I found, & released, a baby thrush in my office!

My room is part of Nissen hut, quite comfortable. The main snag is that there are no baths on the site.

I've come across an officer in our crowd, though he's not stationed here but on one of the other stations, named Brazier. He comes from Bromsgrove and went to school there.

Tomorrow we start 'Salute the Soldier' Week here, & there is a big parade at the Parish Church at which I am preaching. After this I go to lunch with the big wigs – the General who is inspecting the troops etc!

I've discovered that I'm practically unique! There is only one other glider Chaplain in the army & he doesn't glide!

22.5.44

I hope this reaches you in time for your birthday. I also sent some records off from Duke & Forty's last Saturday which should, with luck, arrive in time.

We are now under a very strict censorship, so I have to be careful what I say. I have at last started holding Services in the Station. The RAF Chaplain has provided an altar frontal, crucifix & candlesticks & I borrowed some matting to kneel on &, generally speaking, have made quite a nice little chapel out of a disused hut. We hope, eventually, to make this into a proper Chapel. It is an ideal hut for the purpose with three separate parts which could be Anglican, RC & Non-Conformist Chapels, another excellent room as a quiet room, and a good little office.

I had two flights in gliders last week, one short one & one long one. The latter was topping for we went all over our honeymoon country, & it was grand seeing it again. My pilot was a young subaltern called Brazier who comes from Bromsgrove.

It's been bitterly cold this last week, especially on the days when I had to get up at 6.15! The Senior Medical Officer here was at Charterhouse though not at Saunderites (*one of the School's houses*).

I hitched a lift to Salisbury on Thursday. I got there quite easily in six different vehicles. The first person I saw was an officer who was with me at Hardwick. After lunch, I caught a bus and went to see one or two people at Whaddon. Then I went back and saw the old Prin(*cipal*). He seemed very fit though a good bit older & we had a good chat about various chaps who were at Sarum with me. Then I went to the Freemantles who are still living in their little house on the Close. I took them out to tea & then caught a train back – a very jolly day. The driver of a lorry I had a lift in was a Gloucestershire man & a terrific cricket fan, so you can guess we had plenty to talk about!

I'm sitting out in a field writing this as it is too nice to be indoors.

Old Richards, the RAF Chaplain, although he doesn't know you, sends his salaams on your birthday & condolences for having had to put up with me for so long!

Two censorship posters.

Chig began this letter by referring to the strict censorship which all were called to adopt. Government posters reminded the general public of the need to be guarded and circumspect.

Intense preparations by the Allies for D-Day were under way, hence the essential need for secrecy, and hence the intense flying training going on at Chig's station, at neighbouring stations as well as at many others across the south and east of England.

29.5.44

A new address headed this letter: No 2 Wing, Glider Pilot Regt., A.P.O., England.

It is likely A.P.O stood for Army Post Office, though this was an acronym used more frequently by American Forces.

> First of all you will note the alteration in address. For some reason or other they have changed this to the present one although we haven't moved.
>
> The main excitement of last week was that on Tuesday – your birthday – I did a hitch-hike home! The chances of getting home seemed to be getting less & less, & so, hearing at breakfast that a good lad called Nichols was going by car to

Cheltenham, I decided to have a shot at it, even though I had little hope really of getting there. Anyway, off we went at 10.15. At Cheltenham there was no means of getting on, either by rail or bus, so I walked towards Tewkesbury. I soon got a lift in a lorry, nearly as far as the junction with the Gloucester road. Then along came a private car & I got to Tewkesbury. I was dropped by the Abbey & walked to where the Worcester road turns sharply to the left to cross the bridge out of town. Here I caught a traveller, & he proved an excellent choice for he took me right through to Bridgnorth! – where he turned off my road, for he was going to Wellington & Market Drayton. I walked over the bridge & just by the road that leads up to the town I got a lift in an American Army lorry driven by a negro, & he dropped me at home! This was a pretty hair-raising section of the journey for he drove like John, & hills etc like Wenlock Bank meant nothing at all to him. I reached home at 1.45, 3½ hours after starting & about 90 miles in all. Pretty good going don't you think? Pauline of course knew nothing about this & was nearly as bucked to see me as I was to see her. It really was grand and we just ambled about the garden & leant over the railings & looked at the village. Then we went & had a peep at the Church & brought Jennifer & Jeremy (*Olga's children*) back from school. Of course we met lots of the village, including the Pelhams, & Noel Baldwin heard I was home & came up to see me – he is a good chap. There are nasty rumours floating about Burgess who isn't at all well – one being that he has a cancer. I hope it isn't true for he is such a good chap. In addition it would be extremely awkward for his parish as well as mine if he is crocked up.

Well I had to get back that night, so off I set at 5.00pm. I walked out onto the road & saw a car coming up the hill. It was John Wainwright's so I got in & chatted with him as far as his farm. Then I went very slowly for some time, for I walked to Hartley, got a lift from there to Wenlock & then walked about 2 more miles. I didn't like this as I wanted the early part to be quick for the last part of the journey wouldn't be easy late at night. However eventually an N.F.S. (*National Fire Service* or *Night Flying Squadron?*) car came along & took me to Bridgnorth, & from there to Worcester I caught up time considerably, for an American Military Policeman on a motor bike asked me the way to Bridgnorth. He very decently told me to get on the back – although he was not really allowed to do this & away we went – Bridgnorth to Worcester 45 mins! He dropped me on the outskirts & I went by bus through the town, getting on the Bath Rd one with old Castley who is now living opposite the Norton Barracks turning. There I caught an American lorry & an RAD (?) man got on too. He turned out to be an old St. John's School boy, named Kings. He remembered Mr Bowen & Radcliffe, the Chalks, Tyler whom he used to assist blow the organ, for he failed to get in the choir, you wouldn't pass him (!). We had a good chat & the lorry got to Cheltenham in 40 mins. Here I had to walk out of the town, & then got a young farmer to give me a lift for 6 miles or so. Then when I was walking along the lovely Cotswolds what should come along but the same American lorry on another journey – this time to Cirencester. From there I soon picked up another lift & was back by 9.15! I called at the Richards & they insisted on giving me a supper of bacon, fried bread & 2 eggs (!) with rhubarb pie to top up & a pint of beer. It was one of the best days I've had for a long time.

Yesterday – Sunday – we had two Eucharists in the Camp at 7.00 & 8.00 which I took. Then I preached at a strange Service in a village Church near here at 11.00. It was Matins, to the Creed, then a hymn followed by the first part of the Eucharist. My sermon came after the Nicene Creed. Then a hymn, prayers, blessing & National Anthem (!) & exit choir & majority of congregation.

In the afternoon I went to the Richards to tea & sat on the lawn & listened to the gramophone playing Brahms 1st Piano Concerto. Afterwards I preached at Evensong – Solemn Evensong with incense, Richards in a cope, & procession. We sang 'Down Ampney' & 630 English Hymnal, two of Vaughan Williams' best hymn tunes I think, & we had Attwood's setting of Veni Creator as an anthem which reminded me of the old days at St. George's.

PS. Don't send this letter round the family or anything of that sort, for, although I've betrayed no secrets, it gives the names of several places.

7.6.44

Just a short line in the midst of all the great events that are going on. First to thank you for the book & letter & birthday greetings. Your letter arrived on my birthday & the book next day. Then to say I'm still OK, still in England & likely to be, though I may be trotting about a bit – but I should have been doing that in any case. Thirdly to ask you to forgive me for the delay in writing, which I know you will now know what's been happening. You can't imagine how marvellous this has been – one day I'll be telling you. Heaps of love to you all.

It was wholly unsurprising that Chig's note to his father, though guarded, spoke of "all the great events that are going on" for the previous day, Tuesday 6 June, was D-Day, the day of the Normandy landings. Preceded by air attacks by the RAF and USAAF, thousands of Allied troops, transported by some 4,000 ships and several thousand smaller craft, more than 7,000 vessels in all, had landed on the Normandy beaches of northern France, signalling the start of a major new offensive against the Germans.

In the air attack, some 1,300 RAF planes created the first wave of assaults then 1,000 American bombers followed, dropping bombs on targets in northern France to divert the German forces.

The Normandy landings had been planned to take place in May, at around the time of a full moon, but were postponed by poor weather and doubtful weather forecasts until June and then, originally planned for 5 June, were again postponed, for 24 hours, by bad weather.

Chig's letter to his
father of 7 June 1944.

> 7. 6. 44,
>
> No. 2. Wing
> Glider Pilot Regt.
> A.P.O.
> England
>
> My dearest Father,
>
> Just a short line in the midst of all the great events that are going on. First to thank you for the book & letter & birthday greetings. Your letter arrived on my birthday & the book next day. Then to say I'm O.K., still in England & likely to be, though I may be trotting about a bit – but I should have been doing that in any case. Thirdly to ask you to forgive me for the delay in writing, which I know you will now you know what's been happening. You can't imagine how marvellous this has been – one day I'll be telling you.
>
> Heaps of love to you all,
> Your loving son.
> Rowland

What is remarkable is that with huge numbers of Servicemen (and women) fully at the ready, on stand-by or otherwise actively engaged in countless bases, camps, embarkation ports and beaches not one word of Operation Market Garden leaked to the enemy. It seemed that everyone across the whole nation was holding their breath.

In total some 75,215 British and Canadian troops and 57,500 US troops were involved in the D-Day landings, and another 23,400 were landed by air. No wonder Chig's letter spoke, as it did, of the "great events going on". His previous two letters had hinted also of similar activity. Things were hotting up. As we read on, we will see how this affected Chig.

15.6.44

I'm sorry so to have neglected writing to you lately, but I know you will understand after having seen all the news in the papers.

As you can imagine, my birthday was a pretty exciting day – chaps from here were the first people to go across & there was plenty on in preparations as you can guess. I myself didn't go. I wasn't allowed to, but I had a lot to do & have done a pretty good lot of travelling ……. Our people have been in the news a lot lately. Major Dale in charge of Hamilcar gliders is one of ours. I see the papers say he is a Shropshire man – that is the first I knew about it, though I haven't seen much of him. Then the evacuation of the wounded story that appeared in yesterday's papers took place here. We were swamped with bally reporters spreading themselves all over the place and drinking all our beer. They were just like a lot of pigs escaped from their sty. They ran about everywhere, getting in everybody's way & were a blinking nuisance. Heaven preserve me from reporters!

I have held several voluntary Services for our chaps this last week or so, & have had very good numbers, & many of them made their Communion. I try and get round to bless each of them individually. Everyone is on top of the world here. Some of the stories of people going from here are really marvellous. For instance there was the glider pilot that had to hang on while the tug (the plane that pulls the glider) was in a spiral nose dive through cloud, with one of its engines temporarily out of action. It is a tricky business to follow a tug at any time, but this was really marvellous. They came through all right too.

Then there was the parachutist (*today we would call them para-troopers, but in those early days of the Parachute Regiment they were known as parachutists*), who, when the time came to jump found all his kit had been harnessed to him outside his static line – the line that is attached to the plane & which automatically opens his parachute. This meant he couldn't move. So he yelled to the pilot who sent the rest of the crew back to undo the chap & do him up properly again. The wretched man kept on apologising for the inconvenience he was causing, & eventually jumped 4½ mins after the others had gone. The plane had to make 3 runs over the spot where they had to be dropped, & dropped him bang on it. That takes some courage you know to drop like that in enemy territory, by yourself, 4½ mins after the rest have gone (*the pilot clearly did an heroic job too*).

Then there was the amusing incident of the chaps who went from here who, while they were waiting, brought a piano out on the aerodrome to amuse themselves with, & then wanted to take it with them!

In his drafted autobiography Chig, looking back to those weeks immediately before D-Day, wrote that No 2 Wing "was extremely busy – the Operations staff especially so". He wrote of RSM Briody, an ex-Guards Company Sergeant Major "one of the finest men I have ever known – no regiment could possibly be slovenly with Mick Briody about". As a result Chig firmly believed "The Glider Pilot Regiment was an incredibly smart regiment. It was unique in that all the active personnel were either commissioned officers or non-commissioned officers. They had to become pilots and were therefore given the equivalent rank of RAF pilots – sergeants for second pilots, staff sergeants for first pilots, 2nd or 1st lieutenants for second pilots, 1st lieutenants and captains as first pilots. Before flying a glider they had to be capable of flying powered aircraft. Their job was to fly their gliders, land them behind the enemy lines and then, it was envisaged, they should get back to the Allied lines and Britain as quickly as possible in order to fly more gliders in if necessary. As all had started as soldiers, and as they would obviously have to fight their way back in many cases, their training included that of combat troops as well as skilled specialist pilots. This meant that Glider Pilots (all of whom volunteered for this special service) were picked men – men of considerable character, intelligence and ability."

Almost certainly war-time security was a key reason why Chig's letters to his father were limited in the details they offered – that, and the fact that he was constantly busy and letter-writing, even faithful letter-writing, had to be squeezed in to available moments. This makes Chig's later recollections of this period a valuable record.

"As everyone knows, 5th June was to be D-Day", Chig remembered, "but adverse weather delayed it for 24 hours. On the evening of 5th June I went with John Place (*CO*), John Blatch (*Major, Second-in Command No 2 Wing*), Donald Shuttleworth (*Captain, Adjutant*), and many others to see 6 Dakotas with 6 Gliders take off from our airfield. These six gliders were commanded by Lt. Aubrey Pickwoad, a large, imperturbable young man. They were carrying airborne forces scheduled to be landed close to a bridge near Caen. Two other specially trained glider sections were, at the same time, leaving other airfields, one making for another bridge and one for a very strongly fortified gun emplacement. These places were vital. They had to be taken if sea-borne troops and other air-borne forces were to be able to get a foothold on the British sector of the Normandy coast.

"All the tugs and gliders successfully became airborne and turned in the failing light over the airfield. Suddenly we saw the leading glider flashing a light. 'Good God,' exclaimed John Place, 'Aubrey's in trouble and is going to have to pull off and land. 'No he isn't,' he suddenly shouted, 'he's giving us the V-sign. Oh, well done boy!' And so he was. Aubrey and his fellow glider pilots were able to complete their dangerous task with great success and were back in England at Blake Hill Farm in a day or two".

His recollections continued "Next day C, E and F squadrons flew over to Normandy, as did No 1 Wing, carrying large numbers of men and much equipment. C Squadron with their large Hamilcars, each carrying a tank, were a real surprise to the enemy."

Blake Hill Farm, with its extended sick quarters, had been chosen as the aerodrome to which the wounded evacuated from Normandy would be taken. Many VIPs turned up on the night of 6 June to see how these arrangements worked. With medical staff and nursing staff on full alert, and a fleet of ambulances ready to convey patients direct from the returned Dakotas to the sick bay, plane after plane returned without a single casualty. From the point of view of publicity for their medical planning this aspect was

A timely stop! A Horsa glider made it to the Landing Zone, but only just short of the field wall.

a flop, but it did of course mean that, in the immediate aftermath of D-Day, marvellously few casualties required treatment. Eventually, later that day, a plane brought in a casualty. One unfortunate young man found his glasses had been broken during the invasion, rendering him helpless and of little use – until his spectacles could be repaired! Perhaps this was why the journalists and photographers, referred to by Chig in his letter of 15 June above), were running about and getting in everyone's hair – they were looking for a story and, at that time, there weren't any stories, or not the ones they had expected.

Later, many casualties were flown into Blake Hill Farm and were all visited by Padres Chignell and Richards. Here they were given the immediate treatment that was necessary before being sent on to specialist units which could provide the more specialised treatment required. Of this period Chig remembered: "We would get the name and address of their nearest relatives, to whom we would send a card if the casualty could not manage to fill it up himself. We prayed with those who wished, and a lot did."

Chig's work was set aside briefly around this time when his CO gave him 48 hours' leave to return to Cressage for the funeral of his great friend, and the village's Doctor, Ernest Gittins..

Once the intense D-Day operations were completed things became a little quieter for the GPR, although training continued and plans for future operations were formulated, operations which were thought to be a month or so off. In this lull Chig took time to attend concerts in Swindon and also, at the end of July and coinciding with Pauline's birthday, he was given seven days' leave, which they spent in Abersoch.

22.6.44

I have just had 48 hours leave unofficially. The reason was a wire from Pauline saying that Dr Gittins' funeral was to be yesterday afternoon. A letter she had written some time before saying he was much worse, and another saying he had died, had not reached me. Fortunately she sent this wire. So on Tuesday afternoon I set off at 3.30. I caught an American Army lorry to Cirencester, then an old English lorry to Cheltenham, a bus from there to Tewkesbury, & a lorry from Tewkesbury to Enville, a village near Kinver, & on the road from Stourbridge to Bridgnorth. I was a bit doubtful of a lift from there as the road seemed pretty quiet, but a car soon picked me up & proved to be going to Shrewsbury &, of course, right through Cressage. So I was home by 8.00! Just in time for supper!

If it hadn't been for the Dr's funeral it would have been a grand bit of leave but, of course, that put rather a dampener on it all. Still I'm glad the dear chap's sufferings & those of his wife are over.

Of course I saw pretty well everybody in the village & it was all looking very charming. Pauline has done wonders with the garden & is, herself, very fit & well.

I set off back this morning at 9.20 & the first car took me to Worcester! Then I got a Bath Rd bus & immediately a lift in a lorry to the Cheltenham turning off the Gloucester road, There I had to walk about a mile & then got a lift in an RAF car driven by a WAAF, & this brought me right into our camp – 3 hours 55 minutes all told!

We are very busy with casualties coming in by air. They are not strictly my job, but I go and help old Richards out with them.

I can't tell you much about my journeyings – what they were for or anything like that – at present, but I've certainly been making my acquaintance with quite large parts of southern England lately.

30.6.44

I'm afraid this will probably be rather a scrappy note as I haven't much time to write & am also pretty tired. We've had a lot of casualties in lately & I haven't been getting to bed very early. Still it is grand to be able to help these chaps – some of them are pretty bad.

Last Saturday I had a jaunt up through Worcester to help collect a lot of medical supplies for the sick quarters. When I heard this trip was on I jumped at the chance. It was a grand day, beautifully warm & the journey was very pleasant. We had lunch in Worcester & came back there for tea & had a look at the Cathedral. There was a match going on at the County Ground which brought back memories of good days.

I've come across one or two chaps who were at Hardwick with me &, like me, are only too pleased to have got away from it.

Well I wonder how much longer this European war will go on? Not very long I fancy. At any rate they seem to be doing so well over there they don't need us!

9.7.44

Last week I had three glider trips – none of them long ones though. Still they were quite pleasant & I hadn't been up for some time.

I got talking to a young RAF pilot last night & discovered that he was an old Carthusian. This lad is also the holder of the DFC. He's very full of the idea of teaching aeronautics in schools & wants to do this at Charterhouse.

I had written to Pauline to suggest that she should come down here & stay at the local hotel for next weekend but now I find that there is just a possibility that I might get a few days' leave. Anyway I'm going to try & I hope to know sometime today. The trouble is I don't know who to ask for the necessary authority. Leave is supposed to come from the Chaplains' Dept – my SCF is supposed to grant it – but I haven't got one! There is no such thing in the Glider Regt.

15.7.44

Except for one very pleasant glider trip I don't seem to have been anywhere. However, on this trip I saw quite a bit of England. We went over Basingstoke, then to Reading & Aylesbury & back over Oxford, & it all looked lovely. Oxford, as a matter of fact, is the first town I've seen that really looks delightful from the air.

I did have to go on a trip to Gloucester the other day, by road. It was all very pleasant – the Cotswolds are looking lovely just now. We came back via Painswick & Stroud as the other road was so crowded.

One of the Sisters in our sick quarters has a fiancé – a civilian – who was in Borneo when the Japs arrived, & apart from a communication to his people last August to say he was alive, which came from some Government Dept, she had heard absolutely nothing for 2½ years. So you can imagine her joy when she got a letter from his sister this week to say that they had had two post cards dated last November & December from him. Apparently he is only allowed to write 25 words a month. It must be awful to be in her position.

25.7.44

Chig at last got his seven days' leave, authorised or not! This letter was addressed from: c/o Mrs Thomas, Iona, Abersoch, Caernarvonshire.

I suddenly got news that I could go for 7 days leave starting on Friday, on Thursday morning. So I sent a wire to Pauline to tell her to come home, one to Arthur Cole to say I would take the Sunday Services, and one to the new Secretary of Cound CC to ask for a game of cricket. Then I got a promise from a pilot who said he would fly me up to (*RAF*) Shawbury near Shrewsbury, & so off we went on Friday morning. 37 minutes to Shawbury and 2½ hours from Shawbury to Cressage! I had lunch in Shrewsbury & the 1.15 train was nearly an hour late. I knew I should be home before Pauline & was rather glad for hers would be a tiring journey & I could get the house straight for her. I bought some rations & Mrs Mansfield brought me a loaf & I got some milk & was quite ready for when P arrived on the 6.00 train.

I got my game of cricket which we lost by 3 wickets & I took the Sunday services. It seemed such a pity to spoil P's holiday from housework so we decided to come up here yesterday. It is a long journey. We started from Shrewsbury at 7.50 & went via Welshpool, Dovey Junction & Barmouth, having to change at each of these, but the changes were perfectly easy, our connections were just sitting & waiting in the stations. We stopped at every station but the trains were not too crowded & we got seats all the way, & the countryside – the mountains, valleys & seashore – were absolutely lovely.

This is a pleasant, quiet little spot & the rooms are very nice indeed. We have to get our own food & Mrs Thomas cooks it – she's a good cook too & is very nice.

I have to go back on Friday & have a 13 hr journey before me, starting at 7.45 & getting to Swindon at 8.25.

29.7.44 (Pauline's birthday)

Well, I've had a topping leave with Pauline. Abersoch is a grand little spot & the good Mrs Thomas who runs the boarding house where we stayed is an extraordinarily nice woman who is always doing all sorts of little kindnesses to us. We bathed two or three times and went for leisurely walks along the shore where we saw Ringed Plovers, Dunlins & Oyster Catchers – the latter reminded us of our 1938 Scottish holiday with you, for we saw lots then. We also went to see a very nice old Church at Llanegan, with a beautiful screen from Bardsey Island, a celebrated Celtic Church spot.

I had to leave early yesterday morning & got up at 6.15. The nearest railway station was Pwllheli & the train left at 7.45 so I had to take a taxi from Abersoch.

I took sandwiches & good Mrs Thomas gave me 3 hard-boiled eggs as well as a good breakfast of bacon & egg. My journey was through marvellous country. All along the sea shore as far as Barmouth where I changed. I got a corner seat in a first class carriage both in this train & the next which went through the equally lovely country of Dolgelley (*sic*), Bala, Corwen & Llangollen to Ruabon where I changed again. This time I didn't get a corner seat, but I got a seat all the same for the long journey to Paddington! That was the silly part of the trip, to think I had to go all the way down there! I should have been in London by 5.10 & my train out should have left at 6.35, but we lost a lot of time on the journey down & I only had 5 mins to catch the 6.35. It was absolutely crammed & I was in the corridor all the way. Then I caught a bus back & went to see the Richards who gave me a much-needed drink – I'd had nothing but one cup of tea at Barmouth at about 9.30.

Chig's letters reveal the many vagaries and challenges of using public transport in the war years (since he had given up using his car). On the other hand earlier letters showed how, with determination, it was possible to get about by hitch-hiking – though this was probably easier for Service men and women in uniform.

5.8.44

One of Chig's longer letters. Without much exceptional operational activity to report (or sketch in even the merest details), much of the letter recounted concert-going in Swindon. The London Symphony Orchestra performed three concerts on successive evenings, and Chig managed to get to them all with a small party of friends, although he noted that only one other person, "a nice sister from Sick Quarters, called Hickie" managed all three. He was in his element, as each of the concerts contained work by Edward Elgar

> This letter seems to be nothing but music, but music has been the really great joy of the week. We are getting some gorgeous weather & I had a short flight with the CO in his Tiger Moth earlier in the week.
> We've been getting a fairly regular supply of casualties just lately – they seem to be coming in more workable numbers now.

14.8.44

I did a trip down to Salisbury to marry one of my old Whaddon Sunday School scholars – a girl called Miriam Bartlam. She is one of two children from Whaddon with whom I have kept up a spasmodic correspondence ever since my old Sarum days, & of late I have seen her several times – first when she became a WAAF

& was stationed at Bridgnorth &, recently, because she has been asking my help. Her mother has cancer & is seriously ill & I've been able to get Miriam a four months' release from the Service. I had a very pleasant trip down to Alderbury stopping in Sarum on the way for lunch. It was a pretty little wedding, & the bride was absolutely punctual & it all went off without a hitch. I came straight back & was here just in time for a cup of tea before starting work with the casualties that were coming in. We didn't finish with this lot until about 11.30.

On Sunday I went to Matins at a little village Church near one of our other stations, as I wanted to get hold of the parson & ask if I could use his Church to hold a Service every Sunday at 10.00. It was a charming little Church with a lot of Norman work in it – arches & windows – and the parson was a good fellow. He took the Service & preached well, and he readily agreed to let me use his Church. In the afternoon I played a game of tenni-quoits with some of the chaps & got a bit of fat off!

This is a terrific spell of fine weather – the harvest is going strong down here – but I hope you aren't finding it too trying. It seems to be suiting our Normandy forces though some of these chaps say that the mosquitoes are awful – the insects, not the planes!

18.8.44

I don't know whether you will have got a letter from Pauline before this or not, but there is no need to get alarmed as the show is off for the time being …

Thank you for the cuttings & especially the one about the Guards Chapel. The new Chaplain, Whitrow, who was killed, was my Deputy Assistant Chaplain General when I was at Chilwell & Hardwick – an awfully nice fellow who had been Vicar of a large parish in Winchester before the war. I liked him immensely & got on very well with him. He was one of the best chaplains that I've come across. Incidentally two other chaplains whom I knew well have been wounded, a Ch. of Scot. laddie called Aston who was at Chilwell with me, & an old Sarum man called Hearsey.

I began to learn to fly yesterday! The Wing Commander Flying suggested that I should go up with him in an Oxford for a trip, & then he said he'd give me a lesson. I found I could handle the thing quite well, in ordinary flying – I did one or two quite good turns etc & then he tried me with three landings & take-offs. The landings were – the first quite a good one, we came in smoothly & settled on the runway absolutely right; the second one I bounced the plane a little, but the third was bad – I came in too steep & after correcting that I bounced heavily. As for take-offs they weren't bad, but I found it a great temptation after leaving the ground to point the nose up too steeply.

I've had a letter today from Burgess, who has been looking after my parishes for me. He made a muck of the Services a Sunday or two ago, having gone away on holiday & left someone in charge, he went & locked his garage & the poor bloke couldn't get the car to come over in. Arthur Cole, according to Burgess, has been rude about it & now Burgess says he is going to resign from looking after Cressage & Sheinton. I've seen my CO & he is going to fly me up to see the Bishop tomorrow if the Bish can see me. It's a beastly nuisance & I'm frightfully sorry this crisis has arisen. I think Burgess has been very silly about it & I also fancy that he is using it as an excuse to get out of the work for which he has shown less & less enthusiasm. I don't really know what the solution is, I certainly can't think of anyone to do the job, & I don't want the parish to be neglected, when everything was so promising.

What show was "off"? Why might his father feel alarmed? Typically and understandably Chig's notes fail to disclose the reasons to his father. Perhaps later letters will do so. His reference, however, to the Guards' Chapel related to a newspaper report of it being bombed on Sunday 18 June. Germany's targeting of London with V1 bombs (sometimes called the flying bombs, buzz bombs or doodlebugs, and also as 'Hitler's secret weapon') had begun five days earlier, on 13 June. By the weekend of 17-18 June some 60 V1s were reaching the capital, and that weekend 45 were to strike south London.

With these horrendous attacks beginning just days earlier, few people were aware of the risk, as their existence had not been publicly acknowledged by the Government. Indeed, news of this tragedy was suppressed initially, and it was not until the following month that the Guards' Chapel incident was openly reported in the press (confirmed, as we have seen, by Chig's letter above).

The Guards' Chapel (formally The Royal Military Chapel, St. James Park), the religious home of the Household Division which it served, had (and has) a deserved reputation for the quality of its worship and also its music, often provided by a Guards' band (the Band of the Coldstream Guards was playing on this fateful day). Alongside many Service men and women, the Chapel regularly drew Service families, civilians resident or working in London, and visitors to the capital (from home and abroad). The Chapel, on Sunday 18 June, was packed, many of the congregation wishing to give thanks for the success of the Normandy landings; it was also the anniversary of the Battle of Waterloo. Among the congregation and its wide mix of people were Guardsmen from the barracks and other Service personnel based in London, their families; Free French soldiers and military personnel from Australia and America, local residents and members of the aristocracy.

At around 11.20am the Chapel, which also had suffered hits during the Blitz, earlier in the War, was struck by a V1. The explosion demolished the entire concrete roof, which collapsed devastatingly on the worshippers below. Those killed totalled 121 soldiers and civilians, and 141 were seriously injured. It is said that the only person not injured was the Bishop of Maidstone, who was conducting the Service. When the bomb struck he was standing at the altar, under a huge portico, which survived the blast and so protected him. When the Chapel was re-built (in the 1960s) the portico was retained and incorporated in the new Chapel. Legend has it that the altar candles survived the devastation and remained alight – perhaps a fitting symbol of so much of the nation's extraordinary determination and will.

26.8.44

The main excitement here is that we're 'moving house' next week. There has had to be some readjustment made, & we are moving – that is HQ plus me – to another station about 20 miles away. This will be very nearly 20 miles nearer to you &, with luck, I ought to be able to get over and see you, but I daren't make any promises. Things are moving so fast these days that we may not be there any time. In many ways I'm sorry to be leaving here, for I have liked it very much indeed, & though I shall still be with the same Glider people, I have made some good friends in this Mess who are not Glider people, & also some outside. However, I expect I shall be coming over here quite often, for we are leaving some fellows here who will be under my charge.

Then also, although the Mess at this other station is much better run, & there is some lovely country round about, yet the actual situation of the aerodrome is very bleak, & I sincerely hope we shan't be there in the winter. (I don't think it looks as though any of us will be, at the pace the war is going). As a matter of fact this place we are going to is the station where I have just lately fixed up regular Sunday Services in the little Church nearby. Now I shall have to fix up the same here, though it will have to be in the station Chapel.

I've heard no more about the trouble at Cressage. I hope it is settled for this coming Sunday – 27th – is the last that Burgess said he would be responsible for. It will be very awkward if he persists in resigning. I don't know where on earth I shall get anyone to take charge or to celebrate the Eucharist.

We've had some absolutely soaking weather here, earlier in the week – it leaked through my sleeping hut roof all over the place & I spent one night having to get out of bed & move the bed all over the place in the vain endeavour to find somewhere where it didn't drip on me. Eventually I had to just lie & let it drip on the ground-sheet that I put over my bed. Since then though it has cleared & now it looks as though it is going to be really warm today.

Pauline sent me a box of Worcester Pearmains this week. I don't seem to be getting many of them – they are going down well with the other chaps!

I had a very nice letter from the girl I married at Alderbury the other day thanking me for taking the Service. She said they had spent their honeymoon at Lynton which was a strange coincidence wasn't it?

No 2 Wing HQ – plus Chig – moved to Broadwell, just south of Burford in Oxfordshire. Long after the War Chig remembered the new station "was a similar sort of camp, but I did not get a bedroom of my own and I also shared an office with the RAF Chaplain, who lived with his family outside the camp."

At Broadwell No 2 Wing found itself, like many other military units at the centre of things, in a state permanent 'ever-readiness'. Operations were continually planned, amended, postponed, or cancelled. In part this was due to the rapid advance made by the Allied Forces in France since D-Day, making it difficult at times to coincide airborne forces' plans with land troops' progress. Pilots of No.2 Wing GPR and their RAF and USAAF colleagues must have been constantly on tenterhooks during this period. On the other hand many felt the end of the war was in sight, and any initiatives involved in bringing this to an end were infused with optimism.

"By now the Second Front was becoming very active and mobile," Chig recalled. "Many air-landing schemes were planned, only to be dropped because the ground troops were advancing so fast. No less than sixteen of these aborted schemes were planned around this time; some were only cancelled a few hours before take-off. This was very exhausting and frustrating for the airborne troops, not least the GPR, whose chief responsibility was to plan the actual ferrying of non-parachutists to the selected sites.

"Amongst the operations that were planned was one that still makes me shudder; the dropping of the 1st Airborne Division to cover the total area that they, plus the 82nd and 101st American Airborne Divisions, were eventually charged to occupy. I well remember talking this over with Staff Sergeant Alec Waldron, who had nobly said I could fly with him, despite the fact that his glider was already slightly overloaded. We were going to land in a field on the border of Germany, somewhere to the east of Nijmegen. We thought we might run to the border, and put a foot over it to say we had been in Germany! Fortunately this operation was cancelled – I think only an hour or two before take-off."

1.9.44

> This new move is one of mixed blessings – it is not nearly such a pretty station as the last, but it is much better catered for in the way of entertainments in the evening. There is always quite a good selection to choose from of things to do. So far I've been to a most interesting & amusing lecture on Shaw's "Arms and the Man", and the Music Club which functions twice a week.
>
> We moved in the rain & mud – there is plenty here & the scenery is almost completely lacking trees except in one direction. I'm sharing a sleeping hut with 3 other of our chaps, very nice fellows too. Two of them I've been with all along & the other is an old inhabitant of this station.
>
> You may not be hearing from me for a while, but you will soon guess the reason why.

And then, as a change from the ending he habitually used, he wrote:

> My fondest love to you, Father dear, & to all at Kineton.

Then came a PS.

16.9.44

> I've held this letter over, owing to the last paragraph, & various cancellations. God bless you, Father dear.

13.9.44

> I'm afraid I've sadly neglected you these last two weeks, but things have been so hectic & there has been so much I should have liked to have told you about, but which I am not allowed to, that you must excuse the absence of letters..
>
> However here I am, feeling very fit – just to give you an idea, Pauline sent my old bike to Oxford for me to pick up, & last Sunday afternoon I got a lift in & cycled out straight away, a matter of 20 odd miles, & then on Monday I did another 48, all without the slightest feeling of tiredness. It was all very pleasant, ambling through this delightful country.
>
> Then last Saturday I took another wedding – this time one of the Sisters at my last station. It was a very nice little wedding & there was a small reception afterwards, to which I went.
>
> It has been quite impossible so far to get over to see you, but I still hope to do so sometime. The distance isn't very great, but I don't know whether it will be a very easy road for 'hitch-hiking'!
>
> This is a rotten letter, but there is hardly anything to write about.

"A rotten letter" it might have seemed to its scribe but undoubtedly he was very much restrained, feeling "there has been so much I should have liked to have told you about, but which I am not allowed to".

Rotten letter or not, this note saw an abrupt ending of Chig's war-time correspondence with his father.

Why was this? All will shortly be revealed but, before that, two more letters, albeit in another hand, were among the letters received by George Chignell and collated by him. These were written by Pauline, Chig's wife.

19.9.44

> Dearest Father Chig,
> I'm writing, though I expect you have guessed that Rowland has gone out with his big Airborne Army to Holland.

Things don't sound to be going too badly for them so far from all accounts. Let's hope it won't be for long now & this wretched war will be over & they'll all be home. I'll let you know if I hear any news from Rowland. I don't suppose he'll have much time to write. I don't expect I shall hear for some time as they are dropped behind enemy lines, Letters won't get through either way for a bit. I haven't heard of any different address to write to.

This will be an anxious time for us won't it, but we can but hope & pray.

I'm on my own now as Olga & family went away yesterday, but I've lots of jobs to do to keep me occupied.

The remaining part of this letter is missing but four days later Pauline was writing again.

23.9.44

Dearest Father Chig,

Thank you very much for your letter & Bobbie's (*her sister-in-law Robin*) kind offer. I think I'll stay here all the same. If there is any news it will come here you see.

Things look terribly bad today I fear. It seems impossible for them to go on holding out any longer.

Much love.

Yours affec(*tionately*),

Pauline

What were those things which looked "terribly bad". Why were they "holding out", and where was this?

10

Arnhem: "A Sort of Diary"

The abrupt ending of Chig's letter to his father, alongside Pauline's two anxious notes to her father-in-law, tells a story of its own. Undoubtedly there was much Chig would have wished to tell had security considerations not precluded this. The rapid (though anticipated) change in his own situation and circumstances imposed its own embargo too.

The bundle of Chig's well and widely read and now rather dog-eared letters returned to him, by his father after the War, contained no further notes from him. But that did not signal his writing had come to an end.

On 17 September 1944, along with colleagues from No 2 Wing GPR and many other troops, Chig found himself engaged in "Operation Market Garden".

It was, at the time, the largest airborne operation ever conducted. An Allied military operation, fought in the Netherlands and Germany, its intention was to force a way into Germany over the Lower Rhine. General (later Field Marshal) Bernard Montgomery, Commander of British Forces in Europe, proposed a powerful, narrow thrust deep into German lines, believing this would be far more effective than an advance on a broad front. Accordingly the aim was to seize the eight bridges that spanned the network of canals and rivers on the Dutch-German border, including those across the two arms of the Rhine. This would allow the Allies to encircle Germany's industrial heartland.

The large-scale use of airborne forces, the greatest ever conceived, was paramount to the operation. Thirty thousand British and American airborne troops (including paratroops) were flown in, some 60 miles behind enemy lines, in the area around Arnhem. Their aim was to capture and secure the bridges across those waterways, thus opening the way for a speedy advance by armoured units on into northern Germany. In this they would be supported by General Horrocks' XXX Corps, part of the 2nd Army, which was expected to link up with them within two or three days. Frustratingly, XXX Corps' progress was impeded and proved slower than anticipated.

"Market Garden" was one of the boldest plans of the Second World War. As a result of suspect intelligence (or maybe an unwise use of the available intelligence) the 1st Airborne Division found itself surrounded and pinned down by a larger-than-expected

German military presence. Yet, despite suffering heavy casualties, it gallantly held out heroically for nine days before the survivors – a remnant, almost – were evacuated. Had it succeeded it was expected that Allied tanks and troops would have reached Berlin weeks before the Russians, with the distinct prospect – and eagerly awaited prize – of war being ended by Christmas 1944. Had Operation Market Garden succeeded and all its hopes been fulfilled the fate of post-war Europe might have been very different.

Chig, as we shall see, found himself, even as Chaplain, right in the thick of things in Arnhem. But before departing from Broadwell he noted:

"We were all up early on 17th September and some came to a very early Eucharist I held. After breakfast we went down to the airfield. There were our gliders, all in utterly regular order on the runway, with ropes attached to the Dakotas on either side. Whilst we were waiting to enter our gliders and whilst airborne troops were getting in, I went round to as many of my own men as possible, blessing them in small groups.

"At last we got in and I found my glider had 25 or 30 men of the Border Regiment."

Amazingly, from this moment, in the midst of all that was going on around him, all that he found himself engaged in, he found odd moments to record his thoughts and recollections: "During the following days I jotted down at various times a sort of diary ".

Immediately prior to take-off for Arnhem on 17 September 1944, Officers and Padre of No 2 Wing GPR. Pictured (L to R) are Lt. Martin Culverwell, Lt. S R Maclaine, Major Tony Murray, Captain P Robson, Lt.Col John Place (C.O.), Captain John Hooper, Chig, Lt R A 'Joe' Maltby, Captain Donald Shuttleworth (Adjutant). (photo, without attribution, appears in The Torn Horizon by Chris van Roekel)

"A sort of diary". What follows here, unedited and unexpurgated (and apart from a rare additional explanatory note from Chig's later recollections), is his account of the Battle of Arnhem and of his own experiences there as Chaplain to the Glider Pilots.

DIARY OF THE BATTLE OF ARNHEM.
September 17th–26th, 1944.

By

The Revd. W.R. Chignell, C.F.
No. 2 Wing. Glider Pilot Regt.

17.9.44.

After a good night's rest, we woke up about 6.0 and made our final preparations, including a good breakfast. I found I was very little excited by the prospect of the operation – in fact, I think we were all really rather relieved that at last it was going to come off, for we had had so many disappointments. It was something like the time before going in to bat, though not as thrilling. I spent the time on the airfield before the take-off, going round to as many gliders as possible, and giving the chaps a Blessing.

We took off at 9.45 – a perfectly good take-off – but had some immediate difficulty getting through some cloud. (We found later on that two or three gliders did not succeed in getting through, and had to pull off) A little later on, the tug stalled and we nearly had it, as our speed dropped to 75 m.p.h. We picked up however, and I went and had a look. It was a marvellous sight! We were above the clouds, which looked like a great whitish-grey landscape. All round were tugs and gliders, ploughing steadily along.

It was beginning to get quite exciting – not the excitement of fear, but of pride. I found that the Border Regt. Lieutenant, by the name of Holman who was sitting next to me had been at Jesus with Norman Chignell Jun.

We went over the coast and out to sea. Here, I hoped that all would go well, not being able to swim! Again, it was a marvellous sight! the cloud had gone, and far below was the sheen of the sea, with an occasional tiny boat looking as though it was stationary.

When we got in sight of Holland, we began to get thrilled for we were going to relieve this unfortunate country, and unfortunate it certainly is, at any rate for many miles for the floods are terrible – farms, villages and small towns completely cut off. Earlier, Joe Speller and his bunch of parachutists had passed us, and we saw fighters, and American gliders below us. In fact there were fighters all round us.

We got a terrific shaking up with one burst of 'flack', and S/Sgt. Waldron, our first pilot, nearly had to release for we were tossed all over the place. However he succeeded in righting the glider, and after that everything was quite quiet and uneventful. We made a good landing, and hopped out quickly. After helping to unload we went to our rendezvous, where I heard that 'Joe' Maltby had been killed by 'flack' on the journey over, and I found that the C.O. had had a very narrow escape, as his smock had a bit torn out of the left shoulder. John Blatch and R.S.M. Briody had not arrived. I went to see 'Joe's' body – the poor lad had it in the head and right side. He had died almost immediately. Our other casualties appear to have been slight, though one or two pilots had broken limbs, their gliders landing in the woods surrounding the L.Z.

The first page of Chig's Arnhem diary.

17.9.44

After a good night's rest, we woke up about 6.00 and made our final preparations, including a good breakfast. I found I was very little excited by the prospect of the operation – in fact I think we were all rather relieved that at last it was going to come off, for we had so many disappointments. It was something like the time before going in to bat, though not as thrilling. I spent the time on the airfield before the take-off going round to as many gliders as possible, and giving the chaps a Blessing.

We took off at 9.45 – a perfectly good take-off but had some immediate difficulty getting through some cloud. (We found out later on that two or three gliders did not succeed in getting through, and had to pull off.) A little later on the tug stalled and we nearly had it as our speed dropped to 75 m.p.h. We picked up however, and I went and had a look. It was a marvellous sight! We were above the clouds, which looked like great whitish-grey landscape. All around were tugs and gliders, ploughing steadily along.

It was beginning to get quite exciting – not excitement of fear, but of pride. I found that the Border Regt Lieutenant, by the name of Holmes, who was sitting next to me had been at Jesus with Norman Chignell Jun.

We went over the coast and out to sea. Here I hoped that all would go well, not being able to swim! Again, it was a marvellous sight; the cloud had gone, and far below was the sheen of the sea, with an occasional tiny boat looking as though it was stationary.

When we got in sight of Holland, we began to get thrilled for we were going to relieve this unfortunate country, and unfortunate it certainly is, at any rate for many miles for the floods are terrible – farms, villages and small towns completely cut off. Earlier Joe Speller and his bunch of parachutists had passed us, and we saw fighters and American gliders below us. In fact there were fighters all round us.

We got a terrific shaking up with one burst of 'flack', and S/Sgt Waldron, our first pilot, nearly had to release for we were tossed all over the place. However he succeeded in righting the glider, and after that everything was quiet and uneventful. We made a good landing, and hopped out quickly. After helping to unload, we went to our rendezvous, where I heard that 'Joe' Maltby had been killed by 'flack' on the journey over, and I found that the CO had had a very narrow escape, as his smock had a bit torn out of the left shoulder. (*'Flak', the term commonly used today, and 'flack' are both acceptable forms of the word. Chig's use of the latter is retained throughout.*) John Blatch & RSM Briody had not arrived. I went to see 'Joe's' body – the poor lad had it in the head and right side. He had died almost immediately. Our other casualties appear to have been slight, though one or two pilots had broken limbs, their gliders landing in the woods surrounding the LZ (*Landing Zone*).

The country is very pretty, though perfectly flat, and I have yet to see a typical windmill. Long straight dusty or brick lanes and avenues of trees, seem to be the general rule. The houses are delightful, but though they have a great deal of window space they are usually pretty dark, as they are nearly always built right inside coppices, and the gardens are small or non-existent. We made our way by slow stages, first to a farm, then to a private house, and finally to an unoccupied one. We had to stop every now and then as we had a little opposition, and twice bullets went very close. The people are not very demonstrative, but I think they are pleased to see us, and some have given us apples and pears – though pretty poor ones. Still, they have hardly had (*time*) to recover from the severe pasting our bombers gave the area this morning, and many people had fled. The house in which we made our HQ was empty. I found a couple of eggs and some bread and real butter. The CO was about all in, so I boiled the eggs and we had one each, and a cup of tea. Then we turned in, making beds on the floor with stuff from the beds upstairs. The folk certainly don't seem short of good things – port, cognac, champagne and various other wines, cigars, butter, eggs, bottled and tinned fruit etc., and masses of good quality clothes and household linens.

18.9.44

We got up soon after dawn and had a cup of tea and a slice of bread and butter. There had been a bit of trouble further down in the village where about 150 Germans were holding a hotel. Our artillery went up and knocked the place about so severely that all resistance ceased, and we took quite a lot of prisoners. I collected four chaps and we went off and buried Joe. We meant to find another chap and bury him, but fortunately we decided to go back later on bicycles if possible, as he was a long way off. When we did get back we found everyone on the move, and for some time now I've lost Wing HQ. However, I'm quite comfortable – it's a lovely day. The only snags are that I have apparently lost my kit – temporarily I hope – German fighters have been over and shot up the LZ which we had only left about 10 minutes before, and the second lift hasn't arrived yet. Another 30 M.Es have been over and shot up our positions, but there were no casualties. Now I have found Wing HQ again and they have collected my kit, but still there is no second lift, four hours after we were expecting them, and things are beginning to get a bit awkward, for Jerry is apparently coming at us from three sides, and is forcing our company back.

At last! Thunderbolts and Spitfires, and now the grand old Dakotas and Horsas. What a marvellous sight! And over there to the west are lots more Dakotas and we can see the parachutists dropping. This is about the best sight I have ever seen in my life. These Glider Pilots are marvellous. They are doing wonderful landings despite the difficulty of finding room and the 'flack' which has appeared today – quite heavy 'flack' too. There were one or two exciting landings – one glider crashed right through a pretty big hedge, and another did a marvellous side skid to draw up mostly in a wood, and out came everybody quite unhurt.

Then came Halifaxes and Stirlings – the former with Hamilcars and the latter dropping supplies. Fierce firing broke out over the supply dropping zone. There is not much chance as yet of getting at the supplies. There is also a machine-gun sniping in the wood the other side of the railway, which is causing a bit of trouble. The RSM has arrived – he had to pull off yesterday, but no John Blatch, although he set off again today. Our present HQ is a rotten house badly hit by the Fortress' bombing on Sunday morning. I hope we don't stay here long.

We didn't stay long, thank goodness! But, oh blimey! We did have a march! These packs are the devil's own for weight, and we marched solidly for about 3 miles, mostly in the dark and led by Alec Johnson, (*"Capt. Alec Johnson, a man of 6ft 4" or thereabouts"*) who takes simply enormous strides. We eventually got a very swanky billet, but although we got whisky and the host was very kind, we didn't much trust him, (This, I believe, was a mistake, as we heard afterwards that he was perfectly genuine.) We had a pretty foul night with a heavy machine gun and various other oddments firing all night, including one shot through the kitchen window about fifteen yards off us. The result was that for the second night in succession we got practically no sleep.

What, one might wonder, did Chig carry in his pack?. Like all those on active service his pack would have contained all that was absolutely essential, whilst avoiding the unnecessary. Even so, it seems the packs were 'the devil's own weight'! It is worth bearing in mind that though Chaplains were firmly caught up in the action and sought to assist their colleagues in any way possible, yet they were classed as non-combatants. They carried no weapon, and certainly did not carry the normal armament of the airborne soldier (or indeed of any other soldier). Their kit with which they went into action included the basic accoutrements of a priest in the field: a small Bible, a copy of the Army prayer book, a specially designed airborne Communion set, along with some shell dressings and other first aid kit – plus, of course, their faith, certainly their faith in God, but also their faith in those alongside whom they served.

19.9.44

In the morning I went the round of the chaps – our squadrons had spent the night in slit trenches which they had made in the surrounding woods. When trying to come back I was stopped owing to a sniper in the wood just by our HQ. So I returned with some of the others to their squadron. Foolishly I had ambled out in my beret and battle dress plus a mountaineering stick I got hold of yesterday, and had left all my kit behind. We got strafed by M.Es again and Chris Dodwell got some shrapnel in the shoulder in the next slit trench but one to us. I took him round to his HQ and then towards a Div HQ but met a jeep which took him to a Field Ambulance. Then I found our HQ just moving off to a new place. They hadn't got my kit, so I had to set off for it, but I took two armed

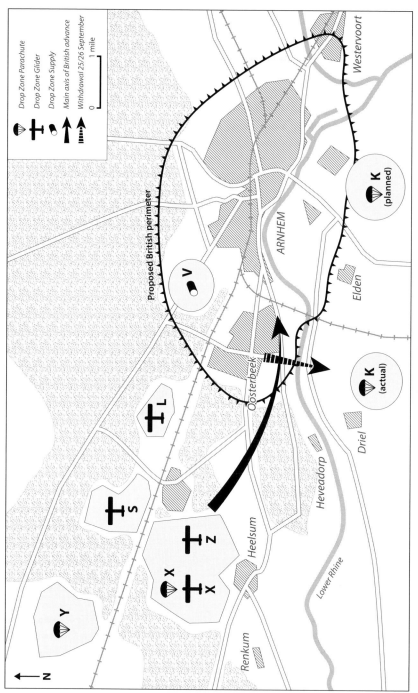

Map of Arnhem.

chaps with me *(one of them S/Sgt Alec Waldron, who would remain a close friend of Chig's long after the War)* just in case there was anything about at the house, or in case the people in the house had turned against us. I got my stuff all right, and back we came, to quite nice but small billets. Here I heard that some chaps had been killed and injured down at C Squadron. I felt pretty tired and so I borrowed a bike. It took me some time to find the place and I passed a prisoners' camp on the way. I found that four chaps had been killed and seven injured by an anti-personnel bomb from one of the enemy planes. We (*"dug shallow graves and"*) got unpleasantly shot up again during the funeral. I got back at last and had most of a tin of sardines and two or three biscuits and a mug of tea at about 3.00pm. It is extraordinary how one can go on quite well with hardly any food. The 24 hr. ration packs are not bad, but why do they put so many sweets in them? Things got a bit sticky as time went on, Jerry apparently bringing up an odd tank or two and fairly heavy guns. While the third lift was coming in there was very heavy 'flack' and he got a few Stirlings, but these chaps were magnificent. One at least was on fire but circled to drop its containers. The gliders had a bad time as we had more or less lost control of the LZs, and Jerry opened up on them immediately they got in.

House used as cover by No 2 Wing GPR until 21st September (and later used by King's Own Scottish Borderers), which clearly attracted a great deal of enemy attention.
(Photo: J van Leusden)

We thought we heard the guns of the Second Army, which was a good sound, but we wanted to hear they were over the bridge which the 1st Parachute people had been holding so magnificently, and we should very much have liked to see some fighter cover.

The evening and the night were not much fun as we were expecting a largish attack from the north, the area where the Glider Pilot Regt was. The GPR was being used as though it was a crack infantry unit – a great compliment!

20.9.44

The attack didn't get very near our HQ, but E and F Squadrons had plenty on their plates, although it was not a full scale attack.

This was perhaps the worst morning so far. Jerry very nearly broke through, and it was apparently only due to very courageous standing up to it by the Glider Pilot Regt and the KOSBs that really held them. They had an odd tank or two and heavyish guns. I did a round of the chaps to see how they were getting on – I believe in going round with my beret and stick as it seems to cheer the chaps to see a 'cherry beret'. I dealt with a few wounded to the best of my ability, and succeeded in getting them onto jeeps and taken to the ambulance posts. Three mortars dropped just on the other side of the road and some splinters came into the room where I was lying. One of the mortars made a mess of the little house opposite, and killed one man and wounded two others. Things got pretty tense again, but after probing about, Jerry moved off from our area for some reason. Still the Second Army have not appeared and still no fighter protection. During the attack this morning some of our chaps began singing songs and shouting at the Germans. Amongst others they sang 'Lili Marlene' and finished up by telling Jerry to come and get her!

I joined up with an RAMC orderly and we did a spot of good work together, and then during some heavy shooting we found a good slit trench and had a cup of tea and a biscuit or two. Then over came, first, Spitfires and Thunderbolts, and then the wonderful old Dakotas as steady as rocks amid the heavy 'flack', and they dropped their supplies, Half an hour later another bunch came over and their stuff came down on the red, yellow, green or blue parachutes right on the proper spot, and they were followed by Stirlings – a grand sight. Finally the Spitfires went to shoot up the AA positions. The 'flack' was very heavy indeed. We all feel much better though are very tired, for we have had hardly any sleep since we've been here. Still the news of the Second Army seems much better and they are really getting round about us. (This news incidentally proved false.)

We seem to have had a fair number of casualties. Briscoe and Brazier of E Squadron both put up a magnificent show – being cut off, they called their chaps and simply charged right through the enemy.

There was more supply dropping, 'flack' and general 'hate'. During the afternoon we moved our HQ again to the next door house, this proved to be a far nicer house, though it was inhabited by Quislings. The son had fled with the Germans, leaving his mother and his wife who had a baby on the day we landed in Holland, together with a nurse. They were quite nice to us, but obviously could do nothing much about it. In the evening we had tinned steak and then went to bed and actually had a quiet night – such as quiet nights are these days! I got a false report of RAF bombing and the Second Army boxing us in.

21.9.44

We got up at about 5.30 and just as we were going to have a brew, a very heavy barrage started and lasted for about three hours. It was nearly all mortars. I only succeeded in getting round to the chaps nearby as snipers had got between us and E Squadron. I spent most of the morning sitting in a slit trench, and we didn't get much in the way of food till mid-day. The news of the Second Army is getting to be nothing more than a lot of bally rumours. Still we aren't doing too badly, and are holding out pretty well. Things have quietened down a bit, though there has been almost continuous gunfire and rifle shooting etc., flaring up in one locality and then in another. We had a good mid-day meal – tinned Irish stew from stuff dropped by parachute. Stirlings came over again at 1.30 and again at 2.05 and a few more at 4.00 followed by Dakotas which, as usual, flew over in formation. We all feel that these Dakota chaps just about deserve the V.C. They fly absolutely straight through the 'flack', for they know if they start weaving then the chances of our getting the supplies they drop are considerably minimised. The 'flack' bursts all round them, and the Germans have obviously got the range and the height at which the Dakotas come in, but the planes drop the containers almost without exception right over the area, and it isn't their fault when we don't get them, for Jerry always puts down a heavy mortar barrage over the places where the containers lie. This was a big supply today, but the astonishing thing is that there has been no fighter cover.

In the evening things began to look very bad. We heard that most of the news about the Second Army was untrue, and that they were held up four miles from the river at Elst. However the Poles dropped at about 1600 hours. Most, or rather all, of us are feeling the strain of little sleep, shortage of water and almost continuous fighting, mortars and shelling. It is not a very comfy feeling to be surrounded for five days as we have been. We all got a bit short with each other, and some of the neighbouring troops retreated by mistake, but we held like grim death. Later on Tony Murray (*Major Anthony Murray, who was awarded the MC for gallantry in this action*) and Tony Plowman (*Captain, second-in-Command of F Squadron*) and the rest of F Squadron had a magnificent show and thoroughly routed a German attack, but Murray got a wound in the throat. (This fortunately turned out not to be serious). There were some wounded in the wood in front of our line which I went off to collect with Martin Culverwell, who held a Red Cross flag in front of me. We made contact with some Germans and they came out and helped us and we helped them with their wounded. They were only youngsters, and one of them was a Dane. We did what we could for the wounded of both sides and brought them back on stretchers to our place. While we were binding up one German, some fool started off with a machine gun, and for a minute or two there was some hectic firing going on round us, but fortunately it soon stopped, and we went off to try and find some more chaps. We found one dead and finding no trace of the other we went back, only to learn that he had returned quite all right with a couple of prisoners.

The evening grew tenser and tenser and some of our chaps had to be moved to new positions. We didn't get much sleep again.

22.9.44

Up early again and a hasty breakfast, then the 'hate' started again almost immediately after the Brigadier (*Brigadier P H W Hicks, Commander of the 1st Air-Landing Brigade*) had been round to say we had got to hold on at all costs, and that the situation was extremely grave. He told the CO to go round and tell the men personally, and so he and Donald and John and I went off with the rather melancholy news. The men took it magnificently and since then have been surpassing their previous efforts. The barrage has been continuous and very heavy. About 10.30 we began to get news that the Second Army artillery was doing some damage to Jerry round our perimeter. First they had knocked out a Nazi HQ to our West, and then they bust up a battery, and at 11.45 the Brigadier came round to say that the Poles had linked up with the armour on the south of the river, and that the 43rd Div were putting in a strong attack to relieve us. We can hear the artillery or something plainly now. All the afternoon and evening we got heavily plastered, or there were attempts at infantry attacks. Jerry has been colossally persistent. He never stops getting at us in some way or another. The news about the Second Army has bucked us up a lot. We had two infantry attempts at infiltration, which both failed, and produced a few prisoners.

We decided to move our HQ again and found a good spot, except that the cellar has too many mosquitos in it. After dark Jerry quietened down at last, and then the Second Army did some shelling, which was a really pleasant sound to hear, even for me a non-combatant. It is awful how blood-thirsty one gets, and how soon you lose all sense of the grace of peace and Christian charity, when you are in the thick of a battle. I find I am just as pleased when I hear of Jerry's being knocked out as anybody. We just sat in the garden and listened and watched the shelling. Then when it stopped, Jerry remained quiet, and we actually went to sleep.

23.9.44

We didn't have much of a barrage during the night, though there was a bit. Then we got more gloomy news, as Jerry woke up and started his 'hate' again, only a very few Poles got across the river last night. Everything is getting serious. We are still getting almost continual shelling, and it seems to get heavier every day. Water is scarce and so is food and some sorts of ammunition. However the chaps are absolutely wizard, quite determined to stick it out, and we can certainly continue to give the Germans a heavy pasting. We knocked out an SP (*self-propelled*) gun this morning, and have also finished two or three tanks at different times, which is pretty good. Tony Plowman got wounded in the arm; he had done a very fine job, and had been a great inspiration to his men. The way he led them in raucous and rude choruses when the Germans were attacking was something worth going miles to hear. (He died later in hospital from shock when the hospital was hit. A good lad was Tony.) F Squadron has had a lot of casualties, and Jerry is still very determined. He has gone on trying to get through first here and then somewhere else, but without success. In the late afternoon we had some relief as Spitfires and Typhoons came over for quite a long time. I must say I should hate to be at the wrong end of a Typhoon! Then over came some supply Dakotas and Stirlings, but the Stirlings dropped all their supplies out of the area, while at least two of the Dakotas were hit and went down in flames. The night was comparatively quiet, and as usual we were quite cheerful and optimistic. In the evening I went to see how the civilians were getting on in the cellar. They were extremely nice people, and one woman, a widow of 36, was educated at Cheltenham (*Ladies*) College. Naturally I found them all a bit anxious.

24.9.44

We woke early and got up and had a short Service in the cellar in which we all joined, RCs and all. I should have liked a Eucharist but that would have meant that the RCs definitely, and the Non-Conformists probably, would have held no part. We had a terrific strafing all the morning and most of the afternoon and evening from shells and mortars, relieved once or twice by our planes – Spitfires and rocket Typhoons, but they were not over nearly enough, and we had a lot more casualties, and were actually forced out of our positions for the first time. This was due to one or two tanks, SP guns, a flame thrower and the enemy's very accurate mortaring. I had two or three dicey journeys collecting wounded, but we usually managed to get the poor chaps back all right. In the afternoon the same went on, and while trying to get a casualty – which we eventually succeeded in bringing back – one of the two with me got hit by a splinter from a mortar which burst 5 yards away. It smashed a small garden statue, and bit of this hit me, but with no damage. We went on, got the chap, and as we were bringing him back, another mortar burst on the roof of the house we were entering. Another lad we left in the garage, and I'd just got a party of stretcher bearers and gone into the house to prepare a place for him in our crowded cellar, while they brought him in, when another mortar burst by them and wounded the lot, together with one or two other fellows who were helping to get the casualty through the door. I had a busy time with these chaps.

Donald Shuttleworth, our Adjutant, had been doing a magnificent job, he never seemed to rest, and is constantly going round encouraging the men. John Hooper too, has been really excellent, and proved himself to be a first-class officer. Donald went off to encourage one group of men during a particularly bad period, and got killed by a sniper – he was a very gallant and courageous man, was Donald. Jerry certainly has the range of our spot, for he has had five direct hits today. However, this cellar has remained all right, though the rest of the house is a complete shambles. I feel very sorry for the young woman who owns the house, and who is still in the cellar, with her two girls, aged 15 and 13.

Towards evening the situation deteriorated considerably and we lost control of the woods, and had to take positions in the houses. John Hooper took over this evening and immediately ordered that every house was to be defended to the last man. In consequence I have had to clear out with my wounded, down to Div HQ where there is a better medical spot with a proper doctor. It wasn't much fun

Final place of shelter (No 17 Hartensteinlaan) for Chig and GPR comrades prior to the withdrawal across the Rhine, showing some of the mortar bomb damage. (Photo: H J Willink)

getting down to HQ for there was a lot of shell fire and mortaring going on. So here I am now, very loath to leave the remaining GPs (*Glider Pilots*) but unable, at present, to get back to them. However, I can be of some use here, which I could not be up there, as I had run out of most of the main first-aid necessities. I hear that Dr Benson, the RC Chaplain, has lost an arm (*his right arm was shattered when he went to assist some wounded men; he underwent an immediate amputation, but died two days later*). Nobody seems to know much about the other Chaplains.

25.9.44

Today proved to be the worst of all, though from my own personal point of view it was one of the least eventful, at least the first part of it. I got some sleep the previous night lying on the floor of the M.I. room, where the atmosphere was terrible. I was not much use early on as I was too tired to move about much, but I managed to do a few jobs to help the MO who was absolutely magnificent. Casualties kept coming in all the time. We had a biscuit each and a quarter of a cup of tea apiece for breakfast, and that had to last for lunch as well. Jerry shelled and mortared us all day as usual, and the snipers around the house picked off quite a number of fellows. There is one somewhere in the trees in front of the main door, and he is repeatedly getting somebody or other as they pass the door. We just cannot find him. It was unsafe to go out unless you had a Red Cross flag and were taking wounded. The snipers even shot a couple of German prisoners in the tennis court where they were being kept. We heard that a battalion of Dorsets had got over the river last night and also some supplies, but as far as I know we never saw the supplies – it was too tricky getting them up here.

In the afternoon I heard we were getting out under cover of the dark – so we now had the prospect of an extremely dicey journey down to and across the northern arm of the Rhine. There were to be some boats, but it was expected that quite a lot would have to swim for it – about 130 yards. Not being able to swim, I devoutly hoped that there would be some boats! In the evening I opened my emergency ration, and some of us pooled our resources in sweets, cigarettes and Horlicks tablets. We drank some pretty foul water, and made as much of a feast as possible. Then I cut off the sleeves of my smock and pulled them on over my boots, so as to deaden any sound I might make on the journey. These hours before setting off were quite the worst in my life. We knew that Jerry was all round with SP guns and machine guns, and that snipers were all over the place in the woods, and also there was a battery that had the range of the strip of shore where we were to embark. We knew we had to do something between 1½ to 2 miles down to the strip, and that the width of our escape route was only a few hundred yards, and even that was not really clear of Germans. We were divided into small groups of about 20 men, and the leader of each group was shown the route to go. As time drew near we were all getting pretty jittery. We tuned in to the BBC at 9.00pm and heard that troops and supplies had got across to us – it all sounded fine! Not much like it was in reality! From about 6.00 onwards Jerry simply poured mortars and shells into our small pocket, which was, I learnt, something about 1,200 yards by 900 yards now, but the Second Army artillery put up a heavy barrage too. At 9.00 No 2 Wing Glider Pilots set off, but they lost quite a lot of men while getting across the common. So heavy was Jerry's fire that we wondered whether he knew all about our plans. Then about 10.15 we set off, after we had some prayers and final instructions.

Tony Murray (Major; Commander of F Squadron), had rejoined us, and our party was led by him and Peter Jackson (*Major Peter Jackson, Commander of E Squadron*). The mortars fortunately stopped, probably because it was raining and we crept through the trees and bushes and over broken boughs and round small craters and indescribable mess. Down we went through the park. Tracers and flares were going up all over the place, and snipers were loosing off from all directions.. then we got on to the road, and our progress became slower and slower as we kept having to stop and get down during a spell of machine-gun firing. Once we had machine-guns on one side of us, and a blasted SP loosing off on the other. We left the road and crawled across two or three fields, and we passed two or three dead. (*In his later recollections Chig recalled: "There were regularly-fired red tracers in two lines firing over our heads from south of the river. Someone behind me whispered 'Where the bloody hell d'you think we are?' An unexpected voice from behind the hedge said 'You keep between the red lights, chum, and you'll be all right'. Each of us hung on to the tail of the smock of the man in front; it was so dark that it was easy to get lost if this precaution was not observed, and the rear man of our party was lost in this way"*). Then we skirted a badly battered village – over what I suppose was a railway line, but I'm not sure, we waded a ditch up to our middles, and we were out on the landing strip – but no boat was to be seen. Just then half a dozen mortars came over and burst about 50 yards away, and we wondered whether we were going to fail after all. Peter Jackson decided to swim, so I left him, and walked back about 150 yards, when I saw a small rowing boat coming in. There was no queue for boats, though there was a big one later on. I got in, and some other chaps came along and we paddled safely and uneventfully over the Rhine.

The first man I saw on the other side was the CO who had swum halfway across and piloted a boat the rest of the way. He and I walked on, being guided every now and then by Tommies in soup-plate hats. Some of them took us in to a barn where they had made themselves very comfortable, and gave us some hot tea. Then we had to walk on for some distance – it was raining steadily and we were pretty tired, but we didn't mind, for the walking kept us warm, and we were on the right side of the Rhine at last. Those who wanted it were given a tot of rum at another rendezvous and a blanket to wear. Then off we went again, some walking, some getting lifts, until eventually we came to an F.A.P. (*First Aid Post?*) and they took us in lorries etc to Nijmegen, which we reached soon after dawn. We crossed the bridge where only a few days before there had been such fierce and gallant fighting, and then we were put up at a Mission Hostel which had been taken over. There we were given a good meal, and then we all went to bed on stretchers. One or two shells came over but we didn't take much notice of them – we were too tired. We got up about 1.00pm, had another meal, and I went off with a few others in a jeep and had a grand hot shower at a nunnery, now used by American troops. Later in the day we changed our billets to an immense and ugly barracks, and there we stayed for two more nights. German planes came over every now and then, and occasionally dropped a bomb or two, which we didn't like, as a reaction was now setting in, and any noise of warfare tended to get on our nerves. Then came the great news that we were to go home – told to us by Gen. Browning himself, and on the Thursday morning we set off in lorries. We did the slow journey down the corridor that had caused so much trouble and Jerry had one last bang at us, sending four or five shells over as we were passing through one village.

The Dutch were grand to us, and we all felt that they were simply delightful. On our journey back we kept receiving gifts of fruit from both Dutch and Belgians as we passed through, not to mention kisses at odd intervals! We stayed one night in Louvain and the following morning went to the Brussels aerodrome where we got into Dakotas, mostly piloted by Americans and set off for England. We struck the English coast near Folkestone, but as the weather was poor, our pilot took us out to sea again, and we went all along the coast past Dover, Deal and Ramsgate, across the Thames Estuary, and landed at an aerodrome in Essex, where we were given a very good and generous reception. (*They had landed at Bradwell Bay, a very busy and strategically-sited night fighter base as well as an aerodrome greatly welcomed by returning aircraft short of fuel or badly damaged*). The airfield was closed in 1946. Then after tea another plane picked us up and brought us back to our stations, a tired but very grateful and thankful group of men. The Arnhem episode can be said to have closed when on the Sunday morning those of us who returned, and who were at this one particular station, had a short Service of remembrance for those who were wounded, missing, prisoners or who had been killed, and also a thanksgiving for our own safe return, in the little church near our camp.

*   *   *

To reach the end of this incredible first-hand report is to sense, very clearly, what a hugely challenging, demanding and unbelievably difficult task the Airborne Forces had faced. Yet there is a sense, too, in which one feels that, almost certainly, it was far, far hairier than Chig's account suggests, his diary account being masked by his typical under-statement, his natural inclination not to 'over-egg' things, and to adopt a "let's get on with it attitude" no matter what came his way. But there can be no doubting the determination and immense, seemingly limitless courage shown by all those involved in the Arnhem action, on land and in the air, including by their Chaplains.

It is striking, in Chig's diary, that he makes the point that he, and his fellow Chaplains, were non-combatants and carried no weapons, yet his story makes clear (wholly unintentionally I'm absolutely sure) their commitment to their fellow men, those whom they served alongside (and to whom they ministered).

In his later recollections of his life, Chig adds a little more flesh to these matters, without giving away his own intense and constant involvement with his men.

He recalled No 2 Wing marching down the road from Wolfheze to the junction with the main Arnhem-Renkum road, and then along that towards Oosterbeek, led by Capt Alec Johnson. Chig wryly noted that he was 6ft 4 inches tall and marched at a good pace which the medium-height Chaplain found exhausting. The immense pack they carried proved a considerable burden. Looking back Chig reflected "I have little recollection of what was in mine. There would have been the emergency rations of chocolate – a special block of extra nutritional value – Horlicks tablets, sweets and a water bag. Then there was a small, sealed container with various tablets, including some for purifying contaminated water, a minute compass, more sweets and a ground-sheet. I had a Red Cross First Aid kit, and my Airborne Communion set, but there must have been plenty else as well to weigh as much as it did."

At a road junction on this march they passed a disabled Volkswagen, in which were three dead German soldiers. "George Pare, Chaplain to No 1 Wing, relates that he later buried these three and that one was Major-General Kussin, Field Kommndantur of Arnhem, who had been returning to Arnhem when he was caught by the 3rd Battalion".

As Chig recounted in his diary he was often to be seen wearing his 'cherry beret' instead of a steel helmet. He later described this as "brainless" but his "pig-headed idea was that I was damned if the Germans were going to make me change it".

As the temperature of battle increased No 2 Wing needed to move its Divisional HQ frequently, sometimes only as far as the next house when the one in which they were based no longer offered sufficient cover and protection. One new HQ for the Wing was a house opposite the Harnstein Hotel, the Airborne Forces HQ.

This house was owned by a Dutch couple, Mr and Mrs Ower. Chig described Mr Ower as a "dear and fine man". They were all to remain good friends long after the war, and exchanged peace-time visits. Of the Owers, Chig recalled they had been "absolutely marvellous. It must be grim to see your house, your furniture and other possessions steadily being ruined or destroyed by both friendly troops and enemy gunfire, yet they never complained and were always trying to help".

It was from this vantage point that Chig had his first sight of a German tank in action. He described it as "like a pre-historic monster, slowly approaching (*towards E Squadron*). It was knocked out by a PIAT (Projector, Infantry, Anti-Tank) gun after what seemed to me an endless wait as it came nearer and nearer and, at last, within good range".

Enemy action pressed on the men of No 2 Wing such that it was necessary to move their HQ to another, nearby property. In this there lived "an elderly woman, her married daughter and the daughter's baby, which was born on the day of our invasion arrival. The girl's husband was an ardent Dutch Nazi. He had fled immediately it became clear that this was a large airborne invasion".

The young woman needed medicine from her doctor, but there was nobody to fetch this and she asked if one of the new occupants of her house might do this. John Place, the CO, insisted on having the girl's note for the doctor translated in case she should be trying to pass information to her husband or to the Germans via the doctor. Mr Ower was called in to translate. He then risked his own life by taking the request to the doctor himself. Chig was greatly impressed by many of the Dutch with whom they made contact, whose lives were in turmoil at the centre of this Arnhem operation.

In the diary account of the Airborne Forces crossing the Rhine, Chig makes no reference to a small but important part he played just prior to that evacuation. His later drafted recollections revealed that he "went to the cellar where Major General Urquhart was, together with his staff. I had, like everyone else, blacked my face and in any case he had never seen me in his life. I asked to be allowed to speak to him and his first reaction was 'Who was this?'. I told him I was Chaplain to No 2 Wing, the Glider Pilot Regiment, and I asked him for permission to say prayers before we set off. This he immediately agreed to. So at about 10.00pm I said prayers and as many as could get into this cellar (*of the Divisional Headquarters*) joined in and said the Lord's Prayer together. Then I gave them a Blessing and went to join the party with which I was to move."

The withdrawal from Arnhem was reported by the *Church Times* (on 29 September 1944), in a piece in which it spoke of the "sorrow and disappointment of the nation". The article ended by saying: "One BBC correspondent, describing the escape, remarked that the men slipped off into the darkness after a prayer by the Padre. The Church may be proud of her clergy who go into the hazards of such battles with their men." The Padre referred to here was Chig.

In all, fifteen Chaplains accompanied the forces taking part in Operation Market Garden. With the Glider Pilot Regiment were Chig, with No 2 Wing, and the Rev'd George Pare, with No 1 Wing. The others accompanied the Parachute Brigade and the Air-Landing Brigade. Of the fifteen, two were killed, three were part of the evacuation across the Rhine, seven were captured and three remained with the wounded at the withdrawal. During the Arnhem campaign Chig did not encounter any of his fellow Chaplains, and circumstances and need dictated (and varied) the role each undertook. As with Forces Chaplains involved anywhere on active service, including modern theatres of war, they sought to support and minister to the men, and encourage them. They often had a particular role in bringing in the wounded, reassuring and heartening them, assisting the doctors and medical orderlies, comforting those near death, scrounging food and water for those unable to do this for themselves, praying with those who sought prayers and generally looking after the spiritual wellbeing of their colleagues, as well as conducting worship whenever it was right, possible or needed. Burying the dead, and conducting brief funerals, was a necessary and too frequent part of their dedicated role.

Looking back on their Rhine crossing and onward progress to Nijmegen, Chig (and almost certainly he was not alone) felt disappointment that the Commander of the Glider Pilot Regiment, who had been at Nijmegen with Major-General "Boy" Browning's Supreme HQ, had not visited his men as they began their trip homeward to England. The Major General, however, did address 1st Airborne's survivors at their billets in Nijmegen. Chig whimsically recorded: "He had us on parade – though a very informal one". It was said that Browning, who would have been very accustomed to addressing committees and boards, as well as soldiers aplenty, "had made many speeches in his time, but never one to an audience such as this. Their mood was dumb weariness, and a tremendous dignity. He realized that they were beyond authority, having no more to give." It was a time for truth for these brave men would see through insincerity; indeed, they were in no mood to stomach such. Browning, though he might have wondered whatever could he say to such men at that particular moment, hit all the right notes according to Chig. Browning "told us how proud he was of us and that we could not have done more". Importantly, too, he told them "arrangements were being made for us to go back to England".

Those were very welcome words. As Chig's later memories indicated: "We travelled down the road that had caused the 2nd Army such trouble and realised what a frightful job they had had with just this one road, raised for much of its distance above the surrounding countryside. We passed through Eindhoven as heroes, and had flowers and fruit thrown at us or thrust on us, and received many kisses from Dutch girls. We stayed at Louvain for the night and then flew back to England, in American Dakotas, from Brussels. We landed at Bradwell Bay and were again feted – so heavily that we found our planes had gone on without us! Fortunately a lone American plane called in and agreed to land us at Broadwell on his journey somewhere further west. On the Sunday, those of us who had returned had a Service in the little church of Shilton just near our camp. And then we were sent on leave."

And so Chig's letters to his father, and his Arnhem diaries end. There can be no doubt that he would have written often to his father in subsequent years, until George's death in 1955, but the letters were not kept and bundled together as had been those written by the newly-instituted country parson who became a dauntless Chaplain to the Forces.

There is just one more letter, contained within the bundle of Chig's letters saved by his family. It was not written by Chig – or to him. It was written to Pauline by Mrs Lilian Hewetson, a friend of Chig's CO, Col. Place. Lilian Hewetson lived, with her daughter Mary, near Blake Hill Farm RAF Station and had been a very kind hostess to several of the men stationed there, Chig included.

Home again. A welcome drink in the Officers' Mess at Bradwell Bay on their return from Arnhem (L to R) Lt E J A Smith, Lt. Don MacAdie, Chig, Captain SG Cairns, Captain Frank Barclay MC (Officer Commanding D Squadron, No 1 Wing GPR), unknown, Wing Commander Paul Arbon DFC (Station Commander), and Lt. Kenneth 'Jock' Strathearn. (Photo, without attribution, appears in *The Torn Horizon* by Chris van Roekel)

The Officers' Mess, Bradwell Bay ca 1944 (by Alan Sorrell).

The letter from Mrs Lilian Hewetson to Pauline Chignell regarding Colonel Place's admiration of Chig.

The Old Bakery,
Ashton Keynes,
Wilts

Oct.13th

Dear Mrs Chignell,

I saw Colonel Place at the beginning of his leave, and he talked so much about Arnhem & said 'The Padre was absolutely marvellous, going about looking after the wounded, never waiting till the attack was over, but helping the men the whole time, quite oblivious of bursting shells all around him – the men simply adore him'. I said 'His wife would like to know that' – & Mrs Place remarked 'Well, he has gone on leave'. I saw the Colonel again this week, and again he said that 'he couldn't speak too highly of 'Wilf', he was just marvellous – smiling benignly amongst the hell all around, & carrying stretchers & cheering the wounded – he had never seen anything like it'.

I just thought I'd tell you in case no one else has!

Please don't trouble to answer this.

Yours very sincerely,

Lilian M Hewetson

There can be little doubt that Pauline Chignell would have received this note with real delight and immense pride – delight that someone had taken the trouble to tell her something that would otherwise have been wholly unknown to her and, even for a woman so gentle, modest and unassuming, who never sought the limelight, heartfelt pride at hearing others' valued opinion of her husband. In all probability, Chig would have told her one or two things about his experiences, albeit carefully edited and sanitised so as not to cause anxiety, but never divulged much more; the exciting and hair-raising part of his adventures would, almost certainly, have remained unspoken at home.

For Pauline, Lilian Hewetson's note would make clear that, despite the understatement and unsensational tones of his letters home, Chig had indeed been playing his part to the full, had been doing a real and proper job, and had been doing it with great gallantry.

From Lilian Hewetson's letter we learn that, in the Army, Chig was known as 'Wilf' rather than 'Rowland' which is how he was known in the family, and how he signed his letters. Is this a reflection of the Army's bureaucracy – on all the forms that he undoubtedly completed (probably in triplicate!) Wilfred would have come before Rowland? Or was it that he wanted to have a different persona in this part of his life, one that was separate from all which had gone before, and from all that would follow?

Our earlier reference to *The Church Times*' report of the Arnhem evacuation may be worth re-visiting, for it contained a broader picture of the Operation and its outcome:

> "The news broadcast on Wednesday evening, that the remnants of the airborne force at Arnhem had been withdrawn, came as a profound shock to the nation, though it was not unexpected. But tempered with sorrow and disappointment was the knowledge that a quarter of the force had escaped in the dark, deceiving the Germans by a master stroke of skill and trickery, and was eventually ferried over the Rhine. This will stand in history as one of the great feats of British armies and has elicited from the enemy a modicum of praise for British endurance.
>
> Lightly armed airborne troops are in sore straits if they are unable to obtain relief from ground forces soon after their landing. Despite their resistance for more than a week, they could not hope to stand out indefinitely, and the High Command was wise to withdraw the remnants before the whole body was liquidated. But by their courage and endurance the Second Army had been enabled to cover three of the four obstacles, Eindhoven, Grave, and Nijmegen, barring its way to the Westphalian plain and the Ruhr. The corridor may not yet be secure and is still exposed to penetration by the German forces, but the bold thrust at the enemy's vitals has kept the battle moving at a time when it threatened to become static."

The article ended with the reference to "the Padre", Chig, leading prayers and blessing the men before the evacuation, and to the pride the Church – and the nation come to that – was entitled to have in its clergy who go into war with their men.

Perhaps we might draw this chapter – in the war and in Chig's life – towards its close, with his own summary of the Arnhem campaign:

> "Argument will no doubt continue as long as the Battle of Arnhem is discussed, as to why it failed. Was there betrayal? Why was not a Dutch Underground warning of a panzer Division re-forming just north of Arnhem passed on from London to Airborne HQ before take-off? To most of us on the ground it has always seemed, I think, that we should have succeeded had the lift been completed in one day. Shortage of tugs has been stated to have caused the triple lift. And shortage of planes was caused far farther back by strikes in the aircraft industry, presumably for more money. If this is right then we get back to the fundamentals – the sin of greed; still very much with us."

The gap between success and failure of Operation Market Garden was small, perhaps as slender as it could possibly have been, and this awareness that they were so close to succeeding remains a frustration for so many who were engaged in that operation. Many years now have lapsed since Operation Market Garden ended in frustration for those who committed so much to it succeeding, and countless studies have been conducted by countless military men and academics. As is often the way in this present day, some of those studies have an element of revisionist history about them, so easy when in possession of all the facts and with the benefit of hindsight with which to juggle them.

Such studies have indicated that intelligence about the greater prominence (and calibre) of German troops in the Arnhem area was known, but was ignored or played down, perhaps because so many operations around this time had been cancelled and there was a keen wish to hasten the Allies' progress into Germany. Perhaps, too, there was anxiety about another morale-sapping cancellation or delay.

Similarly it was anticipated that the Second Army's progress to Arnhem, to link up with those landed by and with the airborne forces, would have been swifter. The urgency of progress towards Arnhem Bridge was essential. That this was not achieved could have been a tactical error. It also was due to stiffer-than-expected enemy opposition. Was the available intelligence as good as might have been wished or, again, was this played down or did it go unheeded?

Others have argued that the landing zones and dropping zones could and should have been much nearer the Airborne Force's intended target of Arnhem Bridge. It seemed that desk-bound RAF planners were given untrammelled influence over choice of dropping and landing zones, when responsibility might better have been in the hands of those experienced at dropping out of the sky by parachute and glider. Success may well have been heightened by having dropping zones and landing zones much closer to their intended target of Arnhem Bridge, rather than opting for caution and safety – and distance – in selecting those landing and dropping zones.

Whatever the arguments, whatever the information and analysis considered at the time, and subsequently, and however reconsidered or diverse the conclusions, there can be no doubting the tremendous and unquestionable gallantry, commitment and unselfish courage, determination and never-say-die endurance of those engaged on the ground and in the air in this Operation. Whenever and wherever Britain's wartime exploits are discussed – both exploits in two World Wars and also in the many subsequent campaigns in which the UK has been engaged – the men who went into Arnhem as part of Market Garden will be held in the highest possible regard.

Col Place, Chig's CO, clearly held him, and all his endeavours and tireless commitment in Arnhem, in the highest regard. He wanted to put Chig up for a DSO (Distinguished Service Order), awarded for "meritorious or distinguished service during active operations against the enemy". However, such an award to a Captain (the customary rank for an Army Chaplain) was considered an extreme rarity. So Chig was put up for an MC. This did not come his way, but his splendid and unstinting service was marked by a 'Mentioned in Despatches' (most usually awarded for gallant or meritorious action in the face of the enemy). With typical understatement he decreed this to be "very definitely as much as, if not more than, I deserved when I think of the acts of utter unselfish courage I saw which went completely unrewarded." He felt that he received this award as a member of the Royal Army Chaplains' Department rather than as a member of the Glider Pilot Regiment and it incensed him, almost beyond words, that (to the best of his knowledge) no awards went to the men of No 2 Wing GPR. "When I remember people like Lt. John Hooper and S/Sgts Alec Waldron and John Ainsworth, and their *continuous* bravery for 9 days, it still infuriates me that some people in an office in London should 'ration' awards for bravery."

Chig's Arnhem diary finished with the words:

> The Arnhem episode can be said to have closed when on the Sunday morning those of us who returned, and who were at this one particular station, had a short Service of remembrance for those who were wounded, missing, prisoners or who had been killed, and also a thanksgiving for our own safe return, in the little church near our camp.

It was as if, in giving thanks to God, he was a drawing a line under the experience. Yet as Chaplain to the Glider Pilot Regiment, Market Garden still had work for him to do.

11

After Arnhem, After the Army: The Padre Reverts to Parson

'Market Garden' may have ended, but still it created work for the Chaplain to No 2 Wing, Glider Pilot Regiment (and doubtless for other Chaplains elsewhere). Following a deserved spell of leave, Chig set about the challenging but essential and important pastoral task of contacting the families of colleagues who had been killed or were missing. Some contacts could be made by letter, others, understandably, were better undertaken by personal visits.

It was indeed a considerable task, for only one in five had returned from Arnhem. Another task was to work for the GPR Association which had been formed to help the families of GPR casualties. This meant often being in London for meetings.

One of Chig's visits was to the widow of Lt. Ralph Maltby. 'Joe' Maltby, the CO's second pilot, had been killed, on the opening day of Operation Market Garden, by the flack encountered by many gliders on the approach to Arnhem. Chig had conducted his funeral near the landing zone, the day after landing.

Mrs Maltby was living at Little Sampford in Essex, and Chig wondered how he might get there. After making various enquiries, which revealed an airfield nearby, he was given a taxi – a Dakota aircraft. Coming in to land, they found a football match under way on the grass landing strip, but the players readily (and perhaps sensibly!) gave way to the plane. Chig disembarked, with his bicycle, waved goodbye to the aircrew and, after reporting to air control, cycled off to find Mrs Maltby. Despite the sad purpose of his visit it was the start of a long-standing friendship between Jean Maltby and the Chignells. Duty done Chig took the train to Liverpool Street and cycled across London to Paddington Station, to catch the train to Oxford, and thence to cycle to Broadwell.

Around this time John Place was replaced as CO of No 2 Wing. Chig, an immense admirer of Place, was incensed at his removal, especially after his splendid leadership under fire in Arnhem when neither the Commander of the GPR nor the Commander of the Airborne Forces had actually been at the "sharp end" itself and when Place had lost both his second-in-command (and best friend) and his adjutant. Chig was convinced John Place had been treated most unjustly. His frustration, real sense of injustice and great disappointment at Place's departure was somewhat ameliorated when he discovered his new CO was to be Lt. Col. S C 'Billy' Griffith, a man of enormous natural charm and tact. Billy was known by Chig as a man of cricket. Before the War Griffith had won a Cambridge Blue as a wicket-keeper and had begun to make his mark with Sussex CCC. It would be with Sussex, after the War, that he established himself as an amateur wicket-keeper-batsman, captain and Secretary. He would also become a cricket statistician's delight when, in the second Test Match of England's Test tour of the West Indies in 1947-48, he played an epic innings. Opening the batting, as three other batsmen were ill or injured, he batted for six hours and scored 140, becoming the first man to score his maiden first-class century while batting in England's colours and the only man to do so on his Test debut. Later he became an outstanding and distinguished Secretary of MCC. To have such a man as CO was certainly to be welcomed, particularly as a man known to have played a heroic part in GPR's role at Normandy and at Arnhem, for which he was awarded the DFC. Soon after becoming CO, Billy was joined by Hugh Bartlett, his almost inseparable friend from Dulwich College days and fellow Sussex cricketer (who also later captained the County), so Chig was in his element as far as post-dinner cricket discussions went.

Billy Griffith had a considerable task on his hands as the Wing needed a large intake of new pilots to replace the losses incurred at Arnhem. These were drawn now

Chig: Chaplain No 2 Wing, Glider Pilot Regiment

Lt.Col S C 'Billy' Griffith, who piloted one of the gliders at Arnhem and was awarded the DFC. Post-Arnhem he became Chig's and the Glider Pilot Regiment's new CO. Billy is pictured here in the Committee Room at Lord's Cricket Ground in his later role as Secretary of MCC.

from the Army and the RAF and they had to undertake what, in other contexts, might be referred to as a crash course.

In January 1945 the Regiment moved to Mushroom Farm Transit Camp, near Withersfield in Essex. It was not a comfortable base, as it had indeed been built to grow mushrooms. The mushrooms had prospered under electric heating but this had been removed and the men's huts now were heated – inefficiently and ineffectively – by coke stoves. Two months later they moved to RAF Keevil, near Trowbridge.

It was from here that the GPR took part in supporting the Rhine crossing at the end of March 1945. Chig did not go with them as it was expected most of the men would return the same day. In truth a considerable number were shot down and casualties were higher than expected.

The ultimate goal that Britain and the Allies had so resolutely been seeking was achieved on 8 May. Nazi Germany unconditionally surrendered. Surrender documents were signed in Reims on 7 May and in Berlin on 8 May. The latter was declared Victory in Europe Day. After all the sacrifices of war and the huge deprivations of war-time, jubilant celebrations erupted throughout the western world and the Commonwealth.

Cricketers, who largely had been denied any serious cricket throughout the duration of the war, were anxious to get back in action. A series of five Victory Test Matches was staged between England and an Australian Services XI, between mid-May and 22 August. The first of these three-day games began on 19 May, less than a fortnight after VE Day, such was the huge appetite for catching up missed opportunities and restoring normality. More than 500,000 watched the five games. Three of the 'Tests' were played at Lord's, one at Old Trafford, and the other at Bramall Lane, Sheffield. Almost fittingly for nations which had been the strongest of allies, the series was drawn with England and Australia each winning two 'Tests' each, the other being drawn.

England's XI for the series included players like Wally Hammond, who captained the side, Len Hutton, Cyril Washbrook, John Dewes, Bill Edrich, Donald Carr, Doug Wright, Walter Robins,, Les Ames, Alf Gover, Errol Holmes. Pitched against them were Australians of equally notable sporting pedigree, amongst whom their captain, Lindsay Hassett, and Keith Miller would be best known to cricket followers today.

To those other eminent names from whom England's team was selected we should add one other name: Lt.Col S C Griffith DFC, Chig's CO. Billy kept wicket in all five Tests. More than that, he arranged for his Chaplain to accompany him to two of the Lord's Tests and also to the Bramall Lane Test. Chig was in his element, delighting in the joyous atmosphere of the historic Victory Tests after all that had gone before in the previous six years.

Around this time Brigadier Chatterton (who had earlier commanded the Glider Pilot Regiment) and his wife invited Chig to visit them in their beautiful home in Stedham, Sussex. The purpose of the invitation became clear when they asked Chig if he would consider taking the living of Stedham, which was in Mrs Chatterton's gift. It was a tempting offer – a delightful parish, with a beautiful church and a handsome

Georgian Rectory. With some reluctance he declined the offer, but it had provided a reminder that now War – in Europe at least – had ended, he soon would be returning to being a country parson again.

Yet there was still work for him as Chaplain to the Forces. After moving, with No 2 Wing, back to Blake Hill Farm on the Cotswolds, and a short leave, he and George Pare, his opposite number in No 1 Wing, went over to Holland tasked with finding, and identifying, the graves of Glider Pilot colleagues who had been killed and buried there. After days spent searching for evidence leading to those graves they were able able to bring back much information. They arranged, too, with the Dutch authorities for the removal of many of the deceased to the Airborne Cemetery once it had been laid out and completed. In between whiles on this trip, Chig was anxious, too, to make contact with the Dutch families whose homes they had used, particularly Catherina van Zanten Jut and her daughters.. They were over-joyed to see him again, in happier circumstances, and welcomed him with kisses galore and, as he said, "awful soup and ersatz coffee – Dutch rations were still both poor and scarce".

In September he was back in Holland, along with John Hooper and Mick Briody, for the first of the Memorial services in the Airborne Cemetery at Oosterbeek. During the ceremony Chig recalled that the sight of "500 Dutch children all standing by Airborne personnel's graves and, at a signal, kneeling and placing a bunch of flowers on each grave was too much for many of us. There were plenty of parachutists, glider pilots and airborne soldiers brushing away tears surreptitiously".

On that trip, aware of the limited food supplies available to the Dutch, he took 250 cigarettes, 1½lbs of coffee, 8lbs of dried milk, 2 tins of cocoa, a tin of Bournvita, 16oz Marmite, various jars of paste, a tin of mustard, half a dozen eggs (Chig was always an optimist!) and a tin of floor polish for Catherina. How warmly welcomed and prized that was, might be gauged from the largesse of the official lunch provided for those attending the ceremony: mashed potatoes and onions.

Demobilisation was now under way. George Pare, his senior in length of service, was demobbed first. The Glider Pilot Regiment was now to consist of one Wing only, and was to serve in Palestine. On 28 February 1946 they sailed from Tilbury on the SS Strathnaver.

A sandstorm welcomed them at Port Said before they made their way to El Qassassin, a vast camp between Ismailia and Cairo. Their stay here was short and uneventful, but it gave Chig the opportunity to visit Cairo several times. Initially he and his batman-driver travelled in a Jeep, but they quickly discovered that no-one in Cairo took the slightest notice of a small vehicle. Adherence to the Highway Code was non-existent! "Every car hooted all the time and the crowded trams clanged their bells continuously. After that we always went in a three-tonner" he recalled. On one occasion Chig found himself lost in a very poor quarter of the city. An Egyptian boy, a Boy Scout who spoke good English, offered Chig help, pointing out that British troops were not permitted in that part of Cairo. Expertly he led Chig through a maze of alleys, where they encountered many unwelcoming, scowling faces and, when challenged, the lad seemed able to satisfy the questioners. On reaching Sheppard's Hotel the young man said his farewells and left. Chig much relieved, thanked him warmly but, good Boy Scout that he was, he refused all offer of payment.

Chig's personal account of this period is strangely silent about the Regiment's active service, though he readily noted the wealth of bird-life and wild flowers. The latter were particularly apparent on his first flight over Palestine and he recalled that "After Egypt it was easy to see why the Hebrews called it 'a land flowing with milk and honey'." Even on the airfield at Qastina, where the Wing HQ was now based, gorgeous wild flowers abounded, there were birds galore, and the camp was surrounded by orange and lemon groves laden with fruit. They also encountered yellow scorpions, lizards (which lived in the corrugated roofs of their huts), chameleons, all sorts of ants, and praying mantis.

During this time in Palestine Chig made several visits to holy places. Once he had a feel for this he began to lead small groups of Glider Pilots on visits to those same holy sites. His first trip to Jerusalem was on Good Friday 1946. His visit there, and to Bethlehem, on this special occasion, made a lasting impression on him. Indeed throughout his time in Palestine he wrote a diary, sending it back with letters to Pauline. Sadly its 188 pages have not been found.

"As long as we stayed on the station, life was secure and pleasant," he later recounted. "We even flew in army and air-force nurses for the occasional dance, for there were no women on the station.

"Outside was not so pleasant. Jewish terrorists were constantly murdering unwary or innocent Arabs and British troops. Occasionally we went off on an expedition to round up suspects. What riled our troops was that, often at risk of their lives and to the relief of many peace-loving Jews and Arabs, they would capture some of these murderers. Then the British Government, sitting safely in Britain, would release them in an attempt to appease offended Zionists."

GPR men were stationed also at two neighbouring RAF stations, Aqir, which was close by, and Kebrit, at the junction of the Greater and Lesser Bitter lakes on the Suez Canal. Chig travelled to Kebrit by train, road and air, depending on what transport was available. Road travel proved interesting. On one journey he and his companions passed a dead camel which, on their return the following day, was a bare skeleton, stripped by Egyptian and Griffon vultures, now gorged and barely able to stagger into the air!

Summer temperatures were so high that transport regulations insisted that vehicles had to be stopped every 50 miles to allow the engines to cool. Chig never ceased to be amazed that, no sooner had the vehicle stopped, than vultures began to appear in what had been, seemingly, an empty sky. A few minutes later the most ragged, most wretched-looking people would appear, begging for food and drink, which they always received. From where had they come? Moments earlier there had been nothing, and no-one, to be viewed across a stony desert extending on all sides as far as the eye could see – often 20 miles or so.

Of his Middle East postings Chig preferred Kebrit. A cool breeze came off the Bitter Lakes and made life pleasant and balmy. Ships passing through the Suez Canal were within hailing distance. The Officers' Mess was a particularly friendly one here, and Mick Briody, formerly the RSM but now commissioned, joined Chig as a very powerful darts pairing especially – Chig recalled – "after two or three vodka and limes!"

Whilst staying at Kebrit on one occasion Chig heard that a ship carrying his sister Margaret and her young son, Hugh, was coming up the Red Sea from India, en route for Britain.

Determined to see his sister, Chig borrowed a huge Triumph motor-bike (even though he had not ridden one since his banking days eighteen years earlier), and headed for the Suez. A launch took him out to rendezvous with the 'Monarch of Bermuda' and, after a loud hailer had bellowed for Mrs Rolfe, his sister Margaret came alongside the rail. It was a huge but joyful surprise to see her young brother again.

Chig's trip back to camp, in good spirits, provided one anxious moment. After stopping in the desert for a sandwich and a drink, he couldn't kick-start the Triumph back into life. Eventually, and to his considerable relief, its engine fired, and he made it back to camp before dark.

His account of this trip to see his sister has a 'gung-ho' feel to it – not untypical of Chig! – but it must be remembered that whilst the motor-bike was an indispensable, convenient, swift and economical form of transport in both towns and desert, riding one in Palestine in those unstable years was a dangerous occupation. Motor-cyclists were easy prey for snipers and those laying mines. Death by decapitation – by a wire stretched across the road – was not unknown.

In contrast to his war-time letters to his father and his diary account of the Arnhem operation, Chig's unpublished biography is reticent about his role – and, indeed that of the GPR – in Palestine. It may be that in his letters from Palestine to Pauline and his father he continued to give details (probably 'sanitised' and 'safe' details of daily life) but his later recollections contain very little about his time there.

Suffice it to say that, unusually for a Chaplain, he again received a Mentioned in Despatches, his second, awarded for distinguished service. We might therefore conclude that his role with the Regiment in Palestine was at least as important, and greatly valued, as it had been at Arnhem, with Chig showing the same level of whole-hearted commitment to the men alongside whom he served, the same gallantry and willingness to go the extra mile. A soldier mentioned in despatches is one whose name appears in an official report written by a superior officer and sent to the high command, in which is described the soldier's gallant or meritorious action in the face of the enemy. Mind you, in his typically self-deprecatory way, he claimed he had no idea why he should have been so recognised, and concluded that his Commanding Officer, Lt. Col Billy Griffith, had nominated him for his service to Billy as his Chaplain during the Victory Test Matches! A jest wholly in character – but doubtless many a mile distant from the truth!

Those who were recognised by a Mention in Despatches received a formal document which read, in Chig's case: "By the KING'S Order the name of Rev. Wilfred Rowland Chignell, Royal Army Chaplain's Department, was published in the London Gazette on 4 April 1946, as mentioned in a Despatch for distinguished service, I am charged to record His Majesty's high appreciation. E Shinwell, Secretary of State for War."

With his demobilisation now close, it was arranged that he should fly back to England. The flight was to be in a Halifax that was due to be broken up, an arrangement which probably didn't generate vast confidence. On the other hand with a choice between getting to England – and demobilisation – or not, Chig was unlikely to go for the cautious option. Confidence was probably heightened though when he realised his travelling companion was to be Major Barry Murdoch who was flying home in order to be married – not something he would wish to miss!

Chig's batman Jackson packed his kit in wooden crates. When he accompanied his belongings to the dispatch centre, the Sergeant there didn't bother to look up until he had finished his writing. When eventually he did so, seeing an officer before him (and a Padre!), he swiftly stood, and apologised. Then his eyes spied the writing on Chig's cases, and noting his name and rank, he also spotted Chig's address: Cressage Vicarage, Shrewsbury. "Cressage, sir" he exclaimed, "do you come from Cressage?" When Chig explained he was the Vicar there he said "I know it well, sir; I used to fish there before the war". Chig knew then that his kit would travel safely to England.

Their flight home along the North African coast, took them above places which war had fixed firmly in the public consciousness like Tobruk and Benghazi. Their route then headed north from Tunis to Istres, near Marseilles, where they stayed overnight. Next morning's flight allowed them to take in the magnificence of the Alps and the Pyrenees before heading for Cornwall and touch-down at St. Mawgan. The onward part of his homeward journey, from Cornwall to Cressage, by train took somewhat longer than the flight from Qastina.

It was good to be home again, though after a short while settling in to life at home he travelled again to Arnhem, on a pilgrimage with Airborne Forces colleagues, to take part in a Service held at the cemetery there. He made time too to visit the van Zanten Juts.

Then, after a brief stop at home, he headed London-ward and, on completing all the formalities of demobilisation, put away for good his uniform and military clothes. Except the 'cherry beret'.

Of his demobilisation leave, part was spent at home, at Cressage, as he unwound and got re-acquainted with rural village life, but he and Pauline made time, too, to holiday in Aberdovey, before fully taking up parish life again and, once more, being Vicar to his flock.

For Chig, one great joy of his resumed role was to arrange for the installation of the 'Victory' bells, the project for which the village had worked so hard in the early days of the war when victory then had seemed a distant prospect.

Life at home seemed wonderful. Yes, there were still food shortages, ration books were required for many food items and for clothing, and the Chignells felt unable to resume running their car, but to be back with Pauline was bliss. Sam, the spaniel adopted when Chig left Chilwell, proved a superb companion and lots of fun.

The summer of 1947 saw Chig resume his active support of Worcestershire County Cricket Club, though an occasional day's cricket meant setting off by train at 8.30am, and not returning until at least 10.00pm.

Later that same summer the Chignells had a visit from Anna-Maria van Zanten Jut, who warmly took to both Chig and Pauline and thereafter became, in Chig's words, "a very lovable and loving 'niece'"

New horizons were opened up for Chig and Pauline by a letter from the Dean of Hereford, the Very Rev'd Hedley Burrows. His letter invited Chig to consider the living of Fownhope with Fawley and Brockhampton, which the Dean declared to be "the most important living in the gift of the Dean and his Chapter". Note those words, for Chig was to hear them again.

Chig and Pauline were both very happy at Cressage and Sheinton and felt no desire to leave but they felt they should properly respond to the Dean's invitation with much thought and prayer, as well as a visit to the parishes. Chig visited by himself and declared Fownhope's church to be "gorgeous – perhaps the finest I ever had in my care". Brockhampton was a modern gem, splendidly furnished in oak in the 'Arts and Crafts' style, yet it had a thatched roof which added greatly to its appeal. Fawley's chapel had a long history and had once been part of a small monastery or convent. Both felt they were being called to this new living and so, immediately after Christmas, they bid a truly reluctant farewell to their Shropshire parishes and moved south to the Fownhope group on 1 January 1948.

Fownhope, alongside the River Wye, a few miles south-east of Hereford, was a lively parish, and an attractive rural village, and there's no doubt that the Chignells were immensely happy during their nine years in this delightful community. They made many good friends there, although traditional 'wisdom' suggested clergy should avoid making close personal friendships within their flock (in order to be *seen* to be treating all their parishioners on an equal footing), but there's no doubt Chig's ministry, and Pauline's affection for their new home, was greatly strengthened by the natural friendship of many of their new neighbours. In Cressage and Sheinton Chig had been able to walk around his two parishes, or cycle when visiting some of the more outlying parishioners. For most of the war period he had given up his car but now, with three widely-spread parishes, he would need to become a car owner again.

Soon after their move to Fownhope, Chig's sister, Robin, suffered a breakdown in her health, and it was felt better for all concerned that George Chignell should come to stay with his son and daughter-in-law at Fownhope Vicarage. Happily the Vicarage, a delightful building, offered plenty of room. It had, too, a most attractive garden as well as large and productive orchard with a whole variety of fruit trees, many of them old and unusual (and tasty!) apple varieties (cider, culinary and dessert apples), which pleased the Chignells no end.

For years George Chignell had fancied he had a dodgy heart, though his old Worcester friend and doctor, Dr Bunting, had constantly assured him there was

Chig during his time as Vicar of Fownhope, blessing the church's new lychgate built in 1953 as part of the village's celebrations of HM The Queen's Coronation.

nothing wrong in that regard. Once he had found his feet in Fownhope, George quickly made the acquaintance of his new doctor. Knowing nothing of George's previous anxieties, the Doctor immediately suggested George should give up smoking his pipe. Chig rather regretted this advice to his father for, as he recalled "Now father could scarcely see to read; we had no television – mind you, nor did anyone else – and no-one can occupy day after day listening to the wireless. The poor old chap went for walks, but found the days very dull, I'm afraid. As the years went by and he came to second childhood it was pathetic to see him. Perhaps his pipe might have shortened his physical life a little, but it might also have given him a small pleasure of his own."

Apart from their natural concerns about George they were in their element in their new parishes and Chig was kept fully occupied. Nevertheless he made time to join Hereford Choral Society, conducted by Sir Percy Hull, an old friend of his father's. Hull was Organist and Choirmaster of Hereford Cathedral as well as Conductor of the Choral Society and Chig found singing under his baton a great joy.

Another great joy, having resumed his active following of Worcestershire CCC, was to begin, in 1949, bringing together his life-long collection of statistics about the County's cricket in a book, which his old friend David Littlebury would publish in 1951. The book, "A History of Worcestershire County Cricket Club, 1844 – 1950", recalled the County's deeds in a year-by-year account in which the most important (and statistically interesting) feats were recounted. With customary under-statement Chig said of his work "The book is not exactly exciting, but it can at least claim to be very factual".

Around the same time Chig became even more involved with Worcestershire's cricket. A parishioner, and good friend, G L 'Peter' Clay (younger brother of J C Clay, the distinguished Glamorgan and England cricketer), was a stalwart secretary of the Herefordshire Gentlemen CC and as such was Herefordshire's representative on the Worcestershire CCC committee. One day he suggested that Chig might take his place, and so began Chig's long spell as a member of Worcestershire's General Committee.

In for a penny, in for a pound! It wasn't long before, having expressed some reservations about the constrained quality of the County's Year Book, he found himself part of the small group charged with improving the annual publication – which is how, as the opening chapter of this book explains, I first came to know Chig.

These cricket interests occupied some of Chig's 'spare time' but another activity which would become an official duty as well as a delight came through his secretary-ship of the Diocesan Missionary Council. Initially his experiences in Palestine and Egypt had led to his being asked to represent the Jerusalem and East Mission in the Hereford Diocese and from there it was but a short step to taking on the work of Hereford Diocese's DMC. He threw himself into these endeavours, constantly and actively encouraging his fellow clergy to support this important work in the mission field. He gave dedicated and faithful service to the Council until he stood down in 1964.

Throughout his ministry Chig recognised the importance, and the value, of contributing to the life of his parishes in a variety of ways. So too did Pauline. Soon after their arrival in Fownhope, Chig became a Parish Councillor. In this role he, with a fellow councillor, Vera Biggs, walked miles and miles of footpaths, Chig often accompanied by Sam. Chig himself covered more than 50 miles of the local bye-ways, so that they could be recorded and marked on a County Council map as the 1951 Access to the Countryside Act ensured that regularly walked paths, recorded on the County Council's definitive map, became the County's responsibility in terms of maintenance and ease of access.

It seemed to be a time of dispute between the Parish and County Councils. The provision of mains water was the focus of one such dispute, with local councillors expressing real concern that this was being unnecessarily delayed by the County. As a councillor, and as Chairman of the School Managers (today they would be called Governors), Chig also battled to save the village school. Being a councillor proved demanding but it was an important way in which Chig felt he could also serve his parishioners and the whole community.

Her Majesty The Queen's Coronation in 1953 aroused much enthusiasm in towns, villages and cities across the whole country. In the week of the Coronation itself Fownhope Church staged special Services. A village tea and sports afternoon was arranged for the children, as well as a tea for the older residents. Festivities included also a village concert. A permanent reminder of the Coronation was provided by the building of a new lych-gate for the Church, Using reclaimed stone from old village buildings, local timber, and traditional crafts and skills, the lych-gate was constructed with two seats and so doubled valuably as the village bus shelter too.

For the Village Concert Chig brought together a Toy Orchestra, a combination of usual musical instruments alongside the more unusual, with talented musicians playing alongside those who couldn't read a note – truly a rural village affair! Chig even wrote a piece of music for the event: "Symphony in C Approximately". The title reflected that this was, most definitely, a 'fun' event. The introduction to the concert went something like this: "Will you allow me to introduce ze members of the world famous Philhadiscord Sumfunny Orchestra. Zer are many orchestras; sum funny, sum are not. Zis is. Each member is supreme with his or her instrument – no-one else can play it like he or she". The preamble aptly set the tone for the occasion. Instruments included those concert-goers might have expected to see and hear: violin ("Mrs Lionel Piggs plays ze second violin. I do not know vat she has done with ze first one, but she is vonderful on ze second"), piano, clarinet, recorders and trumpets – along with home-made tympani (constructed from a garden sieve and parchment) and a child's nightingale whistle filled with water, an ocarina, tambourine and triangle. Though the Toy Orchestra and Coronation Concert was very much 'of its time', it proved a real hit, though whether for its music or its humour (or, just possibly, both!) Chig remained silent. Nevertheless repeat performances were staged, by request, at nearby Brockhampton and Madley. Word must have spread, for they then received an invitation to appear on BBC Midlands TV.

If parish life was not full enough Chig spear-headed two major restorations during his time at Fownhope. The wooden shingles on Fownhope's large spire needed replacing. The £500 cost was quickly raised by parishioners. The work was undertaken by a steeple-jack who used a bosun's chair slung from the top of the spire, and swung from point to point simply by pushing with his feet. No scaffolding, no Health and Safety! Again, very much of its time. Brockhampton Church was re-thatched using Norfolk reed, requiring a staggering amount of reed. Again the cost was £500 and all of it raised promptly by the locals.

During this time Chig and Pauline made a number of holiday visits to Holland, delighted to see the country in happier circumstances than on Chig's earliest encounter. They often met up with the Dutch families who Chig had come to know during the Arnhem days, and with whom firm, warm friendships had been established. On one trip they attended an Airborne Forces Memorial Service, staying with the Owers family, old friends from Chig's time there in 1944.

Towards the end of 1955 Chig's father died. "He had," said Chig, "been a splendid Christian, a devoted husband, a firm but affectionate father and, until he became increasingly senile, a wise counsellor. No-one could have had a better father and so the funeral service at Lillington, where he was buried, as mother had been, was one of joy and thanksgiving with Easter hymns. I have often wondered why Christians

Chig about to conduct Fownhope's Toy Orchestra.

Chig with Fownhope's Toy Orchestra 1954. Pauline Chignell is second from the left, playing the triangle. (J. Soulsby)

who believe in the Resurrection, so often have gloomy and mournful hymns and how easily we speak of the dead as 'poor old So-and-so' as though there is no marvellous hope in our faith."

In 1956, nine years after their move to Fownhope, Chig received another letter from the Dean of Hereford, again inviting him to consider a move to a new living. As he had in similar circumstances nine years earlier, Dean Burrows invited Chig to consider taking "the most important living in the gift of the Dean and Chapter". Perhaps forgetting that he had earlier conferred this title on Chig's present parish, it seemed that Hedley Burrows had now awarded it to the parish of Kington with Huntington on the diocese's Welsh border.

The Chignells were well settled at Fownhope, felt very much part of the community and at home there. They were immensely happy where they were, but Chig again felt he should properly consider the Dean's invitation to take this "most important" living.

He had only once previously visited the little market town of some 3,000 residents on the edge of the Radnor Forest and the hills of mid-Wales. He felt, too, that his ministry to this point had made it clear – to him at least – that he was cut out to be a country priest and parson, a very different task from that of being an urban priest, even in a small market town like Kington.

In the light of these thoughts he consulted his Archdeacon, the Venerable Arthur Winnington-Ingram, a man who Chig respected greatly. Kington, the Archdeacon told Chig, was a depressed little town, whose market had almost ceased to exist and whose railway station recently had been closed. It was feeling sore and neglected. Hardly a ringing commendation, but Winnington-Ingram felt Chig could do a job there and recommended he accept, with the intention of staying there for five years and getting the place back on its feet again.

With this helpful and persuasive advice, and again after much thought and prayer, Chig accepted the living.

Fownhope gave them a heart-warming – and heart-tugging – farewell, presenting them with several gifts, one of which was a cheque for £60, a tidy sum in those times. (equivalent to well over £1,000 today).

That gift of the cheque led to a delightful story. One parishioner had been unable to attend the farewell party but her young daughter, who had been at the festivities, was happy to tell her all about it. "Oh, it was so lovely," she told her Mum, "they gave Mr Chignell £60 to go away!" However the story was recounted, and however sad their Fownhope, Brockhampton and Fawley parishioners were to see them go, Chig and Pauline departed with much goodwill and genuine thanks and good wishes ringing in their ears.

Their new home, Kington Vicarage, stood in three acres of grounds, much of it a splendid garden, which Chig's predecessor, Tom Wilkinson, and his wife had maintained beautifully. The house had an old 15th century part, with further 18th and 19th centuries additions. The more recent parts comprised a large entrance hall with a fine staircase and balcony which led to six bedrooms and storage rooms. The dining room, 28 feet long and with a beautiful oak floor, offered magnificent views over the lawns.

All the rooms were 15 feet high. It was a splendid house, even if the Chignells felt it rather large for the two of them!

The difference in stipend between Fownhope and Kington was then, in 1956, £1 a week, though this additional benefit was quickly swallowed up by the extra expenses of car, telephone, correspondence, heating and lighting of the office and study, and entertainment of clergy and other visitors.

Again, feeling God's call to serve the people there, Chig threw himself into the life of the parishes, in a town situation. As Vicar he was expected to serve on numerous committees and groups, as was Pauline, always a stalwart and faithful yet quiet supporter of her husband's work. As he had anticipated, there were differences in ministry in a market town, even a small one, compared to that in rural villages. Chig felt it was far less personal; it was possible to get to know everyone in a small village (or villages), but that was almost impossible in a town, especially one with numerous civic committees. Whilst valuing this recognition of the Church's public and civic role, Chig also became aware that what one could actually *do* was limited; there was a real danger of spreading oneself too thinly. As one who was by nature (and discipline) a frequent and regular visitor of parishioners he begrudged the time spent in meetings when he would rather have been visiting.

One great joy of the Kington post was that it offered sufficient work for a Curate to be appointed. During his time there Chig trained three Curates, welcoming the opportunity to share with them his vast ministerial experience. Those Curates all became life-long friends, constantly grateful for the sound foundations Chig had offered them.

The first of his Curates was Hugh Sargeant who made an immediate impression on Chig. "It seemed that he, rather than I, did the interviewing" Chig later recalled, albeit with a warm smile on his face. Hugh's confidence and organisational bent was seen also at the rehearsal for his wedding. Hugh was not attached when he first met Chig but perhaps buoyed by the success of his interview he promptly got engaged. His marriage to his fiancée Pauline early in 1957 was to be a Nuptial Mass and was to be conducted by Hugh's father, his god-father, and Chig. "Hugh had it all planned in his mind," Chig recalled, "and the rehearsal was more a matter of his telling us and showing us what to do, than of our showing the bride and bridegroom. We meekly accepted the advice given to us and then sent the young couple off." With their joint and very considerable experience in such matters Chig and his fellow clerics then agreed between themselves exactly how they would share their duties. "It was, I think, a very reverent and worthy Nuptial Mass" he concluded afterwards and when everything had gone to the satisfaction of all concerned, including the young Curate-groom.

When Hugh left to take up a post at St. Magdalene's, Bridgnorth he was succeeded by Richard Smith, a young bachelor who looked younger than his 23 years, who was ordained at Michaelmas 1958. Richard hit it off with Chig immediately, with Pauline too, and they made a good team.

In that same year, the Lambeth Conference was held in London, with Bishops attending from every corner of the Anglican Communion. Hereford Diocese hosted four Bishops prior to the Conference: the Bishop of Northern Michigan, the Bishop of the Niger Delta, Bishop Johnson who had been Bishop in Egypt until he hurriedly had to leave at the time of the Suez crisis, and Bishop Nigel Cornwall, from Borneo.

As a result of his visit to Kington and getting to know Chig a little, Bishop Cornwall enquired whether Chig might consider going to Borneo, either as Dean of Kuching or to a chaplaincy in the oil fields in Labuan. It was a tempting offer for, as a much younger man Chig had seriously considered overseas ministry. Again much thought and prayer was given to the invitation. Chig wrote to the Bishop, who was by now in the USA on a circuitous route home, pointing out that he had given an undertaking, albeit an unofficial one, to stay at least five years in Kington, five years which were not yet up. He also advised the Bishop of his and Pauline's age. The Bishop sent a charming reply, saying he had no idea the Chignells were both in their fifties and that he felt this was too old for the tasks he had in mind. So ended what was to be Chig's only chance of serving overseas, apart, of course, from his Army chaplaincy in Egypt and Palestine.

Towards the end of 1961 a United Society for the Propogation of the Gospel mission evening was held in the parish, with a film showing the Society's work in what was then British Guiana. At the evening's end Chig noticed that Richard seemed unusually quiet and thoughtful. Next day Richard said "I can't see any reason why I shouldn't go overseas. Do you think I ought to offer myself to the USPG for this?" Chig's heart leapt for joy, indeed he did well not to become airborne himself such was his delight. If *he* couldn't go overseas himself, how marvellous then that his *Curate* wished to go. Chig gave him every encouragement and in 1962 Richard set off for British Guiana, where he spent several years doing wonderful work for the mission charity.

This additional role of training Curates, ensuring they gained plenty of good experience, was something Chig took to like a duck to water, and he ensured their training was first-class. In return, their respect and regard for him turned into friendships which extended way beyond their curacy time in Kington.

For Chig parish life in Kington continued much as in his previous parishes, though with the greater involvement in civic life. There were many good people in Kington, and many good supporters of the Church. It was good to have Churchwardens who were such stalwarts and on whom he could happily rely. His shared ministry with his Curates brought him much joy. Along with the regular round of worship, on Sundays and in mid-week, and visiting parishioners (in their homes and in the cottage hospital) there would be all the customary activities of Sunday School, youth groups, choir and choir practices, study groups, confirmation classes, mothers-and-toddlers groups and the like, along with meetings galore and the annual fixtures such as the Church fetes, eisteddfods and concerts (for Chig happily involved himself in the musical life of the town and parish), together with his role as a school governor. In addition to his own parish duties Chig was made Rural Dean of Kington for his last three years there, which brought with it pastoral oversight of his clergy colleagues, with whom he was on good terms and with whom he enjoyed mutually supportive friendship, as well as a pastoral and watching brief on the other parishes of the deanery. This included making arrangements for continued ministry when there was a vacancy in one of the deanery's parishes and, in this, Richard Smith proved a tower of strength.

The Curate's post vacated by Richard on his move to Bristish Guiana was soon filled by John Davis. John was a Herefordshire man who had studied at both Durham and Oxford universities, and was steeped in Old Testament and Hebrew studies. Chig could recognise a brilliant intellect when he saw one. Whereas it had been his policy to ask his Curates to share their sermons with him before preaching them, he never had the nerve to ask the same of John! When Chig suffered a couple of lapses of health, John came up trumps and was a splendid help, taking on far more than might otherwise have been expected of him

During their time in Kington, Chig and Pauline celebrated their silver wedding anniversary, in 1961, a landmark they marked by a trip to the Holy Land. Chig found it a real joy to re-visit – now with Pauline alongside him – many places associated with Jesus and the Bible accounts, a number of which he had visited during his time as a Forces Chaplain in Palestine. Their actual wedding anniversary found them alongside the Sea of Galilee. Chig's account of this visit, which moved them both enormously, had an interesting footnote which again offered a sign of the times. In those days before jet travel, their flight from the aerodrome at Jerusalem made an unscheduled touch down in Damascus to collect more crockery and cutlery (proper crockery and cutlery!) as there was insufficient for all the passengers on board!

Alongside his parish duties, Chig remained an effective and enthusiastic Secretary of the DMC. In such spare time as he had he continued to follow the fortunes of Worcestershire CCC. With Kington being closer to Worcestershire's New Road ground than Cressage, it was easier to get over to watch the County more frequently. To watch many a grand game in the company of committee colleagues he now knew as friends provided a relaxed contrast to life in the parish.

Nevertheless the living provided its irritations and challenges, too. One cloud which hovered over his time at Kington was an on-going dispute with the Diocese about the Vicarage. The Diocese wanted to build a new Vicarage in the vast garden (at a cost of some £12,000), with the probability that the then Vicarage, a fine old house, would be pulled down. Chig, with the advice of an architect friend, believed the present Vicarage could be up-graded at a significantly more modest cost (perhaps £5,000). After much heat, and strong feelings on both sides, the Diocesan Dilapidations Board (what a wonderful title!) reluctantly agreed that the Chignells should continue to live in the old Vicarage so long as Chig remained Vicar of Kington, but they would spend no money on repairs. For a time Chig and Pauline continued to enjoy this lovely but too-large house, but the disagreement clouded, on a personal level at least, the latter part of his time in Kington. The last straw came in February 1964. Heavy snows settled on the Vicarage roof and, when they began to thaw, the melted snow leaked through the roof in several places. It was more than Chig could do with his buckets and tin baths to keep up with the trickling floods. Perhaps it was time to move on.

Shortly before this thought gained legs, the Bishop of Hereford invited Chig to become a Prebendary of Hereford – an honorary Canon – and so to have a prebendal stall in the cathedral. A mark of distinction, it was usually accorded to a senior member of the clergy who had given distinguished or long service to the diocese. Chig recognised the honour being conferred on him. Yet, characteristically, he felt unsure that he was deserving of this and unsure about accepting the invitation. After much thought he eventually persuaded himself that he should accept, in part as an encouragement for both the Diocesan Missionary Council and also for his Kington and Huntington parishes. Ironically, within a few weeks he was neither Secretary of one (having stood down after thirteen years) nor the Vicar of the other!

Of their time in Kington, Chig was clear that there was indeed much for which they were truly grateful. They had splendid friends there; a church which also had many good friends and supporters in the community and a church life that grew stronger and stronger; and the backing (and friendship) of excellent Curates who had blossomed under Chig's guidance; a most attractive (if large!) vicarage; and wonderful countryside and wildlife all around them. They enjoyed many blessings there.

Many years later, Pauline – who had a gift for finding the right word or phrase in summing up a situation – said "There were too many people who thought they were very important". Chig felt she had, again, hit the nail cleanly on the head. Perhaps it had been time to go.

Their next move was to be to Whitbourne, a rural parish on the other side of the diocese, on the Herefordshire-Worcestershire border. Recognising the closer proximity to Worcester and its county cricket ground (10 miles away only, much closer than in any of his previous parishes) Chig – typically – wondered if this might be a reason to turn down the move; the County Ground's proximity might prove too great a temptation and distraction from parish duties!

Such thoughts may have been heightened by the improving fortunes of Worcestershire CCC. In 1963 they won their way to the first-ever Final of the newly-instituted Gillette Cup, against Sussex, at Lord's. By now, Chig's former CO, Billy Griffith, was Secretary of MCC (as well as a former Sussex player and captain), and generously he invited Chig to his Secretary's Box for the Final. A fellow guest, and another man of Sussex, was Billy's great friend and another of Chig's former Glider Pilot Regiment colleagues, Hugh Bartlett. Chig recalled that Hugh, himself a former Sussex captain, "generously wore both a Sussex and Worcestershire favour on his coat!" If Worcestershire was unlucky in that first Lord's Final the following summer of 1964 saw the County enjoy greater success. Chig was in his element – and yet, with a firm self-denying ordinance, mostly kept his cricket-watching to his days off!

For the first time in its ninety-nine year history the County headed the 1964 Championship table as County Champions. Their success was sealed in their home game against Gloucestershire, three days fondly remembered by all who were there. Chig – to his frustration – was not there! He and Pauline had a niece staying at the time, along with her family, and when offered the choice of a visit to cricket or to mid-Wales they opted for the latter. Chig's characteristic generosity to his guests meant he never saw a ball of that historic game. There was some compensation in 1965 however when Worcestershire again proved themselves Champions in winning the title again. Avoiding the temptation of being constantly at the County Ground, Chig did manage to squeeze in a good deal of that summer's cricket at New Road. To retain their title Worcestershire had to win their last match of the summer, against Sussex at Hove. That afternoon Chig was out, parish visiting, but came in to find that the scheduled radio coverage of a Test Match had been temporarily set aside to cover the Worcestershire-Sussex nail-biter. In his excitement as Worcestershire inched nearer the title, he failed to hear the announcement that the BBC's commentary was being transferred to another wave-length and so Chig was left in frustrated anticipation until the six o'clock news confirmed what he hoped to hear!

Kington had sent Chig and Pauline on their way with undoubtedly genuine good wishes, "an unexpectedly large cheque and some delightful smaller presents" when they left the Borderland parish in the autumn of 1964.

Chig believed he was going to Whitbourne as Rector of an enlarged benefice, comprised of the parishes of Whitbourne, Tedstone Delamere with Tedstone Wafre and Edvin Loach, Upper Sapey with Wolferlow, Thornbury with Edvin Ralph and Collington. These were to be united as a group of parishes with Chig as Team Rector assisted by two Vicars (at the time there were three clergy looking after these other parishes, though they were all sick men and not in good health). In fact, nothing came of that plan until *after* Chig had retired, so it was as Rector of Whitbourne that he was installed.

Whitbourne was a small parish of 500 people, many still involved in agriculture in the 2,500 acres the parish covered. The Church of St John the Baptist was largely 13th C and, a couple of miles away, on Bringsty Common, was a chapel of ease, a 'tin tabernacle' (known locally as Bringsty Iron Church), with what Chig described as "a grand little congregation of real country folk". The village had its own school. In many ways it was a typical Herefordshire village in that its population was scattered, with "four or five hamlets with the odd farm and cottage lying between each hamlet. Most of the land belonged to Whitbourne Hall estate and much of the remainder to Whitbourne Court". It was a joy for Chig to be back in proper rural ministry, the ministry for which he seemed so fitted.

One adjustment Chig and Pauline had to make was in what today would be called "down-sizing". All their previous vicarage homes had been huge buildings, and the furniture they had acquired and bought had been appropriate to those places. Whitbourne's rectory was of 1950s design and much smaller. Most of their familiar and comfortable furniture had to go.

It was during their Whitbourne years that I first got to know Chig, and so to be aware of how greatly loved he was – by church-goers *and* by those who seldom darkened the church's door, and how faithfully and generously he looked after all his flock. As always he was devotedly supported by Pauline, 'Mrs Chig', who in her own quiet, unassuming way entered fully into village life.

As in all his parishes Chig took a keen interest in the church choir, as well as other musical activities in the community. He saw a benefit in some modest, but very useful, re-ordering of the church, and got the churchyard tidied up. They worked hard to improve the parish magazine and introduced the "Whitbourne Whistle", a weekly news-sheet. Its circulation was soon greater than the number of houses in the village! Soon he was invited to write a weekly "Christian Viewpoint" column for Berrow's Worcester Journal, the local weekly newspaper which served a very wide area and readership (and was the oldest weekly newspaper in the world). Life as a parish priest and country parson was full – and good!

Many country clergy find (or they did in Chig's time) that a responsibility for local glebe land was something they still carried, though in most cases the dioceses took responsibility for the larger tracts of farming land and commercial properties. As incumbent, Chig discovered that he 'owned' 150 yards of fishing on one bank of the River Teme. It was let to a fishing club in Birmingham. This became apparent when the agent acting for the club came to pay the annual rent of £10 on its behalf. He also made a personal donation of £10 to Church funds – nothing like keeping in with the Rector! At the same time he advised Chig, rather surprisingly, that the club would not want the fishing again. Chig therefore decided to let the fishing to a colleague on the WCCC Committee, a Bromsgrove solicitor, who offered to pay £50 p.a. for it. Towards the end of the year Chig was visited by three members of the fishing club saying they had come to renew their lease. When he explained to his visitors what had happened, and explained that he was now to get £50 p.a. for the fishing, they were infuriated. Their anger was not with Chig but with the agent who had acted for them, for they had been paying him £50 p.a. to secure the rights. Clearly this sum had not reached Chig!

One new and added dimension to his work came through an invitation from St. James' School in West Malvern. The Headmistress, Miss Southgate, wanted to appoint a priest to take Confirmation classes for her girls, and Chig had been recommended to her.

At that point he knew nothing about the school, but quickly discovered it was a small but prestigious girls boarding school, with a high reputation. After interview by the Headmistress, to whom Chig warmed immediately, and by the Dean of Gloucester (vice-chairman of Governors), he was invited to take on this role. Of this he later said "So began some of the most rewarding work I have ever had the privilege of doing". As part of this he instituted a Quiet Afternoon shortly before the girls were due for Confirmation. The first was held in Whitbourne Church and it quickly became a much-loved and appreciated part of the girls' Confirmation preparation. Often, within a week or two of his classes starting, the girls were asking "Please, Preb Chig, when are we having our Quiet Time at Whitbourne?", and ages afterwards letters to him from old girls referred movingly to what a special landmark the Quiet Day had been in their school days.

A little later Miss Southgate asked Chig if he might be willing and able to teach Divinity a couple of times each week. This had some appeal, for Chig's stipend had dropped by £200 p.a. with his move from Kington to Whitbourne, but the greatest appeal was sharing the 'Good News' and assisting the young ladies on their Christian pilgrimage. He was, however, unsure about accepting and suggested that the Headmistress should first consult the Bishop of Hereford, Mark Hodson about calling on Chig's services, not least because St. James' was not in Chig's parish, neither indeed was it in Hereford Diocese!

A phone call from the Bishop to Chig made clear that his lordship had no objection in principle to him taking on this work, whilst pointing out that Chig had no more qualification as a teacher than did the Bishop himself. Bishop Hodson stressed that he felt duty bound to convey this to Miss Southgate.

When Chig next saw the Headmistress she reported she had indeed heard from the Bishop, and she showed Chig the letter with which she would respond to Bishop Mark. It read "My dear Lord Bishop, Thank you very much for allowing Prebendary Chignell to come to teach Divinity at St. James'. You mention O and A levels. I am not interested in Prebendary Chignell getting my girls through them. What I want him to do is to help them get to the Kingdom of Heaven ..... ." What a wonderfully robust – and visionary – response!

And that became Chig's programme for the next eleven years, way beyond his retirement as a parish priest.

In this new and wider role he was again much-loved and highly regarded and respected by his charges, so-much-so that in ensuing years (and in retirement) he was frequently invited to conduct girls' weddings, some of them 'society' weddings.

In other ways life in Whitbourne continued much as it had in his earliest days at Cressage and Sheinton. The number of regular communicants was increasing, as was the parish's support of the Church overseas. There was the regular round of Sunday Services as well as baptisms and weddings – which almost always provided Chig with opportunities for reaching out more widely into the community – and many funerals too. Meetings without number featured in parish life, as they do for most clergy. Chig took on a Ladies Choir (this was in retirement) and wrote and produced Passion Plays but central to all his work in the parish was his pastoral visiting, to which important work he dedicated considerable time. Almost always a parson's visiting is reflected in both his knowledge and understanding of his flock and in *their* involvement with their Church. In some cases this will be by direct personal support and church attendance, in others by a willingness to help the Church when tasks need doing or funds need to be generated. The number of house and cottage doors must be countless which received that lusty reverberating knock – Rat-tat-tat-tat! – with which Chig first introduced himself to me.

In addition to his clerical vocation he also served the village in other ways, as a member of the Parish Council, though even there his thoughts and decisions were coloured by the faith so central in his life.

Away from the parish he served on the Bishop's Council, a major strategy-deciding body in the diocese. With his knowledge and experience of the Holy Land he was asked to lead Christian pilgrimages there. In all these ways, life as a country parson with a real sense of the Church's role in the world, was very full.

Full though it was, Chig and Pauline were profoundly happy during their Whitbourne years.

Amidst the delightful and generally harmonious tenor of parish life came one distressing moment for the whole family in 1966. Having no children of their own Chig and Pauline were immensely fond of their nephews and nieces, particularly his sister Robin's daughters, Susan and Judith, and Pauline's sister's offspring, Jennifer and Jeremy. Without showing particular favouritism they saw a good deal of Jennifer and Jeremy. During the War years the children and Olga had often stayed at Cressage Vicarage. Following the death of her husband Arthur, and then their dear mother, Olga had decided to move nearer her sister. In fact she found a house not far from Whitbourne Church. Jennifer had entered nursing, training at St. Bart's in London before going to Canada to specialise in neuro-surgical nursing. Her brother had entered the ministry and was serving as an assistant curate in Woolwich.

Olga and Jeremy set out on a Lake District holiday that Easter together with a cousin, Nancy, and her husband 'Chang' and their family. The five men of the party: Jeremy, 'Chang' and his sons, Gavin, Adam and Giles, had set out on a mountain walk, with no intention of undertaking any serious climbing. However, they soon encountered thick mist and ice. Conditions deteriorated to the extent that they roped themselves together. Unfortunately, rather than offering protection it meant that, when one slipped and fell, they all fell. One of the party was sufficiently unharmed to be able to rush for help, but when the rescue party succeeded in finding them only Giles was alive. It was a devastating time for the whole family. Jennifer immediately flew back from Canada to join her mother and Nancy, Chig and Pauline and other family members for the three funerals. Jeremy's cremated remains were later laid to rest in Whitbourne churchyard, and Jennifer gave up her work in Canada so that she could continue her nursing in England, nearer to her mother. This meant that on visits home she saw more of Chig and Pauline too.

Music continued to be a greatly enjoyed relaxation for Chig and Pauline, whilst he continued to relish his role on Worcestershire CCC's committee and delighted in their second successive Championship win in 1965. This, happily, was the Club's centenary year. As Year Book Editor Chig ensured this repeated success in its one-hundredth year was marked by a special souvenir edition of the Year Book.

A year or two later Chig's love of the County Cricket Club, and his continued interest in its playing statistics, resulted in his second book about the County's history "Worcestershire Cricket 1950-1968: The Kenyon Years". Chig dedicated this new work to Don Kenyon "Leader of Champions and Champion of Leaders". In 1969 Chig's contribution to the County was marked by his appointment as a Vice-President, an honour the County guards jealously and one which Chig greatly appreciated. If that could – for him – be topped, it was in 1978 when the Club elected him President, a role he was invited to fill for the next three years. Mind you his humour came instantly to the fore on his appointment. "With my three immediate predecessors sadly dying in office," he noted, "perhaps the Club felt a clergyman had a better chance of completing his term of office." Humour aside, he valued the role enormously and gave it his all though, frustratingly, health problems in this period occasionally limited his participation.

Chig (on left) with his spaniel, supervising the planting of a copper beech tree by Don Kenyon, in 1968, to commemorate Don's outstanding service to Worcestershire CCC as County Captain from 1959 to 1967, during which the County won successive County Championships in 1964 and 1965. Watching proceedings are Jack Sellars, Gilbert Ashton (then President WCCC), Norman Taylor and Arthur Ross-Slater.

Chig, ca 1969, at the time of the publication of his second book on Worcestershire CCC. (Pictures by *Worcester News*)

Of this particular period two small opportunities gave him much pleasure. It had long been a custom of WCCC that, on the opening day of the season, the wife of each new President provided a special floral arrangement for both the Ladies Pavilion and for the Committee Room. Cricket did not feature high among Pauline's interests, but as a faithful and devoted supporter of her husband's activities and as a superb flower arranger (as well as gifted painter, embroiderer, and cook along with many other talents) she – despite her natural modesty – was more than happy to maintain this delightful tradition. But there was another string to this bow. A Whitbourne parishioner and great friend of the Chignells was Michael Jefferson-Brown, a leading daffodil breeder and grower, and a more than useful flower arranger himself. The start of the cricket season (Worcestershire's opening match was against the Pakistan touring team that year) coincided with daffodils being at their Spring-like best, and so Michael provided armfuls of his own beautiful flowers with which Pauline could weave her magic. Her two wonderful displays won many warm compliments, even from hard-nosed 'unfloral' committee men.

The second particular pleasure offered was that the final year of Chig's presidency coincided with his old Glider Pilots' Regiment Commanding Officer, Billy Griffith, serving as President of MCC, the Club he had served previously with such distinction as its long-time Secretary. Billy, with typical generosity, invited Chig to his President's Box for one day of the Lord's Test Match that year. With his characteristic modesty, Chig was pleased to accept but felt he might be out of his depth among the cricketing 'grandees' so arranged to visit Billy's Box for the afternoon session. As might be expected he was warmly welcomed by his host who, Chig noted, seemed especially pleased to see him. The reason for this swiftly became apparent when Billy said "Come and meet this woman, another of our guests. She talks politics all the ruddy time and doesn't seem interested in the cricket at all." So Chig met, for the only time in his life, the Rt.Hon. Margaret Thatcher, Prime Minister and First Lord of the Treasury. She didn't talk much cricket with him either! Nevertheless this visit to the President's Box at Lord's, as a guest of the President, his old war-time chum, was for Chig as near to 'heaven on earth' as he might have thought possible.

Another cricket milestone had brought him great pleasure in 1977, just prior to his taking up the Presidency of WCCC. Worcester Nomads CC, the club he had formed long ago back in 1927 along with Douglas Rowe, David Littlebury and Don Arbuckle, celebrated its Golden Jubilee. Raymond Illingworth, of England and Yorkshire (and Leicestershire) fame, was the principal speaker. Chig was invited to speak too, with his old friend Don Arbuckle in the presidential chair. It was a delightful evening which kindled many treasured and happy memories. He was especially pleased to see the club in such good and vibrant heart. Today it is one of the most successful teams in the County, now with its own delightful ground at Bransford, west of the city, and with a deserved reputation for its extensive work with young cricketers. At the time of writing the club has just won promotion from the top division of the Worcestershire County League to the Birmingham & District Premier Cricket League. Chig would have been thrilled.

Reverting just briefly to Chig and his friendship with Michael Jefferson-Brown, Chig was walking in the village one day, on his priestly duties, when Michael's van came to a skidding halt alongside him. "I'm so glad I've seen you, Chig," he said, "You're the very man I want to see". Then, in his lovely, slightly hesitant and apologetic way, he continued "Jean and I have got a new daffodil which we think is rather nice. We are wondering whether you would allow us to call it 'Chig'? Would you mind?" And later, in his daffodil growing grounds he showed Chig the medium-sized flower with its pure white petals, primrose cup, and a delicate scent. Would he mind indeed!

Michael's generosity was to the fore again when Chig and Pauline celebrated their Ruby Wedding anniversary, in 1976. Among Michael's considerable talents was the gift of painting. As an anniversary gift he and Jean presented Chig and Pauline with one of his own paintings. It was of hillside fields in Whitbourne, known locally as Vineyards (tradition indicating this is what they used to be). It was a painting which gave them unfailing pleasure, pleasure which, since Chig's death, I too have constantly enjoyed now that it adorns a wall in our sitting room.

Chig was a man whose outward appearance was that of someone "rude with health", which he so often was, but as he got older he suffered one or two lapses of health including, latterly, heart problems. These were not life-threatening, but certainly slowed him down and sensibly made him a bit more circumspect. In some ways Pauline – in my memory a delightful 'Mrs Tiggywinkle' character – had never seemed as robust but was one of those who happily soldiered uncomplainingly on, but advancing years slowed her down too. In particular arthritis and eye problems made life frustrating and sometimes difficult, such that she was not always confident about travelling far and wide as they had done through much of their earlier married life. She became more of a home bird, happily so, and remained resolutely cheerful and full of joy.

After much discussion between them both, Chig announced to the parish that he would retire on 10 June 1973, by which time he would be 65.

A small cottage in the village had become empty in 1968, and it remained empty and unsold for some time. Chig and Pauline wondered whether it might be a suitable buy for their retirement although, at that point, the only thing it seemed to promise was an unpromising prospect. When Pauline had a good look around the vacant cottage she began to visualise the potential it had and, cutting a long story short, they bought Little Stocking, the first property they had owned

Builders and bull-dozers and two years' patience saw the restorations completed, and the garden and orchard uncovered from its weed blanket,

Priest and parson. Chig, shortly before his retirement in 1973.

sufficient that the cottage could be let until Chig and Pauline were ready for their retirement move.

Those who know the ways of the Church of England may be surprised that Chig had opted to stay in his own parish. As with doctors (GPs) who retire, there is an expectation that clergy will retire away from their last parish. Brutal though this may seem, especially where the professional has lived and worked among good friends, it does avoid the scenario where the locals constantly want to turn to the 'old hand', who they know and trust, thus not allowing the new person to establish himself – or herself – and to create their own mark and space in the church and village and in community life.

Chig had felt reasonably sanguine about staying in Whitbourne, however, since umpteen discussions, at diocesan and local level, had pointed emphatically to the sort of parish re-organisation which the Bishop had spoken of when Chig first came to the village. This time, it seemed, more parishes were to be united *and* a new Rectory built elsewhere, outside Whitbourne and nearer the middle of the patch. Chig was sure he would not be treading on any new incumbent's toes and, indeed, he saw that he might be able to help his successor by offering an occasional retirement ministry to people and a community he knew like the back of his hand. How could this not be helpful?

Those re-organisation plans, it appeared, had not been carved on tablets of stone. There was indeed some re-organisation of nearby parishes on Chig's retirement but it was not as extensive as he had been led to believe. A new Rectory was built too, yet not in one of the other villages but just up the lane from Little Stocking. The best laid plans of mice and men … !

His Bishop was certainly not enamoured with Chig's retirement arrangements but, having made them in good faith, Chig was not minded to change them. House prices had rocketed since they had bought Little Stocking and so there was no prospect of their selling Little Stocking and buying a similar property elsewhere. Whitbourne it was to be.

In such circumstances great sensitivity would be needed on the part of the retiring cleric. Though Chig was minded to exercise such sensitivity, it was hard for him to think that he couldn't or shouldn't help out by taking Services occasionally (he might have opted for regularly!). It was hard, too, for parishioners not to turn to someone they had got to know and love. Chig came, albeit gradually, to recognise his changed place in the new scheme of things and, by such goodwill and the goodwill of those who succeeded him as Rector, anticipated problems were minimised.

For these reasons Chig resigned from all Church committees and felt it appropriate too to stand down from the Parish Council, the Gardening Society and other non-church groups too.

Prior to the arrival of his successor, Godfrey Simpson, who had just completed a curacy in nearby Leominster, Whitbourne Church undertook a fund-raising campaign, under Chig's lead, to fund repairs and maintenance which the most recent quinquennial inspection had declared essential. The congregation, supported by other villagers, also undertook a massive spring clean of the church, so that all might be ready for their new incumbent.

Chig took his final Service as Rector of Whitbourne on 10 June, which was followed by a marvellous social evening, for which the village hall was bursting at the seams. Parishioners had decorated it magnificently, as they had a wonderful cake which illustrated various aspects of Chig's and Pauline's lives. All sat down to a sumptuous meal, before the presentations, and then the speeches. "I was much too moved to be coherent," recalled Chig, "and was very nearly in tears of gratitude for their amazing generosity and still more their love, forbearance and never-failing help and inspiration over the years of my incumbency and our joyous service together."

After they had moved into Little Stocking Alec Waldron and his wife Hilda came to stay. Alec, of course, had been first pilot of the glider in which Chig had flown into Arnhem. Their friendship forged then in the red-heat of war had long continued; they had visited each other often, and occasionally holidayed together.

In retirement Chig continued his chaplaincy at St. James' School and, with greater free time, he was able to offer more pastoral care, for the girls and for the staff. This proved to be a mutually fulfilling ministry, which continued until 1977. Looking back over his years with the school he said "I still find myself amazed that God should ever have directed me to a different type of work to that which I had tried to do for so long. It had been a wonderful privilege."

It was in this period, and occasionally afterwards, that Chig was sometimes invited to conduct the wedding of former St. James' pupils. I fondly and amusedly remember one such occasion. The wedding was to take place in the small Church adjoining one of Worcestershire's 'stately homes' where an Old Girl was to marry the son and heir of that aristocratic household. The wedding went well, and Chig was invited to stay to the pre-wedding breakfast Reception immediately following the ceremony. Here he enjoyed the company and politely enjoyed a glass or two of champagne. His route back to Herefordshire took him past the County Cricket Ground at Worcester, where the County was playing. It was too good an opportunity to miss. Chig, still in his 'Hereford blue' prebendary's cassock, could settle down for an afternoon's cricket-watching in the Committee Room among old friends who were delighted to see him.

Now Chig enjoyed an occasional beer when watching cricket, but was never one to drink to excess. Hospitable friends, some of whom had not seen him for a while, seemed determined to make up for lost time. I can still recall the picture of Chig, late in the afternoon, standing with his back to the wall, in mid story and surrounded by friends, when gently he slipped down the wall into an amused, slightly embarrassed, and giggling heap. Champagne and bitter combined had taken their gentle toll. With no trouble we got him on his feet again without further ado, and when eventually it was time for home I took his car keys and drove him back to Little Stocking, accompanied by his occasional and good-humoured "Silly old fool". That, too, was what Pauline said smiling benignly when I returned him home, by now restored (almost) to his usual self.

Chig as President of Worcestershire County Cricket Club making a presentation to Basil D'Oliveira in September 1979 to mark Basil's retirement as a player. Looking on is County chairman Geoffrey Lampard.

Chig with Basil D'Oliveira, John Arlott who was guest speaker at the dinner to honour Basil, and Geoffrey Lampard.

Gardening, which Chig and Pauline had always enjoyed, could now be given more time. So, too, could Chig's visits to the County Ground to watch Worcestershire, especially in the three years of his Presidency of the Club. Together he and Pauline slipped naturally into retirement mode without the angst and 'withdrawal symptoms' some encounter. One new occupation, which both enjoyed, came about because of Pauline's failing eye sight. Chig began reading to her in the evenings and over the years they managed all the Dickens' novels, as well as Dorothy Sayers, Helen McInnes, and Wodehouse galore, Don Camillo and much else besides. A particular enjoyment for Pauline was Chig's attempts to fit his voice to the characters, and her amused delight when he forgot which voice he was meant to be using!

Another new activity in retirement brought about an extension of his love of music, when Whitbourne WI asked him to help set up a ladies choir and to train them and conduct them. This provided, for them all, many hours of satisfaction and fun over the next few years.

He was still conducting the choir in 1981, but by this time he and Pauline had come to the realisation that Little Stocking, with its ¾ acre of garden and orchard, was

President of Worcestershire CCC 1978-80, with the County team, April 1980:
Front row (L to R) John Inchmore, Glenn Turner, the author, Norman Gifford (County Captain), Chig, Alan Ormrod, Ralph Matkin (Chairman) Ted Hemsley, Vanburn Holder; Back Row (L to R) Barry Jones, Phil Neale, Jim Cumbes, Paul Pridgeon, Martin Weston, Hartley Alleyne, Dipak Patel, David Humphries, Henry Horton (Coach).

becoming too much for them. They also recognised the looming problem of loneliness when one or other of them died.

In the autumn that year a cosy little bungalow, Dene Hollow, in the middle of the village, became available. In the course of conversation with the neighbours, Chig discovered one of them, Hilda Mitchell, was an Executor of the widow whose home Dene Hollow had been. "You'll be looking for some nice neighbours" Chig said. "Yes," was Hilda's response, "and we know who we want." "Who?" asked Chig. "Well, *you and Mrs Chig*!" came the reply.

A seed had been sown. They put Little Stocking on the market, determined to sell it to someone who would want to play a full part in village life. The auction of Dene Hollow was to be held on 17 December, and there had been considerable interest. About a week before the auction Hilda phoned the Chignells and suggested that if a sensible offer was made she felt the Agent would consider a pre-auction private sale. Chig wasted no time and immediately phoned the Agents outlining the sum they were prepared to offer. The Agent laughed good-naturedly and said "Well, Mr Chignell, we have come to the conclusion that we are fighting a losing battle. As far as we can make out the whole of Whitbourne is determined that you and Mrs Chignell should have Dene Hollow!" Chig later discovered that three people in the village had been tempted to make an offer, but decided against this when they knew the Chignells were interested. "It made us feel very grateful and humble that people should be so overwhelmingly kind to us" Chig said.

And so Dene Hollow became their final home, a manageable, comfortable and happy home for them both, surrounded by their favourite pictures, with their vast record collection to hand, with splendid and kindly neighbours next door, a garden they could enjoy without being slaves to it, and a gorgeous view across the rolling Herefordshire countryside. And where, un-noticed, the 'cherry beret' hung unshowingly and unmentioned, yet proudly, in the hall.

They were to enjoy almost nine years together at Dene Hollow. Towards the end of that time I had been asked by Chig to hold power of attorney for him, and a farmer friend and neighbour to do the same for Pauline. This to them seemed a sensible precaution in case the time came when they could not sensibly or easily look after their own affairs. In the end neither arrangement needed to be triggered.

Pauline died in 1990, aged 83. Her funeral service, though in September, included her favourite Easter hymns reflecting her firm and staunch faith. I was honoured to be asked by Chig to play a part in the Service, though it seemed to be a part that – in a lovely and understandable way – had strings, his strings, attached.

Chig, throughout his ministry had never – well, hardly ever – given a eulogy at funerals he had taken, believing it is God's view of a person which is important rather than the well-rounded paeons of praise of simple men. So I was instructed there was to be no formal Address.

But in the days leading up to the Service some gentle (and some firmer!) hints were dropped that it might be permissible to say this or include that about his beloved Pauline. There was still to be no Address though. To meet these wishes we agreed that

Retired, relaxed, remembering, reminiscing and rejoicing at how good life had been to him. Chig in retirement at Dene Hollow. (Picture by *Worcester News*)

it might be appropriate to say these things as part of the introduction to the prayers – and so the non-Address was born!

I was touched when, some days after the Service, Chig expressed his warm gratitude, and said how much he had appreciated the 'non-Address'. And now, would I do the same for him when his time came!

The loss of Pauline, his help-meet of 54 years, a devoted and loving and greatly loved wife and companion, who had so unstintingly supported him through so much of his full and active ministry, was a devastating blow – the Pauline to whom his gratitude knew no bounds. Yet he was fortified and upheld by his innate and instinctive Christian faith. This was to help him soldier on resolutely until his own death on New Year's Day 1994.

Some months before his death, fearing that his health might fail and he might not be able properly to look after himself, he had chosen to move to a residential care home, Highwell House, on the outskirts of Bromyard, a handful of miles from Whitbourne. Here he was very happy, visited by old friends and neighbours and former parishioners, until days before his death when his health gave rise to concerns and he went into Hereford County Hospital. Even in hospital we talked of God working his purposes out in a discussion in which he seemed to link Shadrach, Meshach and Abednego with his admired friend and gardener (and former Para) Bob Philpott along with (for reasons no longer clear to me) Midland Bank Personal Finance Services! The typically robust deep-throated Chig chuckle and laughter about this caused all heads to turn to our corner of the ward.

In Chig, in his full and varied life, and in his service to his parishioners in Lightcliffe and Huddersfield, in Fownhope, Brockhampton and Fawley, in Kington and Huntington, and in Whitbourne; in his gallant and dedicated service as a Chaplain to the Forces and, especially, to the Glider Pilot Regiment; and in his loving partnership with Pauline, God had indeed been working his purpose out, working his purpose out in this lovely, lively-minded, caring and considerate man, a splendid and resolute parson, pastor and priest, with a wonderful vision of life, and a good-humoured zest for life.

At his funeral in Whitbourne Church, for which he again provided firm instructions for both Richard Smith (his admired former Curate) and myself – and allowed Bob Colby, Rector of Whitbourne, to be privy to them as well – my non-Address concluded "His faith in God, through Jesus Christ, was so very strong that he has been waiting – in recent months not altogether patiently! – to meet his Creator and to be lovingly re-united with Pauline".

Whitbourne Church was full, and among the congregation were four ex-Glider Pilots and their wives, among them Chig's old friends Alec and Hilda Waldron. A short time after the funeral Alec wrote a brief obituary in which he summarised Chig's time with the Airborne Forces and his time with GPR in particular and noted his "rare distinction of twice being Mentioned in Despatches, for distinguished service in Arnhem and subsequently for his war service as a dedicated, brave and much-loved Padre".

"On a more personal note," Alec continued, " he had the remarkable quality of combining his deep religious conviction as an Anglican priest, with an out-going and approachable personality, accessible to all irrespective of rank, creed or indeed no creed at all! He was an excellent cricketer and hockey player, and a talented and knowledgeable musician". This was a sincere and heartfelt tribute to Chig from one with whom he had shared so much, at a critical time in their lives, at a critical time for the nation and the world.

There is a lovely and powerful saying, which I firmly believe to be true, that states "A man's life is never ended until all the lives it has touched have ended too". Chig touched so many lives, in so many and varied ways, ways which have been deeply and eternally appreciated. Through them he, and his cherished memory, lives on. He lives on, too, in his life's story and in the letters and diary shared here, the story of Wilfred Rowland Chignell, country parson, priest, pastor, prebendary, and padre – 'sky pilot' – to the Glider Pilots of Arnhem.

Acknowledgements

This book would not have been written without the considerable help and support of others, and to all who have so readily provided assistance and encouragement I am most grateful.

Particular gratitude goes to Susan Paxton, Judith Ellicott and Jennifer Hirst, Chig's nieces who, from the start, generously have given their backing for his story to be told. Sue and Jenny had invited me to help with their uncle's effects following his death, in case there might be anything of cricketing importance. There wasn't, but it was then that we discovered the bundle of letters. Recognition was swift that here was a story that deserved a wider audience. The story's writing has taken far longer than I intended or hoped, as other commitments kept interrupting but, throughout, the backing of Sue, Judy and Jenny and their interest and wish to see it come to fruition has been a constant encouragement. Sue helpfully also provided the two photographs of Chig as a young boy.

I am grateful to Paul Handley, Editor of the *Church Times*, who unhesitatingly allowed me to quote from their article about the immense, and often unsung, contributions of Chaplains to the Forces who, in war and peace, minister alongside their Service colleagues.

Keen interest shown by Michael Best and members of the Fownhope Local History Group spurred me on when they heard about the book. They also pointed me towards previously unseen photographs of Chig, and readily gave permission to use some from their publication *Fownhope Remembered*.

David Blake, Curator of the Museum of Army Chaplaincy, at Amport, Hampshire, offered valuable advice, particularly at a time when my search for photographs of Chig had stalled. Dr. Marjollin Verbrugge, Archivist at the Museum of Army Flying, Middle Wallop, Hampshire was similarly helpful, and I am grateful to both for their knowledgeable help.

Chris van Roekel's book *The Torn Horizon: The Airborne Chaplains at Arnhem* (published by Jan and Wendela ter Horst and Chris van Roekel) provided valuable background information, and Mr van Roekel, long associated with the Airborne Museum Hartenstein in Oosterbeek, generously gave permission to use two otherwise unattributed photographs of Chig, one taken just prior to the departure for Arnhem on 17 September 1944, and the other (taken at Bradwell Bay) on his return, both of which appeared in *Torn Horizon*, as well as permission also to include from his work two other photographs, taken by J van Leusden and H J Willink.

Good detective work by Gill Carpenter, in the Reference and Local Studies Library of the Central Library at Halifax was appreciated when she kindly located the wedding day photograph of Rowland and Pauline Chignell. This had appeared in the *Halifax Courier* in June 1936. Thanks are due to Gill for locating a copy, and to John Kenealy, Editor of the Haifax Courier, for permission to reproduce it. The Rev'd Dawn Hyett also kindly agreed to encourage Whitbourne residents to search out any photographs of Chig and Pauline they might have.

The more recent photographs of Chig are included by kind permission of the *Worcester News*, part of the Newsquest Media Group, and its Photographic Editor, Jonathan Barry.

My reading on Arnhem and 'Market Garden', in addition to *The Torn Horizon*, included: *Arnhem: The Battle for Survival* (J Nichol and T Rennell; Penguin Books), *The Glider Gang* (Milton Dank; Cassell Ltd), *Arnhem 1944* (W Buckingham; Tempus Publishing Ltd) among other works and I was grateful for the insights and background 'feel' these offered.

And then comes the team at Helion. Duncan Rogers and his team have been both friendly and professional, immensely encouraging and realistic, in their support and guidance and I am aware I have certainly been in very good hands and here readily acknowledge my great debt to them.

It was Rev'd Canon Dr. Michael Brierley, Precentor of Worcester Cathedral, who suggested I might offer this work to Helion, advice which was most welcome, helpful and timely, and which has come to this happy fruition.

To all, then, a very warm and deeply grateful 'thank you'.

Last, and most certainly not least, I owe a huge debt of thanks to Eileen, my wife, for her boundless and unstinting support, not only for my involvement in this work but for so much else besides. There is no way, however hard or eloquently I try, that I could fully or properly express my very real gratitude to her, and I can only hope she senses some part of the immense depth of this gratitude – for so much.

Mike Vockins
Birchwood, Herefordshire
Spring 2017